For every adult
who believes
that to play is the thin~
try these for starte

☐ Kitefighting with a ground-glass-coated string and a kite you assemble for yourself.

☐ The Freudian truth behind jump-rope rhymes.

☐ The world's largest Monopoly game, with a real jail and giant dice thrown from a fire escape.

☐ *Bite the Dog*, yo-yoing's most risqué offering, which requires a pair of very baggy trousers.

☐ Complete rules for marbles (including the call "Grindings!" that allows you to work your opponent's shooter into the ground with your heel).

☐ The Third Commandment of Frisbee: "Never precede any maneuver with a more committal comment than 'Watch this!' "

☐ *Nurdling*, the tiddlywink term for putting opposition winks too close to the cup for "potting."

☐ And so much much more, in a book that is as much fun to read as the fun it describes.

The Mature Person's Guide to Kites, Yo-Yos, Frisbees and Other Childlike Diversions

Paul Dickson

A PLUME BOOK
NEW AMERICAN LIBRARY
TIMES MIRROR
NEW YORK AND SCARBOROUGH, ONTARIO

NAL BOOKS ARE ALSO AVAILABLE AT DISCOUNTS IN BULK QUANTITY
FOR INDUSTRIAL OR SALES-PROMOTIONAL USE. FOR DETAILS, WRITE TO
PREMIUM MARKETING DIVISION, NEW AMERICAN LIBRARY, INC.,
1301 AVENUE OF THE AMERICAS, NEW YORK, NEW YORK 10019.

Library of Congress Catalog Card Number: 76-48584

Frisbee is a registered trademark of Wham-O Mfg. Co.
for flying discs used in sports games.
Rules to Ultimate Frisbee © 1971, 1976
by CHS Varsity Frisbee Team, used by permission.

 PLUME TRADEMARK REG. U.S. PAT. OFF. AND FOREIGN COUNTRIES
REGISTERED TRADEMARK—MARCA REGISTRADA
HECHO EN FORGE VILLAGE, MASS., U.S.A.

SIGNET, SIGNET CLASSICS, MENTOR, PLUME and MERIDIAN BOOKS
are published in the United States by
The New American Library, Inc.,
1301 Avenue of the Americas, New York, New York 10019,
in Canada by The New American Library of Canada Limited,
81 Mack Avenue, Scarborough, 704, Ontario

Book design: Martin S. Moskof & Associates

First Plume Printing, March, 1977

1 2 3 4 5 6 7 8 9

PRINTED IN THE UNITED STATES OF AMERICA

This book is dedicated
to all the kids I know
regardless of age . . .
and especially to Andrew.

10-1-83

Leroy—
I've had this
book for you for quite
some time. Now, as you prepare
yourself for a few years at Stanford,
and life in California, I'm sure you'll
find it helpful with the problems you're sure
to encounter! Good Luck and Have Fun—
Love
Toots

Acknowledgments

A number of sympathetic people helped me in this rite of second childhood. Some that I would like to single out for their extra special help are Robert M. Ingraham of the American Kitefliers Association, Jo Cahow of the International Frisbee Association, Donald F. Duncan, Jr., Roger W. Howdyshell of Marble King, Inc., Dolores Brown of Flambeau Products and Walter T. Lease. I would also like to thank my wife, Nancy, for her many hours of help.

Contents

From this instant, there's nothing serious in mortality. All is but toys.

—*Macbeth*

Chapter 1

Up from Adulthood

M. BRADLEY. CO.SC

In the nature of an introduction . . .

Play is a necessity of life for children, youth and grown-ups . . . Therefore give to others the opportunity for play and don't neglect to play yourself.

Play is purposeless, yet it can be made to bring together all possible purposes. The experiences of an unrestrained yet legitimate act of play outweigh the educational goals which man substitutes for play. Down with play which has worthwhile, reasonable considerations!

Play as a counterweight to work is not only a means of preserving health, but it is also a necessity for a life which does not wear itself out in the sole pursuit of requirements. Without play, there is no complete life for man.
—H. Hetzer (1935)

One needn't be a sociologist or Eric Sevareid to have realized by now that there has been an unmistakable upsurge in adult fascination with pleasures normally reserved for the young in recent years. Bicycles, amateur magic, Laurel and Hardy two-reelers, ice cream parlors, early rock 'n' roll, vintage comic books, Monopoly, and so much more are in renaissance and appealing to a broad clientele, which is only partially composed of those below the age of consent.

Five basic, often related reasons suggest themselves for the trend:

The Nostalgia Boom that Won't Go Away. It began in the troubled days of the late 1960s as an escape from all that was going haywire and stuck with us as it became apparent that some of those oldies dragged out of the attic for a good nostalgic shudder (W. C. Fields, Flash Gordon, the Marx Brothers, N. C. Wyeth, Tarzan, Humphrey Bogart, Maxfield Parrish—just to name a few of the people who have come back) had substance of their own which was doubly underscored in the plastic age of Ronald MacDonald, G. Gordon Liddy, Mr. Zip, General Westmoreland, and the New Christy Minstrels.

The New Adulthood. It has also come to pass that conventions have loosened to the point that the old facade we were supposed to maintain as adults is melting away like so much wax. Lawyers attend Star Trek conventions, M.D.'s fly kites, professors collect turn-of-the-century postcards with Santas and Easter bunnies on them, Cornelia Vanderbilt Whitney dotes on a dollhouse for several adult years, Senator Barry Goldwater proudly shows off his personal collection of over 300 Indian dolls, noted conductors don Beethoven (or whomever) sweatshirts for jogging in, hard-earned cash is laid out by working people for Captain Midnight Decoder Whistles and Shirley Temple mugs, men and women (and an occasional child) jostle with one another for elbow room at conventions of model railroad buffs, and boys in their thirties and forties negotiate long and hard trades to fill roster gaps in their collection of 1951-series baseball cards—all without fear of being called childish or juvenile.*

In some cases the transfer from the realm of the child to that of the adult has been carried to the extreme of adults trying to take over completely. Although it has recently opened its membership rolls to kids, for quite a while the American Kitefliers Association was for *adults only*. Another case in point is the famous Museum of Childhood in Edinburgh, Scotland, where children are barely tolerated but not welcomed. ("Does the proprietor of a zoo expect to be visited by lions and tigers?" its curator has asked rhetorically.) Or the new adult toy stores like Second Childhood in New York, where the barrier is price, as most kids can't hope to compete with the likes of Dustin Hoffman and Elliot Gould, who go there to add to their respective collections of vintage toy clowns and wind-up cars.

The Desexing of Diversion. As more old roles and images continue to fade there is new opportunity and freedom to savor pleasures once denied. The woman barred from boys' games as a girl can now take a belated whack at stickball, just as the liberated lad with kids of his own can now throw himself into jump-rope games that he feared trying at twelve lest he be taunted as a sissy.

The New Rationale. For those who still need the crutch of reason to act childishly, there is a growing body of justification and sophisticated terminology which can be attached to the pursuit of old-fashioned fun. Should you, for instance, need an excuse to buy that bike of many speeds that Santa never brought

you, it is easily justified as "a nonpolluting, energy-saving device for exercise and transportation." And if your humble passion is filling shoeboxes with old postcards you can tell yourself and others that you are a serious deltiologist replete with a subscription to *Deltiology* magazine and membership in the Deltiologists of America—a package with a scholarly/professional aura usually reserved for Egyptologists and urologists.

Other people need the assurance of art, taste, and pretentious names to rationalize their spending of time, money, and attention on playful things. Accordingly kinetic light boxes, rhombic hexadrons, Kinautic Waves, toy sculpture (like William Accorsi's imaginative circus figures), and more have been created for them. In the process whole sections of places like Brentano's and Georg Jensen's have turned into adult toy stores. The most interesting thing about many of these objects is the rationale which comes with them. For example, tens of thousands of those sets of metal balls suspended from a rack by acrylic thread (that get clicking with precision when one of the balls is allowed to hit the others) have been sold solemnly as a demonstration of Newton's Third Law of Motion to people who haven't the vaguest idea what the first two are.

The Safe Haven. In a world where everything is a revolution (as in the sexual, communications, or computer revolutions) or a crisis (energy, economic, environmental, and so forth), we are in legitimate and increasing need for safe havens—worlds in which one is in control and there is no "future shock" or rapidly changing set of rules to contend with.

In practice these worlds often hark back to our youth and simpler times when we lorded it over electric-train layouts devoid of labor strike, featherbedding and Penn-Centralian mismanagement; managed doll houses in which the residents were free of mortgage, taxes, termites, and orthodontist's bills; and entered ourselves in yo-yo contests with real prizes, easily understood rules, and no Little League adults running around telling us exactly what to do as if they had a corner on "good sportsmanship." Even

---

* For a long time and until not too long ago, only a few intrepid adults were willing to openly express their fascination for childish things. A pioneer icebreaker in this regard was August Mencken of Baltimore, whose enormous and valuable collection of toys was left to the Smithsonian on his death in 1967. He got interested in toys in the 1930s when he happened on and became fascinated with an old toy steam engine which had belonged to his brother H. L. Mencken. Today's toy collecting elite is the 200-member Antique Toy Collectors Club of America which is primarily composed of professional men who spend heavily for their addiction. A member has to die or sell his collection before a new member can enter.

The Air King Game.

No. 4341

A safe way of navigating the air. No broken bones.

Price, each, $0.12; postage, $0.08

OUR DONKEY

Hopes to be invited to a multitude of evening parties this season, believing that his popularity in the past will insure for him a warm welcome. The Game of Re-tailing the Donkey retails for a small sum, but it is not always a small matter to do the job in good shape. The game is printed on heavy buff paper, 24 by 40 inches, and contains the donkey, twelve tails, two prizes, words and music for a donkey march, and the latest improvements in the rules.

SAMPLE BY MAIL FOR TWELVE CENTS.

MILTON BRADLEY CO., Springfield, Mass.

(Courtesy of Milton Bradley Co.)

the darker side of those pastimes—cheating (fudging) at marbles and the close-to-the-surface hostility in many jump-rope chants—is nothing compared to the darker side of the adult world.

There are no doubt more reasons, but as it is a phenomenon which is more fun to take part in than analyze and since we have covered the major points, let us move on to the subject at hand.

Instead of wrestling with a precise and long-winded discourse on what the subject of this book is and is not, these two lists will do the job quite nicely:

This book is not about	but is about
Golf	Marbles
Hunting	Kitefighting
the NFL and PGA	the AKA and IFA (The American Kitefliers Association and the International Frisbee Association)
the Oakland Raiders	the Toucan Terribles
High-jumping	Jumping rope
the Rose Bowl football game in Pasadena	the Rose Bowl Frisbee Championship in Pasadena
Billy Jean King and Hank Aaron	Jo Cahow and Irwin "Skeeter" Beebe
Financially Troubled Abercrombie & Fitch	The prospering Go Fly a Kite Store
Gerald Ford's football days	Thomas Jefferson's marble collection
Second and third base	Boardwalk and Park Place
Ski wax	Yo-yo wax

It is also about such diverse things as: kite-making, paper airplanes, designing your own games, yo-yo tricks and secrets, "Guts" and "Ultimate" Frisbee, the world's rarest marble, tiddlywinks, the "true" meaning of children's jump-rope rhymes, the world's largest Monopoly game in which a real jail was used, collectors of rare and "antique" Frisbees and other flying discs (some dating back as far as the late 1950s), the scheme to fly a kite across the Atlantic, the fabled Duncan demonstrators and other yo-yo pros past and present, the massive 1970 "kite bust" in Washington, D.C., the Nantucket Kiteman and

Kitelady, the rise of the skateboard and the concurrent fall of rollerskates, the war-game boom, the U.S. Navy's $375,000 Frisbee study, and much, much more, including important how-to information on the objects and activities featured.

So much for the *what* of it. Now for the *why* of it as a final item on the agenda before getting underway. First and foremost, there are those qualities which have attached themselves to kites, yo-yos, marbles, and the rest which provide inner satisfaction, true diversion, tension relief, and countless hours of fun. There is no need to dwell on these virtues as there is so much testimonial to their effect spread throughout the rest of the book, but it must be said now that furthering them is the book's main purpose. Then there are the special dividends paid by some but not all of them—the *bona fide* exercise that some of them provide, those that enhance coordination, those that get you outdoors and so forth—and the very special extras which come one-to-an-object, like the vicarious feeling of flight that is a major attraction of kiteflying.

While these are the major, rather obvious reasons for a book such as this (especially the part about having fun), there are other less obvious points, too. One of these is that each and every activity featured is mercifully cheap and therefore puts diversion on a new plane at a time when things like sailing, skiing, and golf are already frightfully expensive and getting more so each day. In contrast, getting started in the three sports in the title plus, say, marbles and jump rope would require a bargain budget like this:

Kite, good beginner's model	$2.00
Kite string	.59
Yo-yo (say, the Duncan Imperial)	1.29
Three extra strings and yo-yo wax	.49
Frisbee Pro	1.49
Jump rope	1.98
Bag of marbles	.49
Grand Total	$8.33*

* These are manufacturer's suggested retail prices which can be cut by shopping discount stores and by making substitutes such as

Another factor involved is giving these humbler sports their due in a world where the sports pages are all but completely given over to big sports, big money, and big athletes and where there is seldom a column inch to spare to keep us posted on the exploits of "Bunny" Martin (the nation's leading independent yo-yo pro), Will Yolen (the kite boss of Central Park), or Dr. Stancil E. D. Johnson (who has formed the Olympic Frisbee Federation to lobby the Frisbee into the world games). Why is it that headlines are made when some oaf with extra glands heaves a shot for a new record or some sportsman with the courage of a $500 rifle brings down a huge deer; yet some kid who has battled his or her way to a city yo-yo championship is lucky to rate a one-line filler. It is a sad state of affairs, indeed, when in 1975 an American marbles team of five boys and a girl, all in their teens, was able to finagle their way to England to wrest the world's team championship from the British for the first time in history and the conquest netted at best a line or two of wire-service copy in most major metropolitan dailies.*

Still another factor has to do with the preservation of these humble pastimes which from time to time become threatened by outside forces. Unlike pro football which has Pete Rozelle to go to Congress to spell out the real and imagined threats to that sport, there are few powerful voices for the activities featured in this book. Fortunately these pressures have not yet proven fatal in any one case—the yo-yo came back from the brink of extinction in the late 1960s, and the

kite has stayed aloft despite a spate of antikite laws enacted in the name of "progress"—but they are still very much present and the more adult practitioners there are the greater their chances for long-range survival. Currently there is much evidence coming in to suggest that the playing of marbles is in decline in the more heavily populated parts of the country. A major reason for this is simply that the bulldozer of progress is eating up more and more of the turf where marbles are played. Great centers for urban marbling, like Baltimore's Mount Royal marble pits and many of the vacant lots of Philadelphia, which produced so many champs, have fallen prey to those who are out to pave us over in parking lots, malls, and roads. Meanwhile the picture is getting bleaker in the suburbs, where the remaining vacant lots are being filled and the adults who lord it over parks have, perhaps unintentionally, banned marbles by their insistence that all surfaces be covered with grass unaware that marbles require the stark nudity of dirt. Even the backyard spot of ground where no grass used to grow is now threatened by the new miracle grasses which are guaranteed to grow anywhere. As more people become alert to the glories of marbles and the forces that would destroy them, the better their chance for survival.

Then there is the consideration of history. The Bicentennial Era which is now upon us is putting history in a special spotlight. But the result so far has been to give the impression that history is almost totally composed of noble ideals, major events, great turning points, and immortal figures. What this book hopes to convey in its own way is that part of the historical brew is also little events, asides and digressions, minor figures, and achievements devoid of ideals. This little quiz (*answers below*) drives the point home quite nicely by singling out a few of the many little-known facts revealed in the book:

1. What was Andrew Johnson doing when he was told that Abraham Lincoln was dead and that he was now President of the United States?

2. What act did Abbie Hoffman perform in public to get him cited for contempt of Congress?

3. What area of invention did Alexander Graham

---

the Festival All Star Champion Yo-Yo, which performs as well as the Imperial but is not as attractive and sells for $1 (and gets discounted to as low as $.69).

* To its credit, one newspaper, *The Washington Star-News*, reacted on its editorial page to the "mere paragraph" the event had been accorded on its sport's page. It said in part:
> [There was] No word as to whether the game was Ringtaw, Nine Holes, Hit and Spin or something else. No description of the play. Were steelies used as laggers, bull's eye aggies for shooters? How about hunching, squibs, babying up? Did they play for keeps?
> We ought to be answering these questions instead of asking them.

(Courtesy of Milton Bradley Co.)

Bell move onto after he had perfected the telephone?

4. How did members of the French nobility show their contempt for the Revolution as they were being hauled away to the guillotine?

5. How did the Brothers Wright first get the feel of flying?

6. What company annually prints more "dollars" than the U.S. Bureau of Printing and Engraving?*

Finally, there is the matter of further blurring the artificial distinctions between the adult and juvenile worlds which was spoken of earlier. Not only does this seem to be the once-and-future trend but one of the past. One of the greatest groups of kitefliers in American history was the adult-dominated Franklin Kite Club (named for the nation's most famous kiteflier) formed in Philadelphia in 1835; in England, time was (and still is in some towns) where marbles were predominantly a plaything of adults and prior to World War I in France there was the prestigious Société des Amateurs des Jouets et des Jeux Anciennes, whose purpose was to play with tops and other traditional toys.

Although little remembered today there were times when the simplest of toys captured the fascination of the nation's adult population. One such toy was a simple offering called Pigs in Clover, which was invented in 1889 by a master toy inventor named C. M. Crandall (whose obituary in *The New York Tribune* carried the line, "In his day he probably furnished more pleasure through toys and puzzles than any other person in this Century.").

The game was simply a round piece of wood six inches in diameter which contained four concentric grooves, each with a hole in it, and a center or "pen" two inches in diameter. The object of the game was to put four marbles in the outer ring and work them all into the pen. That was all there was to it. Within weeks of the first game on the market, there was a

* The answers: (1) He was playing marbles. (2) He "walked the dog", with his yo-yo in front of a committee investigating his activities. (3) Inventing kites. (4) By yo-yoing in the carts that were carrying them away. (5) With kits of their own design. (6) Parker Brothers, the company that manufactures Monopoly.

full-blown national craze for it. In a few short months millions were sold and the company that produced it, the Waverley Toy Works, and its distributor, Selchow and Righter, were never able to keep up with the demand.*

One of the many contemporary accounts of the effect it had on adults was contained in this report from Washington which appeared in *The New York Tribune* of March 13, 1889:

Senator Evarts was walking down Pennsylvania Avenue last Saturday when he was approached by a street fakir who proceeded to enlarge upon the beauties of the "Pigs in Clover" puzzle of which he had a basketful for sale. Sen. Evarts bought one of the puzzles to get rid of the fakir. . . . That evening he began to drive pigs for the first time in his life. . . . Perhaps the fact that there was no end to his labors reminded him of one of his own wonderful sentences, but be that as it may, he worked at the puzzle for several hours.

The next day he carried the puzzle to the Senate chamber . . . pretty soon Sen. Vest meandered over to the New York Senator's desk . . . borrowed the puzzle and took it into one of the cloak rooms. Then he was soon joined by Sen. Pugh of Alabama, Sen. Eustis of Louisiana, Sen. Walthall of Mississippi and Sen. Venna of West Virginia.

They all became greatly interested in "Pigs" and a page was sent out to buy a half dozen of the puzzles. When he returned with them the five dignified senators sat down in a circle and began a pig driving match. They worked for half an hour at it and finally Sen. Vest announced in a triumphant tone that he had driven his last pig into the pen.

A day later *The New York World* reported on what was going on in New York:

Pig driving has become the fashionable occupation of Gotham. Everybody is crazy over it from the Society Belles on Fifth Avenue down to the little cash girls and from the Wall Street bankers to Italian bootblacks in the City Hall Park. Statesmen, diplomats, lawyers, judges, doctors, merchants, financiers, and railroad presidents are just as much interested in the new puzzle as their clerks and office boys, and by general consent it has been pronounced the greatest sensation of the day. Barnum's greatest show on earth is nothing to it. . . .*

Before the fad had run its course in July of the year in which it was invented, Pigs in Clover had been found in the hands of notables and lesser mortals from San Francisco to London including those of a New York minister who contended that he was actually amusing a child, not himself. The mania expressed itself in so many ways. When, for instance, a store in Cleveland put a life-size replica of the game, complete with real pigs, in its window, the police had to be called to restore order.

It is a return to such days that this book hopes to bring about.

Without further preamble, now let us move on to our collection of dazzlingly simple and inexpensive recreations starting with a major examination of kiting—giving details of the adult leaders of the kite movement, retelling the history of the kite, and offering practical information on kite architecture, construction, and flight.

---

* Lightning struck twice for this distributor when more than half a century later it was given a new game called Scrabble to handle.

* Both these newspaper quotes come from *Toys in America* by Marshall and Inez McClintock, an invaluable reference which details more than one such craze. Published 1961, The Public Affairs Press, Washington, D.C.

Chapter 2

World on a String

Once harsh invective, "Go fly a kite!" has become the call to worship for a dedicated band of paper aviators, who, if given their way, would make the emotional high of kiteflying the National Pastime.

There's no such thing as an unhappy person who's flying a kite.
—Headline used by The Wall Street Journal *(March 16, 1973)*

It's one of those special early days of spring when the warmth comes in on a breeze and the winter blahs are blowing away with it. It's one of those days when everybody's a hack poet stringing clichés together and you want to celebrate, so you ante up for a simple two-stick kite, the simplest, most primitive means of flight. Call it the collective unconscious, instinct, or whatever, but you are out to communicate with the sensed, but unarticulated, gods of an ancient sky cult, and you're putting your soul out at the end of a string to let it soar as souls have soared for countless centuries.

You are not alone.

America's enthusiasm for kites is on the rise and seems to go higher with each fresh gust of wind. A kiteflying movement is in the air. Behind the movement are men, women, and children who have come to the united opinion that the kite string is the inside line to adventure, scientific discovery, aeronautical creativity, and just plain fun. Many in the movement are proselytizers who encourage everyone from small children to pensioners to share the extraterrestrial high of kiting.

To this point the movement has been generally unobtrusive; still it has all the trappings of more prominent movements that make the headlines—heroes, leaders, purveyors, polemicists, rallying points, rallying cries, and organization. All of this is dedicated to an object so refreshingly simple that its whole theory can be stated in a few direct sentences: *The kite is a tethered airplane which stays aloft because of the movement of air around its flat or curved plane. The plane is held in place by a bridle, which is a string or strings attached to the user's main line. A tail or other stabilizing influence keeps it from foundering.*

The phenomenon is being expressed in a number of ways. Between forty and fifty million kites are sold each year with countless more being constructed by do-it-yourselfers. While there were only three or four kite manufacturers in the United States a few years

Kite festivals, which were rare just a few years ago, are now held in dozens of cities in the U.S. and Canada. Above, a scene from one of the nation's oldest festivals, which is held annually in Long Beach, California. (Courtesy of Kite Tales *magazine.)*

Flying Machine.

No. 4355

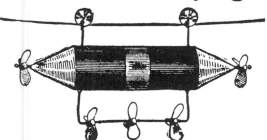

This new and attractive toy is an excellent imitation of the modern machines for navigating the air. The toy, unfortunately, needs a string to make it fly, calling for some skill and causing considerable amusement. Price, each, $0.25

Put up one in a carton.

While there has never been a better time than the present in terms of the array of kites which are available commercially, the same cannot be said for other flying novelties such as this intriguing two-bit offering of an earlier era. (Courtesy of Milton Bradley Co.)

back—mostly making Hi-Fliers, Redmen, Cloud-busters, and the other simple, diamond-shaped, two-stick models of everybody's youth selling in the two- to four-bit range—there are now dozens, some of which are making sophisticated items with names like the Scott Sled, the Super Tetra, the Super Bat, the Para-foil, and the Kitty Hawk. Many of these new kites sell for $5 or more, and a few special crowd-pleasers, like the King Dragon, fetch more than $100 a copy. Major and minor kite shops have sprung up all over the country—to say nothing of the many other stores, from big city department stores to seaside boutiques, which now stock sophisticated versions of what was until recently a dimestore item—and New York's pioneering Go Fly a Kite Store now offers close to a hundred different kites from around the world in addition to kite accessorites and kite-making materials.

Spring kite festivals (popular in the 1920s and 1930s), which had all but died out a decade ago, have multiplied in recent springs to the point where they are now staged annually from Honolulu to Boston to Toronto. These rites of spring have been able to draw crowds in excess of 5000 when the winds are right. There has also been new interest in the scientific potential of kites, with the U.S. military and the National Aeronautics and Space Administration, among others, experimenting with them. On another front there is a new appreciation for finely designed and embellished kites. In recent years, several gallery exhibits have been mounted in which the kite was regarded as an art object.

Not only is there now the American Kitefliers Association (AKA) to head the movement, but local groups are popping up such as the Maryland Kitefliers Association, which sponsors its own events. There is an ever-growing body of kite literature, starting with the ever-so-important *Kite Tales*, the slick and infor-mation-crammed quarterly of the American Kitefliers Association. Then there are the newsletters put out by the local societies and the books—a good shelf's worth—that have come out in the last ten years which appeal to the hard-core kite buffs. These volumes

range from Charles M. Schulz's *Go Fly a Kite Charlie Brown*, featuring the infamous kite-eating tree, to T. Horoi's *Kites*, which has been called the most beauti-ful kite book ever published (its only other drawback beyond the status-symbol price, $32, is that the text is in Japanese).

In all of this, however, the most important and revealing aspect of the movement is the group of indi-viduals who nourish, lead, and help it grow. As a group they are to a person *bona fide* adults (all over thirty as a matter of fact) who are for the most part otherwise employed in the working world, generally little-known outside kite circles (loops?) and kids at heart. Picking out the two or three most important—let alone *the* most important—would be a tough as-signment. Consider the credentials of the following leaders.

Paul Edward Garber. Now in his late seventies, this former curator and now Historian Emeritus at the Smithsonian Institution's National Air and Space Mu-seum is one of the most important forces in modern kiting.

Garber's singular passion for kites stems from his childhood fascination with things that flew. At five he was almost pulled into the ocean by a large kite he was flying, at nine he made it his business to go and see the Wright brothers' first test flights for the Army, and at fifteen he became airborne in a homemade glider of his own design. His particular interest in kites as a subspecies of "things that fly" began one day when he was quite young and found himself unable to get a homemade kite aloft near his home in Washing-ton, D.C. A tall gentleman with a beard stopped him, adroitly adjusted the kite's misplaced bridle and gave him a lecture on the theory of kiteflying. Young Gar-ber then released the kite and it went straight into the air. "The man," recalls Garber, "was Alexander Graham Bell—one of the greatest of American kite-fliers."

Today Garber knows as much about kites as any other person in America. His first book on the subject was published in 1931, and he is still writing on the subject. He has designed and built many of the kites now in the Smithsonian's extensive collection, including a painstakingly researched replica of Ben Franklin's original "electric" kite. He has given hundreds of lectures on the subject, run kite-design workshops, and given countless impromptu lessons when he has happened on man, woman, or child having trouble launching a kite.

He is also a kite innovator of long-standing reputation. His most famous kite, the highly regarded Navy Mark 1, was designed during World War II while he was serving as an officer on the aircraft carrier *USS Block Island*. Garber was put off by the fact that the only way the ship's gunners had to practice their aim for the very serious business of defending the ship from attacking aircraft was to try to "hit" the puffs of smoke left in the air from previous rounds. Most of the time they had no way of knowing whether or not they had hit the quickly dissipating puffs. Garber's solution to the problem was a large, diamond-shape kite of his own design and controlled to simulate the moves and evasions of an attacking plane. It was a boon to the gunners of the *Block Island* whose aim was sharpened with every practice session. Next, Garber took it upon himself to sell it to the Navy's top brass, which was easy after he had lured a key admiral to the roof of a government building where, with very little coaching, the admiral was able to spell out his name in the sky with the kite. Before the war was over more than half a million Mark 1's were made, of which sadly only a few still exist. Though Garber himself is too modest to brag about it, those who have flown it rate it as a top performer which is so docile and controllable that virtually anyone can write in the sky with it—including, it is said, the crossing of T's and the dotting of I's.*

* Garber, who holds the patent, has been approached on several occasions by those who would manufacture them again for nonmilitary users but turned them down because their plans did not conform to his rigid specifications nor will they include spare parts. As Garber puts it, they want to impose built-in obsolescence on his kite. (If you've really got to have one, the plans are in the April 1945 issue of *Popular Science*.) Meanwhile, I have gotten late word from Paul Garber that his son is planning to manufacture the Mark I sometime in the near future.

Garber's greatest contribution to the sheer fun of kiting began in 1967 when he arranged for the Smithsonian to sponsor its first Kite Carnival. The initial event was such a success that it is now an annual rite of spring in the nation's capital. Weather permitting, the Carnival is held on the fourth Saturday in March on the windward side of the Washington Monument. The Carnival itself is preceded by three indoor sessions on the first three Saturdays in the month, during which Garber talks on the history, design, and construction of kites and holds a kitemaking workshop.

The annual event has become at once the Super Bowl of kiteflying and, to quote *The Washington Post*, one of the Smithsonian's "most endearing features." It has become *the* place to come to show off your kites and the ability to fly them. The kites liable to show up at a given Carnival range in size from tiny acrobatic kites to dining-room-table-size offerings. Imagination is the order of the day here, so one should expect anything. At recent Carnivals such oddities as an airplane kite made from cardboard mailing tubes, an easy-to-launch but hard to control monster made up of clear plastic pillows and a large fish kite reeled in and out on a large fishing rod were to be seen. Box kites, winged box kites, Indian fighter kites, Scott Sleds, and all the other classic configurations are, of course, well represented. Most of the kites are homemade and decorated in ways ranging from subtle to outlandish.

An important aspect of the event has been its influence in giving others inspiration to sponsor their own events. Of course, not all of the growing numbers of kite events stem from Garber's Carnival—Long Beach, California, will stage its fiftieth consecutive event in 1977—but many do. Austin, Texas, holds a big one each summer; Baltimore has one the last Saturday in April, and another takes place each August at the base of the Bay Bridge in San Francisco. Both Boston and Santa Barbara hold their respective "Day of the Kite" each May, and a major event, the Pathfinders Kite Festival, is held each March in Burbank. The New York City Parks Department holds an

Paul Edward Garber, the great kite innovator and promoter. (Courtesy of Smithsonian Institution.)

Kite champ Will Yolen being interviewed in Central Park while flying a kite. Yolen, who runs the International Kitefliers' Association, is the sport's tireless top promoter. (Courtesy of Will Yolen.)

official "opening day" for the kite season each March in Central Park. The Canadian Kiteflying and Kite-fighting Championships are held in Toronto each August, and at least a half-dozen events take place in Florida annually in locations from Jacksonville to Boca Raton. In addition, many colleges and universities sponsor kite contests—often as a result of design projects by engineering, design, or architecture schools. The University of Detroit, Pratt Institute, and the University of Virginia all have standing traditions of a "kite day" each spring.

Garber's fascination and delight is infectious, and he alone has converted many a land-bound adult to the sport. He has a way of expressing his love of kites in simple terms such as with this anecdote he has told many times. He was driving from Norfolk, Virginia, to Washington toward the end of World War II to make a delivery of Mark 1s when he stopped in Richmond at a playground where a group of kids were flying kites. He took one of the Navy kites out of the back of his Jeep and proceded to give an impromptu demonstration. Over to one side of the playground was a crippled boy in a wheelchair. Garber recalls, "I gave the boy the kite to fly and after a few minutes he had complete control. Then he called across the playground, 'Hey look, I can't walk but I can fly.' " Later he had to explain to the Navy why his shipment was one kite short.

Will Yolen. He is the outgoing, now-retired public-relations executive who has done so much to publicize and dramatize kiteflying as an adult sport. As kitedom's self-appointed ambassador of good will, he started the International Kitefliers Association or IKA (not to be confused with the AKA), which now has more than 30,000 members. Yolen explains, "As we have no dues, meetings, publications, membership requirements or officers other than myself, the IKA is really more of a good will gesture than a real organization; but it does help give people the sense that they are part of the movement."

Yolen adds, however, "The IKA does have an annual meeting which is unannounced, unpublicized and unofficial; yet which attracts a thousand or more peo-

The legendary Kiteman and Lady of Nantucket at play in the fields of their island. This couple left New York City to set up their kite shop and have since created a line of kites which have few equals worldwide. (Courtesy of Al and Betty Hartig.)

ple each year." The meeting is held every January 17 (which as every ardent kiteflier knows is Ben Franklin's birthday) at the Sand Castle Motel on Ben Franklin Boulevard in Sarasota, Florida. In keeping with the general tone of the IKA, there is no business discussed at the meeting; only socializing and kiteflying are permitted. The meetings which Yolen and his late wife began in the late 1960s have produced their share of records and vital statistics — Yolen himself got a train of 178 kites up on one string in 1974 (a world's record which stood until later in the year when William R. Bigge, a physicist working for the National Bureau of Standards, put 261 up on a string), and several sets of kite lovers have met at the IKA meeting and later married.

His greatest claim to fame as a kiteflier, however, is as the world's kitefighting champion, a title he brought back from India with him in 1961 after defeating the Maharajah of Bharapur in a long battle. (The object of a kitefight is to cut your opponent's kite down with your cutting string — usually a short cord coated with ground glass.) He reports that he has since defended the title against scores of challengers.

Despite his many triumphs in organized kitefighting tournaments, one of his most important bouts to date was definitely unorganized. As he told it to me a few years ago, some young kiteflying pals of his from Harlem told him that he must do something about "The Razor Blade Man." This villain, who had brought his kitefighting ability with him from Puerto Rico, was operating from the roof of a building on 110th Street and was slicing down kites in the neighborhood with a razor-studded knife. With a clear mandate from the kids, Yolen let the word out that he was challenging "Razor Blade," who in turn passed on word that he accepted. The contest was to take place in Central Park. On the prearranged day Yolen, with his most prized fighters, and the terrorizer from Harlem had at it for a long time, and as the sun began to go down it looked like a stalemate. Yolen, however, knew his turf and had observed on other evenings that there was a slack in the wind at dusk. He got his kite far above the other, the slack came, and

Yolen dove without mercy on the floundering razor kite, rendering it impotent with one clean slice of his cutting string which glistened with ground glass.

Yolen has also been one to promote the social value of the kite. As he has concluded from many an afternoon of kiteflying in Central Park, "It's a hell of a good way to meet people of the opposite sex and sure beats gambits like walking dogs. When someone sees you with a kite, the odds are that they see you as a free spirit." (Precedence for the kite romance goes back to Asian antiquity and legends in which runaway kites led couples to their first meeting. A Thai legend tells of an Oriental Romeo, kept apart from his Juliet by warring families, who gets to her and makes off with her on the string of a kite which has been flown into her garret. Still in the romantic vein: horror-film buffs will recall that giant kites were employed to catch lightning to supply the charges of electricity that put the breath of life into *The Bride of Frankenstein*.)

Al and Betty Hartig. The fabled Nantucket Kiteman and Kitelady, with their island kite operation, have become proof positive that the world will beat a path to your door if you build a better kite. The Hartigs produce and sell a line of kites that includes the Red Baron, American Eagle, Bat, Ace, and Valkyrie, all variations on the Delta wing design, which have become among the most demanded kites in the world. Only about 30,000 of the cloth (cotton and polyester) and wood kites have been made since they moved to Nantucket in the late 1960s to become kitemakers, but many thousands more could have been sold, since orders have exceeded production from the beginning. The Hartigs, who make their living from the kites, have turned down a number of offers for expansion and mass production, including, according to *The Wall Street Journal*, an opening offer of $150,000 for the rights to mass produce them.

The Hartigs, by the way, got into kites because of a water shortage in New York in 1963 which dried up the sailing pool in Central Park. Al, who had been an avid sailor of model clipper ships, turned to kites as a means of riding out the drought.

Dominia Jalbert. A Canadian-born kitemaster, his

Parawing undergoing wind-tunnel tests to determine its potential as a vehicle for bringing returning spacecraft to touchdown. (Courtesy of NASA.)

The Parawing, a Parafoil variation, has attracted much attention as a flight vehicle of the future. Here it is shown at work in a NASA experiment in which it is gliding to earth carrying a much heavier object. (Courtesy of NASA.)

Para-foil, a large soft kite of nylon honeycombed with air pockets, has been instrumental in attracting kite interest from large institutions like the Weather Bureau, the National Aeronautics and Space Administration, and the Air Force. The kite has tremendous lifting power and looks somewhat like an inflated aircraft wing. *Kite Tales* has called it the greatest kite ever made. Small versions are made for kiteflying hobbyists while the larger ones are being used or tested for military and scientific applications.

● Para-foils are being used in the Rockies to send weather instruments or seeding material into the skies that are too turbulent for manned aircraft.

● They have been used for high-altitude air-pollution research in Canada.

● Researchers have demonstrated that the kite can be used for "controlled" drops of cargo up to 2000 pounds. The potential application here would be for dropping fragile military goods in war zones.

● Scientists at NASA's Goddard Space Flight Center have been considering the use of gigantic Para-foils for aircraft emergencies. In such an application a plane suffering a mishap could be gently floated toward the ground as the pilot releases his kite.

● It is being considered by the space agency as a "vehicle" for landing space capsules.

● Its application as a parachute has been hailed as the most radical departure in that field since Da Vinci sketched the first one in 1495. In tests it has proven itself able to glide horizontally four feet for every foot of decline, which means that a pilot bailing out at 20,000 feet is able to travel sixteen miles in any direction. With practice, pilots have learned to make precise turns while attached to them and to break themselves for a soft landing.

Despite hardships along the way (including a heart attack and a fire that destroyed his first factory) Jalbert continues to manufacture his kites in Boca Raton, Florida.

Another name that deserves mention in the same breath as Jalbert's is that of Francis Rogallo, who actually pioneered the first flexible kites—i.e., those without hard frames—in the 1940s. Like Jalbert's

Francis Rogallo, kiteflier, space scientist, and father of hang gliding, is shown here with the Rogallo Wing, which is now used primarily for sport but which may have other applications in the future. (Courtesy of NASA.)

Para-foil his Flexi-wing has been adopted for a number of scientific, military, and space-related applications. A few years ago NASA awarded him a cash prize of $35,000 for his kite and other contributions to aeronautics.*

Edward A. Aff. A now-retired vice president of the Federal Reserve Bank of Philadelphia, he is, more than any other person, responsible for bringing adult interest in kites into the open. In the mid-1960s during the course of a speech he was giving, he offhandedly allowed that he was a kiteflier and said that it was a great hobby for adults who wanted more fresh air and sunshine. His confession and word of advice attracted the attention of one of the wire services which sent his message across the country. The story attracted piles of letters from similarly inclined adults and resulted in a number of requests for him to speak elsewhere (on kites, not finance). Aff and others, like *Kite Tales* editor Robert Ingraham, who was convinced that he was "the only kiteflier in the world of advanced age," were now aware of one another and their correspondence with each other led to the formation of the AKA.

Ray Holland, Jr. Founder and owner of the Airplane Kite Company of Roswell, New Mexico, Holland is an aeronautical engineer of many inventions (including a patent on an element of the docking device used in the Apollo Program) who has created more new kites than any other modern person.†

Although he began designing and flying them years before, he has only been in the kite business full time since 1967. His Blackhawk, which roams and soars like a hawk, is his most famous offering. (One reason for its fame are the many stories about the reactions of bemused hawks and frightened birds of other species to its hawkish silhouette.)

Fumio Yoshimura. He is a New York artist whose medium is "kite sculpture"—gigantic wire, cloth, paper, and wood kites which have hung, among other places, in New York's Museum of Modern Art and Museum of Contemporary Crafts. He is just one of a number of artists who are to varying degrees "into kites." Others include Al Hansen, painter of bright "pop" kite paintings, Tomi Ungerer, the well-known illustrator and satirist who is an imaginative kite designer, and the late Ullis Sines, who designed a large series of caricature kites.

These artists and more were combined in a major show which began in New York in 1968 at the Hallmark Gallery, which then moved to other cities. The show, "Flying Kites," featured more than two hundred kites, including novelties like Yoshimura's wind tunnel, in which seven tiny kites were flying. The lasting impact of the show has been to establish the kite as an art form.

Sergei Condrashoff. This Victoria, B.C., biologist became so upset with all the war toys that were being marketed, that he decided to make kites as a protest against them. He explained his choice of the kite as a vehicle for protest to a reporter from *Canadian Panorama* magazine this way: "A kite is freedom. With it a man can vicariously send himself aloft and have a taste of what it is to soar. Yet he is still tied to the earth. That's man's dilemma—his fear of personal freedom and his need for it. From this fear comes aggression. From that comes war. My kites are a protest against war."

Condrashoff and a partner, Frank Annis, formed Condor Industries (which, one must admit, sounds like the name of a weapons conglomerate) and have been doing big business with the Space Platform, an unusual kite which Condrashoff spent months designing and refining. It is a small foot-square kite with an X-frame, tripod bridle, and long plastic tail. And though it doesn't look like much on the ground, it is something else in the air.

One Condor Platform enthusiast has gotten his up to 9000 feet—an amazing feat for a small kite—and another reports that he tied his to a fence and it

---

* Rogallo's award led to an interesting tax precedent. When the IRS tried to tax him on his award, the matter went to court. The judge ruled in his favor, holding that "It rubs against the grain of this court to 'award' something with one hand—unsolicited—for scientific achievement and then reclaim 50% . . . with the other."

† My criteria for this is that he has the most kite patents to his credit (seven). Other Holland patent applications are pending.

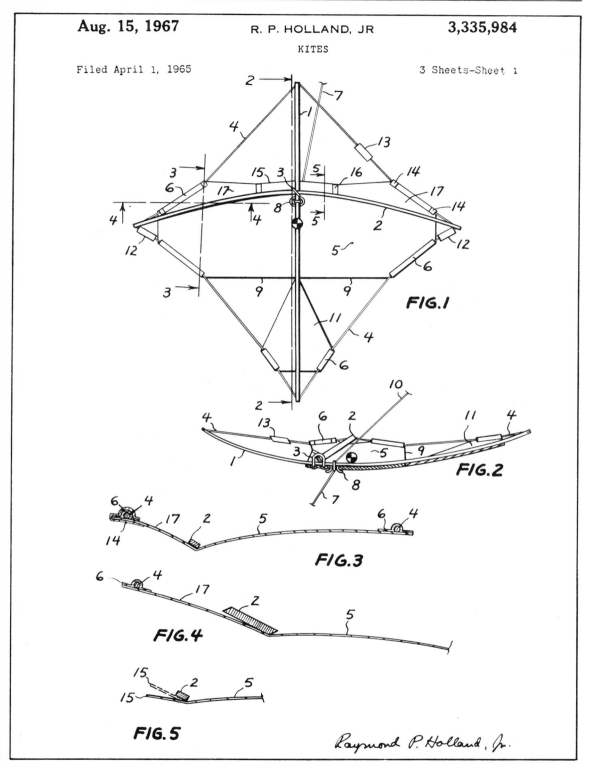

Aug. 15, 1967   R. P. HOLLAND, JR   3,335,984
KITES

Filed April 1, 1965   3 Sheets—Sheet 1

FIG./

FIG.2

FIG.3

FIG.4

FIG.5

Raymond P. Holland, Jr.

These Da Vinci-like renderings were part of the case that kite inventor/manufacturer Ray Holland, Jr. made for one of his growing collection of kite patents. This particular patent, 3,335,984, covers more than a half-dozen of the models he manufactures. (Courtesy of Ray Holland, Jr., Airplane Kite Co.)

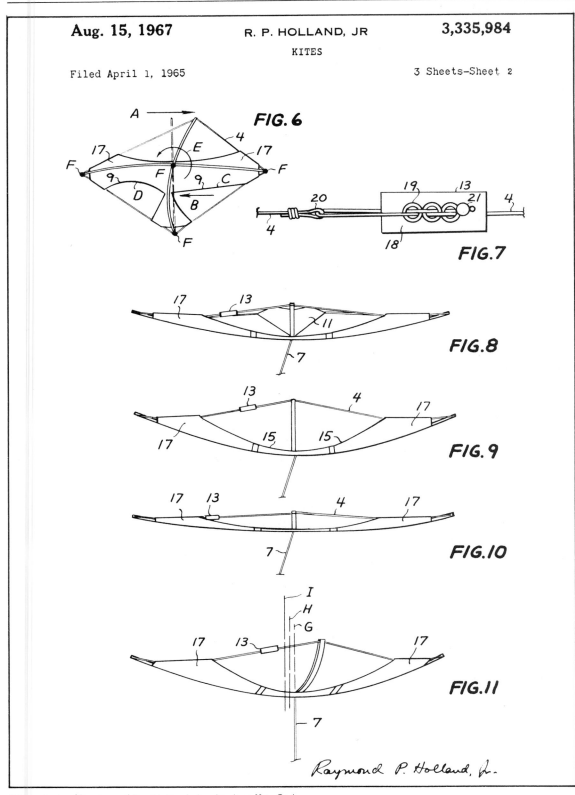

FIG. 6

FIG. 7

FIG. 8

FIG. 9

FIG. 10

FIG. 11

Raymond P. Holland, Jr.

Kite patents. (Courtesy of Ray Holland, Jr., Airplane Kite Co.)

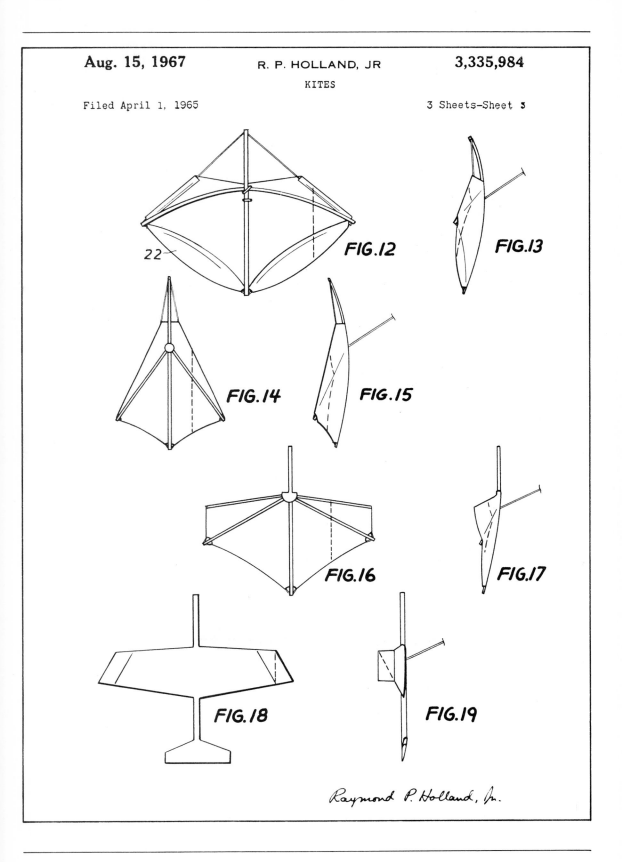

FIG.12

FIG.13

22

FIG.14

FIG.15

FIG.16

FIG.17

FIG.18

FIG.19

Raymond P. Holland, Jr.

The late Surendra Bahadur demonstrates flying an Indian fighter kite to youngsters in Central Park. (Courtesy of Go Fly a Kite Store, Inc.)

stayed up for four days. Condrashoff routinely sails his at 3000 feet, virtually putting it out of sight. The review it was accorded in *Kite Tails*, from editor Robert M. Ingraham himself, no less, was all raves. It said in part, "this little rascal of a kite will outperform any flat kite in the world." Seasoned kite buffs have added it to their kite quivers as a high-performance acrobatic kite. More than 400,000 of them were sold in the first two years they were on the market, with quite a number of them going to dealers in Japan, which is something akin to Japanese hockey sticks becoming big in Canada. It is also one of the easiest kites to get off the ground, normally requiring no running start—making it the ideal kite for handicapped kite buffs like Condor co-owner Annis who wears a leg brace. Condor's initial success with the Space Platform has led to newer offerings, including an eighteen-foot Snake Kite and a Three-Cell Box Kite.

Although it is doubtful that Condrashoff has cut deeply into the sales of war toys, his experiences amply demonstrate that people still come up with new kite designs that can capture the imagination of the kiting community worldwide.*

The Bahadurs. Two members of the same family from Rampur, India, Dinesh and the late Surendra Bahadur, and Surendra's widow, Andrea, have together done the most to vary America's kite tastes and make them truly international.

It all began in 1964 when Surendra opened the Go Fly a Kite Store in New York City, which for a few years was the only store of its kind in the country. He not only stocked and sold kites from all over the world but became a major force in popularizing them first in the city and then beyond as more people heard of the unique store. He formed his own Go Fly a Kite Association of 37,000 members (mostly his customers), ran countless kite demonstrations and workshops, was one of the founders of the City's May Kite Festival held in Central Park's Sheep Meadow, and wrote and

lectured widely on kites and kite design. The business, which started on a kite string, succeeded and kept moving to larger quarters. Extras were added such as the Go Fly a Kite Truck, which was a kind of emergency vehicle which pulled into Central Park on weekends to sell string, reels, and other essentials.

Surendra died at the age of forty four while on a business trip to the West Indies in 1971. The business continues to prosper under the direction of his widow, the former Andrea Davenport, who is as avid a kite-flier as was her husband. She has even taught a course on kites at the New School for Social Research in New York.

Shortly after the Go Fly a Kite Store opened, Surendra wrote a booklet on kites which contains these lines:

> Although the United States has extended more than two billion dollars in aid to India for the development of the Indian economy there are some areas in which America is sorely underdeveloped in comparison with ancient, modern India. One of these is the highly skilled and competitive art of kite flying.

Because of him the United States has made a start at catching up.

While the Go Fly a Kite Store has and continues to be the mecca for kite enthusiasts on the East Coast, there was until very recently nothing like it in the West. Into this void has come Dinesh Bahadur, Surendra's nephew who had worked from time to time at his uncle's store. Although engaged in other pursuits, like earning two M.A.s (one in political science and the other in English literature), his love of kites won out over other interests, and in 1973 he opened Come Fly a Kite, Inc., in Ghirardelli Square in San Francisco, where kites from more than thirty nations are for sale in an art-gallery atmosphere. The kites he offers range from a half-dozen or so of his own design (including a twelve-ounce multicelled box kite which is supposedly a gem to fly) to fighting kites made in India by the man, now over 80, who first taught Dinesh to fly a kite. It would appear that he was well taught as he has rolled up a long list of kite

---

* This is a good time at which to point out that at the back of the book there is information galore on catalogs, stores, associations, handbooks, contests, and prices. For instance, Condor's address is given for those interested in the company's latest catalog.

honors, including the fighter-kite championship of India at the age of twelve, later the Japanese kitefighting title, and a number of top prizes at U.S. kite events, such as the Ben Franklin Day Festival in Philadelphia.

Dinesh, like his uncle before him, has become an articulate spokesman for the sport and seems to be able to turn poetic at the mention of the word "kite." For instance, here is how he describes his first time, when as a young boy he was given a kite line to hold: "I grabbed the string and when the tension came into the line I felt my heart fly up beyond the buildings. I didn't even know there was anything on the other end of the line. It was like being born again as a bird."

And there are so many more . . . Pat Hammond, a Texas housewife who traipsed all the way to Washington, D.C., to take top honors in the prestigious Smithsonian Kite Carnival with a kite called Red Tail in the Sunset. Ms. Hammond has an interesting theory, which is that if you name your kites they will fly better. Among her favorites are Kite Smith, Soar Grapes, Upward Mobility, and a novelty kite of her own design fashioned from an old girdle called Of Corset Flies. . . . David Checkley, who gave up being an architect to create The Kite Factory in Seattle. Today he, his wife, and a team of handicapped workers produce one of the best and most prestigious lines of kites on the market including a nylon Jalbert Parafoil, the Allison Flexible Kite, and a high-performance box-kite variation with the NASA-like designation, Maneuverable Tethered Airframe. Despite the fact that his kites are not cheap (selling at prices up to $30) and are mostly sold blocks away from the dimestore (Neiman-Marcus, Design Research International, and "other fine stores"), he has not lost sight of the next generation of kitefliers. His "Fly Me" kits, used to teach kids the rudiments, cost $4.95 and contain 40 kites. . . . The late "Sir" Walter Scott who became the self-proclaimed "boy wonder" of kiting while in his 70s. He was a portly, dashing man of wealth from Columbus, Ohio, who singly and along with his running mate, Benn Blinn, of Columbus staged some of kiting's more outlandish experiments.

After many tries the two of them almost succeeded in sending a waterproofed box kite tethered to a sea anchor across the Atlantic. It was an "almost" because part of the floating anchor made it to the English coast without the kite, which had to have been lost close to where the anchor (which could have never made it on its own for any distance) was picked up.*

And so many others . . . Clive Hart, the Australian English professor whose definitive *Kites: An Historical Survey* (Praeger, N.Y. 1961) has brought about the day of true kite scholarship . . . the many celebrities—John Glenn, Joseph Wood Krutch, June Lockhart, Charles Schulz, and Burl Ives, among them—whose interest in kites has added glamor to the movement . . . Anthony "Tony the Kiteman" Ziegler of Monroe, Michigan, who has put on more one-man kite demonstrations than can be easily recalled (a pet stunt is sending up a small dummy which, on signal, parachutes down from the kite.) . . . the late F. Rankin Weisgerber, a millionaire industrialist from Detroit, who because of his many travels was able to fly more kites in more different nations of the world than any other person in history.

Yet while any one of these people—and others besides—could make legitimate claim to being of great importance to the movement, they would probably all agree that the man who has done most to put it all together is Robert M. Ingraham. In a word, he is the "glue" of the movement.

Here is, in his own words, how his particular case of kite mania was contracted and grew:

I became interested in all things that fly after seeing my first airplane at slightly less than age five. It was a Curtiss Pusher flown by Ruth Law Oliver which landed under emergency conditions in the center field of the race track at the fairgrounds in Hornell, New York, November, 1915. She was freezing to death.

From that time on I could think of nothing but flying

* Scott was a great devotee of a kite he popularized which has come to be known universally as the Scott Sled. He has often been incorrectly identified as its inventor. It was actually created by William Allison of Dayton, Ohio, who holds the patent on it.

Ed Grauel (left) and Wyatt Brummitt (right) are examples of the innovative types who make the American Kitefliers Association hum. Both men, retired executives with Eastman Kodak, have already assured themselves niches in kite history. Grauel has invented several new kites—the Bullet, Balloon-Keeled Delta and Channel-Keeled Delta—and is a regular writer for Kite Tales magazine. Brummitt is a kite photographer of note who wrote Kites, a small book which has become the classic on how to work in the field. (Courtesy of Kite Tales magazine.)

Bob Ingraham in control of a 45-square-foot Jalbert Parafoil which he reports nearly put him in the hospital before its habits were learned. The site shown is the football practice field at Western New Mexico University where most AKA experiments and tests are conducted. (Courtesy of Kite Tales *magazine.)*

Three kiteframes, finished and unfinished, in Bob Ingraham's stable of kites. Most kitefliers of note are also kite builders. (Courtesy of Kite Tales *magazine.)*

and, because of the limitations imposed by age, the times, etc., devoted my main interest to kites which I could construct and fly.

At 16 years of age, and still building and flying kites, I attached myself to a barnstorming group as an airplane ride salesman, covering towns in parts of New York and Pennsylvania on summer weekends, and became the most successful such salesman in all history. I could talk the most fearful farmer from his Model T and into our decrepit biplanes in record time. On many days I would turn over from $600 to $700 in currency to my bosses from my coverall pockets. For all of this I got a free ride in the airplane for every five rides I sold but that got so heavy they were spending all their time giving me free rides so I went on a commission basis . . .

My burning ambition at that time was to learn to fly and get a license for a career of romantic aerial adventure but it never came to pass. The Depression killed that dream and I remained basically a kiteflier. I can fly a plane and have even flown and landed sailplanes but no longer care about getting a license. Kites are more fun anyway.

I continued my kiting into married life but suffered from that strange stigma attached to adult kiteflying and did so more or less in secret. People could see my kite but had difficulty in locating me in remote areas. When I gained a son and daughter I had what was then considered a good excuse for kiteflying but they eventually left me and I headed once more for the remote boondocks—this time in New Mexico where such things are plentiful. Nowhere in the world are the cities so far out in the country as in the Land of Enchantment.

In 1964 I read a small AP story about Edward Aff, vice president of the Federal Reserve Bank of Philadelphia, who flew kites and went about lecturing about them to service clubs. . . .

The rest is history. Ingraham wrote to Aff and in short order a circle of nine adult and very serious kitefliers were in contact.*

The nine formed the American Kitefliers Association, and its two most important jobs, president and

* The nine: Ingraham, Rogallo, Blinn, Yolen, Scott, Weisgerber, Ziegler, George M. Endicott, and F. C. Jewell.

editor of *Kite Tales*, were awarded to Ingraham, who still wears both hats. With great personal devotion, a major assist from his wife, Hazel Ingraham (AKA executive secretary), and help from his many friends, he has built AKA from a small group of nine in 1962 to a roster of over 2500 members today who are located in all fifty states and twenty-six foreign countries. New members are coming into the fold at the rate of about twenty a week. This empire is ruled from the Ingraham Home in Silver City, New Mexico, where until recently he ran an office-supply company. Now in his sixties and retired, he devotes even more of his time to AKA and *Kite Tales*.

His magazine underscores his devotion as it has continued to improve with age. The first issue, which came out in 1962 and was called *The National Kitefliers Quarterly* (the name *Kite Tales* was adopted for the second issue), was a crude, mimeographed, hand-stapled offering of which only twenty-five copies were published. It evolved into a part mimeographed, part offset magazine and then in 1969 into a commercially printed, slick magazine. Each issue is a rich mixture of kite-related information ranging from hard-nosed technical articles to tidbits of gossip from around the kiting world. In style it is breezy and far from stuffy and has been known to be downright sensational, as shown by such headlines as, "X-22 Destroyed in Crash Dive" (X-22, an Ingraham experimental kite with over 400 pounds of lift) or "Jack Aymar Fights Back—Eddy Diatribe Caused Righteous Wrath" (Ingraham had let criticism of the venerable Eddy kite creep into his pages). New kites are carefully reviewed, news is given of local chapters and their activities, advice for special situations is given (like winter flying or flying around large bodies of water), and kite trivia of every description is published—one finds, for example, an item in the autumn 1973 issue that reads in full, "The first description of a kite in the English language appeared in a book by John Bate published in 1654 entitled 'Mysteries of Nature and Art.' "

Ingraham also keeps things perking with his editorials. Sample:

Kites are for all seasons. Why, after three thousand years and for no good reason whatsoever, are kites flown mostly in the springtime?

AKA has put up a good fight to stop this foolishness and point out that kiteflying is fun anytime the weather is suitable for it. For the most part this is almost anytime other than spring!

As a kiteman, Ingraham is both a collector of fine kites and an ardent flier/experimenter/designer. He designed and produced a special seven-foot-span Delta of nylon to celebrate the tenth anniversary of the AKA (all proceeds from its sale go to the AKA), which is already regarded as a classic. His experiences are broad (a Rocky Mountain golden eagle once attacked his X-22) and his likes and dislikes are clear. For instance, he fumes at "art" kites—those beauties that don't or can hardly fly—and for this reason he has been less than carried away with some of the gallery showings of kites.

Overall he has put in thousands of hours getting the AKA and *Kite Tales* aloft and keeping them there. Putting it all into perspective, he takes it all seriously but not too much so. Awhile back he said of his membership, "it [the AKA] is composed of some interesting people, also some wealthy ones." And of himself, "I am poor. I do all the work for absolutely nothing. I am stupid."

(Before continuing, a sense of journalistic fair play compels the author to admit that he is, and has for some time been, a card-carrying member of this group, whose avowed purpose is putting the nation under the string.)

Upward Forces

Meanwhile, it must be mentioned that the movement has been substantially aided by other forces. One has been the influence of new materials. Strong, light plastics and synthetic fabrics have made possible so many designs not feasible in paper or cloth. Synthetic lines, monofilament and braided, have perhaps been more important as they have, for so many, replaced the crude twines and cotton lines which produce so many kite-destroying "break aways," which in turn discourage kitefliers. Another factor has been the aeronautical research of the space age which has yielded bits of information here and there which have worked their way into kite design—a good case in point is Ray Holland, who helped design the U-2 spy plane before moving up to kites.

On a more specific level there has been the influence of the line of kites which were introduced in 1963 by Gayla Industries of Houston, Texas. These were the first inexpensive, widely distributed plastic kites which deviated from the traditional paper two-stick design, thereby helping show a lot of people the possibilities of kites. And since they were far more durable than the paper kites, kids and adults alike were finding they had a toy for all seasons.* What's more, the Gayla kites hastened the advent of other good beginner kites from the likes of the venerable Hi Flier Manufacturing Co. of Decatur, Illinois. (When one adds the seminally important Gayla line of 1963 to the 1964 founding of the AKA and the 1964 opening of the Go Fly a Kite Store, the 1963-64 period is one that takes on great importance.)

But new technology, products, and influences are only a part of the story because as the movement has matured so has its respect for the past risen to new heights. Heroes who had been long forgotten are being remembered again. A good example of this is a journalist and inveterate kiteman named William Eddy of Bayonne, New Jersey, who among other things established himself as the most resourceful of all kite photographers (having taken many important photos of New York City and vicinity in the 1880s and 1890s from cameras suspended from kites), helped develop a system for sending messages ashore from ships by means of a kite attached to a buoy, and designed the classic kite which retains his name to this day. The Eddy kite, which is a variation on the basic two-stick but with a curved cross-stick, was remarkable for its time—and still is as a matter of fact—for its stability, which allows it to fly without a tail. Eddy's

* The author prizes a Gayla Sky Raider bought in 1967 that still flies.

fascination with large kites, large numbers of kites in trains, and such things as kites carrying fireworks produced some legendary breakaways and accidents. Once when a set of eight kites broke loose on Staten Island he chased them first by ferry and then by train—and retrieved all eight.

As a respect for the past is so much a part of modern kiteflying, it is only fitting that we move on to an account and appreciation of some of the great kites and kitefliers of the past.

The world's most important kite periodical. (Courtesy of The American Kitefliers Association.)

Chapter 3

External Soul

. . . An unstuffy treatise on the historic, symbolic, religious, scientific, and political aspects of kiting

My kite rises to celestial regions, my soul enters the abode of bliss.
—From the writings of a ninth-century monk.

Scholars—who often let us down in such important matters—are at a loss to point to the exact origin of the kite. One oft-heard claim is that it was invented by Archytas of Tarentum, a Greek scientist; but there seems to be more evidence to support the counterclaim that it originated in ancient Asia, and probably in China. In any event, the kite has been around for at least 3000 years and probably longer, which has given rise to still another hard-to-prove claim— that it is the only plaything that predates the doll. The matter of who actually invented it notwithstanding, people in both hemispheres got a lot of early use out of their kites.

In ancient Asia the kite played an important role in magic, ceremony, and religion. Pacific folklore is flying with kites which are variously worshipped as gods, seen as agents of gods, or used as vehicles for communicating with gods. In fact, among certain peoples only priests and chiefs were allowed to fly kites. In one region of Polynesia a sky cult used kites to commune with Rongo, Tane, and Rehua—their sky gods.

Another common religious use of early Asian kites was as agents in matters of divination. For example, land was often divided by the "will of the gods" expressed at the precise point that a kite, controlled of course by the gods, touched ground. So much faith was invested in the divine powers of kites that a New Zealand anthropologist has found that as late as the early sixteenth century kites were still used in his part of the world to solve murders. A kite sent aloft in the name of the dead person would be watched to see who it hovered near and that person would in turn be killed.

Outside religion, many other early uses were found for the kite in Asia. The Chinese commonly fitted kites with whistles, vibrating strings, and other simple musical devices which were played by the force of the wind. Kites found early military utility in China when in about 200 B.C. General Han Hsin is reported to have flown a kite to the wall of an enemy palace to measure the distance to it so that a tunnel of the correct length could be dug to get beyond it. Later, in

Chinese bird and dragon kites from a 19th-century engraving. As the picture shows, kiteflying in the Orient is a pastime that has been dominated by adults. (Courtesy of NASA.)

1232, another Chinese general may have been the first to order an airborne leaflet drop. He successfully got some of his captured soldiers to revolt and escape after encouraging them to do just that in a message attached to kites which were flown across enemy lines and cut loose over the POW compound. For their part the Japanese pioneered in the use of man-carrying kites for military observation and infiltration. Japanese kitemakers have always prided themselves on their ability to make large and powerful kites, with the result that kites in this country have found such workhorse applications as getting bricks to workmen building tall structures, and on several occasions enabling a robber to enter a palace.

Fishermen in the East have used kites in several ways: as a means to get one's line out a great distance, as a way to buoy a line to keep it from sinking too quickly when fishing for gar and other fish that stay close to the surface, and (using bird kites) as a lure to give large fish the impression that a large bird has spotted a school of smaller fish.

Still others in Asia used their kites variously to terrify their enemies, exorcise demons, serve as bait for the winds that would drive away flooding rains, create rain, predict the weather, scare birds away from crops, and finally, entertain and satisfy themselves. A British minister writing of his experiences in China in the 1860s tells of between thirty and forty thousand men, women, and children in the hills outside one town participating in one of the "Kites' Day" celebrations which had begun to become popular in that country during the Sung Dynasty (A.D. 960-1126).

Over time the role of the Asian kite became more directly associated with amusement, celebration, and dexterity. Children in Tibet learned to tie heavy kites to their waists when they rode about on their ponies, so that when a really good gust of wind came along, they would be lifted into the air for a pleasurable ride followed by a soft landing. In Malaya the kite was found to be a suitable vehicle for relaxation and celebration after the rice harvest; in India the first day of spring became the day that all young boys flew kites from the roofs of their homes; and in Bangkok the same day was welcomed with a mammoth kite fight.* Kitefighting came to be seen as the highest test of skill

and developed in China, Japan, India, Korea, Malaya, and Thailand. In most cases a special cutting line with particles of glass or porcelain glued to it was used to bring down an opponent, but others have learned to do the same thing with small blades attached to the kite frame, the friction of an unembellished string alone, or the unsubtle force of collision.

A good glimpse at the exhilarating business of fighting a duel with a kite as your proxy is afforded in this description of the sport in Dinesh Bahadur's native India, which appears in the beautifully illustrated and well-written catalog from his Come Fly a Kite Store in San Francisco.

> In Indian kite fighting contests or "penches," a special thread called "manjha" or "reel" is coated continuously with various secret formulas of powdered glass and used to cut a rival's line. . . . Penches are often spontaneous encounters, a pleasant duel among rivals. . . . In the contest, the most successful kiteman can cut down as many as nine kites, but the supreme act of skill is to capture a free flying kite by artfully entangling the loose string and gently bringing the lost kite to the ground. During the excitement of the pench, boys race madly after drifting victims, grown men run off roof tops in their enthusiasm and all fighters mix together in hectic aerial combat. A victory is admirably concluded when a winner cuts his own kite free as a souvenir for the spectators.

Beyond their social role and utility, kites from the Eastern Hemisphere are, as the eminent kite historian Clive Hart has pointed out in his definitive *Kites: An Historical Survey*, the most elegant and beautiful. Hart, who has studied all kites, finds endless variety and imagination in such artful Oriental classics as the Malaysian figure kite, Maori bird-kite, Oceanic fishing-kite, Thai fighting-kite, Japanese fan- and devil-kites, and so many more. On the other hand, Hart

* Read into it what you will, but this large-scale confrontation is called the "Battle of the Sexes" and pits small, agile, and unarmed female kites against large male kites with sharp cutting lines. The female's only hope in bringing down a male is to move in such a way that the male becomes tangled in his own line.

terms western kites "technologically more important, if less attractive. . . . "

Western Breezes

Save for the kite traced to the aforementioned Archytas in about 400 B.C., there is no other evidence that kites of any kind were flown in the West until the fifteenth century.* Despite their late arrival, once Westerners got familiar with them they began to run up a long string of lofty kite accomplishments the highlights of which are laid out here in their natural chronological order.

1749. Two Scots, Alexander Wilson and Thomas Melvill, were the first Westerners to use a kite in the name of science when they sent a string of thermometers aloft for high-altitude temperature checks.

1752. During June of that year Benjamin Franklin and his twenty-one-year-old son William went into a field outside Philadelphia as a thunderstorm approached to prove the electric nature of lightning with a "common kite" made from a square silk handkerchief. He put his kite up into the storm and nothing happened at first, but then suddenly he noticed that the loose strands of string on the kite line were standing erect. He knew that electricity was present and confirmed it by getting a spark when he put his knuckle close to a house key he had attached to the line with a silk ribbon. Franklin later told the great English scientist Joseph Priestley why there was no audience at this first electrical demonstration: he feared ridicule if the experiment had failed.

1753. As news of Franklin's experiment spread through the international scientific community, others tried it for themselves including at least one, a Rus-

sian, who was electrocuted in the process . . . possibly giving him the dubious distinction of being the first kite fatality in the western hemisphere.

1759. Still another dubious distinction. A Frenchman named de Romas who had conducted a number of electric kite experiments may have been the first and last person ever to have his kite ripped to pieces by an angry mob. While waiting for bad weather so that he could create sparks for scholars in Bordeaux he stored his kite in a local café. The common folk who were fearful of this man's magic to begin with, became fearful that the kite would cause lightning to hit the café.* Remarkably, that is exactly what happened and the completely unnerved residents of the area descended on the café and destroyed the kite.

ca. 1825. A resourceful school teacher from Bristol, England, named George Pocock began experimenting with a kite-drawn carriage. He routinely got the apparatus to do what a horse could not do: reach speeds of up to twenty miles an hour for long stretches of the Bristol to Marlborough run. In one extraordinary demonstration his son got the carriage to leave the ground and scale the brow of a cliff. Kite historians have long given credit to Pocock for the first "man-carrying kite" outside of Asia despite the fact that his own book on the experiments says, "the first person who soared aloft in the air, by this invention, was a lady. . . . " Clive Hart, who has done much research on Pocock's work, has identified the lady in the quote as his daughter.

1848. A kite became the agent for laying the first line for the suspension bridge across the gorge at Niagara Falls. Because this was to be the first bridge and because the river was clogged, there seemed to be no way for workmen to get the first cable across.

---

* Older histories of the kite claim that an ancient Roman vase in the National Museum in Naples which depicts a woman with a triangular object at the end of a string is a small kite. This was believed to be so for more than a century until the noted British aviation historian C. H. Gibbs Smith came along in the 1960s and proved the "kite" was actually a large spinning bobbin.

* Fear of de Romas would not seem to be all that unjustified. In one of his little demonstrations he showed how powerful electricity was by killing a dog with a great electrical arc brought down from the skies by a kite.

One of the legendary Weather Bureau kites which were once used to collect wind, temperature and pressure measurements. (Courtesy of National Oceanic and Atmospheric Administration.)

Then an idea hit the chief engineer, who offered a reward of $10 to anyone who could fly a kite to the other side. The sum was claimed by a lad of thirteen named Homan Walsh. A light line was tied to Walsh's kite which was retrieved by workers on the other side of the gorge who sent back a slightly heavier line. The process was repeated with heavier and heavier lines until there was enough strength to pull the first cable across.

1864. The Union Army found use for the kite as a means of offering amnesty to Confederate troops willing to surrender. Here is how the *Scientific American* described the operation:

> A common boy's kite is sent skyward and rebelward whenever the wind is favorable, having two strings, one strong and the other weak. To a particular weak spot in the weak string a bundle of printed promises of amnesty is fastened. When the kite is high enough and soaring far within rebel lines, the stout string is slackened and all the strain is brought upon the weak. Instantly the cord parts at the tender spot, and the proclamations "thick as autumnal leaves which strew the streams in Valombrosa," shower gently o'er hill and plain and forest top, where the rebels can pick them up. Is not that a brilliant thing, and worthy of universal Yankee ingenuity?

1876. Chinese kites are put on exhibit at the Centennial Exposition in Philadelphia (some of which are now in the hands of the Smithsonian) increasing American interest in kites.

1891-92. Eddy creates his bow kite.

1893. Lawrence Hargrave, an Englishman residing in Australia, invents the box kite. This classic found almost immediate application among meteorologists who liked its stability and lifting power. It also played a major part in the development of some of the earliest airplanes, many of which have been described as powered box kites.

ca. 1893. The U.S. Weather Bureau became an active user of kites, mostly for sending meteorological instruments up. By 1898 there were some seventeen official government "kite stations" located around the country, replete with steam-driven windlasses for reeling them in and out and people who could regularly get kite trains up to altitudes in the neighborhood of 10,000 feet.

1894. Capt. B. F. S. Baden-Powell, a British Army officer who was the brother of the founder of the Boy Scouts, devised a man-carrying kite considered to be the first reliable kite of its type. Later the British were to use kites of this type to hoist up observers during the Boer War and to transfer mail between Navy ships.

1898. Alexander Graham Bell began his work with tetrakites.

1899. The Brothers Wright began using kites to learn more about and get a feel for manned flight. Their first important kite was an ingenious biplane kite, which taught them much about lift. Their first true airplane was essentially a modified form of the Hargrave box kite able to carry a human.

1901. The first record of an American woman to fly by kite took place when Almenia Rice, a circus performer, was lifted from the pavement of Tremont Street in Boston. A year later a Frederick, Maryland, woman named Ida Zimmerman took an even longer kite ride.

1901. Marconi made his first transatlantic radio transmission with the aid of an antenna carried to a height of 400 feet by a box kite.

1901. A Texan named Sam F. Cody, a friend though no relation to "Buffalo Bill," in a combined show of Yankee ingenuity and publicity stunt for a Wild West Show he was performing in, crossed the Channel in a kite-drawn boat. In terms of kiting

As is well known, on a winter morning in 1903 this airplane rose for a few moments over the beach at Kitty Hawk, North Carolina, accomplishing the first heavier-than-air flight in history. What is less well known is that Orville and Wilbur Wright learned the rudiments of aeronautics at the end of a kite string. (Courtesy of NASA.)

innovation, ability, and showmanship, Cody was a match for his fellow countryman Eddy.

1905. Cody used one of his "Bat" kites (double box kites with wings) to send a British lieutenant to a height of 1600 feet—a record that stands to this day.

1906. A great photographic feat as George Lawrence hoisted his enormous panoramic camera ("piano sized" by one account) on a string of seventeen Eddy kites to capture the devastation left by the Great San Francisco Earthquake.

1910. Government weathermen loft a ten-kite train to a new altitude record of 23,835 feet.

1914. The educational, moral, and metaphoric value of the kite is demonstrated in a thesis, "Kitecraft and Kite Tournaments," by Charles M. Miller, a Los Angeles school official. At one point in his book he—like the Asian ancients—shows how the kite can be used to divine a child's later life:

The string is often a source of great annoyance, it snarls up and some lads will cut out the hard knots, but others will tackle the knotty problems and untangle them. They will do the same with knotty problems in life later on.

He comments at another point:

Remember it is not just the pretty kite soaring high in the sky! Remember there is a BOY at the other end of the kite line. BOOST FOR HIM!

1931. A feat that has only recently been bettered: another team of government weathermen got the lead kite in a train up to 31,995 feet.

1933. The Weather Bureau closed down the last of its kite stations as other more efficient but less romantic means of collecting meteorological data are found. The Golden Age of government-sponsored kiting is over.

1945. The Allies uncovered a hitherto secret, Nazi instrument of war: a 145-pound kite for lifting observers from the turrets of submarines. Some 200 of these mammoth Teutonic kites were made. There is no record of how many observers were lost.

1945-48. Rogallo invented his flex-wing . . .

. . . which brings us back to the modern era and, in turn, to the kite revival now underway.

In addition to these milestones there is, of course, much more to the story. Most important, recalling these great events neglects to account for the hundreds of thousands of people who have not set altitude records, advanced the progress of aerodynamics, or invented a new kite, but who have been content quietly to fill breezy afternoons with soulful, free, vicarious flight.

For the average person with above average sights, there is one more kite hero who must be mentioned. Unlike Eddy, Bell and Cody, the hero in question is fictional, the main character in Somerset Maugham's *Kite Story*, who gets carted off to jail because he refused to pay alimony to his ex-wife for a simple reason, "She smashed my kite." At the end of the story the author tries to explain the behavior of his kite-loving character and says in part:

. . . Perhaps it gives him a sense of power as he watches it soaring towards the clouds and of mastery over the elements as he seems to bend the winds of heaven to his will. It may be that in some queer way he identifies himself with the kite flying so free and high above him, and it's as it were an escape from the monotony of life. It may be that in some dim confused way it represents an ideal of freedom and adventure.

Save for a few ill-advised phrases ("in some queer way" and "in some dim confused way," to be specific), Maugham gives us the philosophy of so many kite-fliers and in the process leads us to one of the great issues of kiting.

The Politics of the Kite

For the simple reason that kiteflying has long been a humble but clear symbol of individual freedom, suppressing it for whatever reason (save for one clear exception which we will come to in a minute) is a telling signal of repression. Once this is understood, then one has the essence of the politics of the kite. Oversimplified? Not really.

● In Japan, where kiting is both an art and a national pastime, kites have been banned twice in modern times: once during the pre-World War II buildup so that people would keep their minds on their work and then again at the end of the war by the American Occupation Forces because they were judged to symbolize Japanese nationalism. (When unfettered by such restriction, kites are flown to show joy and pride. When, for example, Japan was admitted to the United Nations in 1957 a group of men built and flew a five hundred-pound kite to celebrate.)

● In pre-Revolutionary France—1736 to be exact—kites were banned because the monarchy feared riots breaking out, as they had in the great kite competitions common in France in the early eighteenth century. Although the Revolution effectively swept the ban away, it did not deter the kite-detesting Napoleon from having kites cut down by his aides whenever he spotted one near him.

● A broadcast monitored from China during the Cultural Revolution contained the rationale for a 1966 kite ban: ". . .we must guard against the handful of reactionaries creating counter-revolutionary power failures, thus making full opportunity of kiteflying." As the Cultural Revolution faded, kites began creeping back into the skies and in November 1972 Reuters reported that the skies over Peking were "blooming" with kites.

Meanwhile, the last century has seen an upsurge in antikite legislation, often prompted by the supposed needs of "progress" (protecting power lines, airlanes, military security, and, earlier, the horse-drawn carriage and the overhead trolley line). In Britain they have been banned above 200 feet—particularly restricting when one realizes that kites have been lofted as high as fifteen miles. Until rather recently there were two stiff antikite laws on the books in New York City, an outright ban in force in the District of Columbia, and the Federal Aviation Agency had a particularly unreasonable package of antikite regulations including one forbidding kites to fly within 500 feet of a cloud—giving the distinct impression that clouds are Federal property.

However, there is good news because antikite provisions are, generally, falling like so much dead timber.

The first event of significance took place in New York City in 1965 when Will Yolen succeeded in wiping two antikite laws from the books in a coup that blended political maneuver and civil disobedience. When John Lindsay announced his first candidacy for mayor, Yolen said he would help. His way of helping was to take to Central Park with a huge French military kite trailing an eight-foot long banner reading "Vote for John Lindsay." A mounted policeman told Yolen he was under arrest on two counts. He was charged with illegally flying a kite in the park, under a nineteenth century law enacted to protect horses from kite-fright, and with violating a law of long-obscured purpose which prohibited kites with commercial or political messages from flying over the city.

Yolen went to court three times and with the help of the American Civil Liberties Union and Lindsay, who wrote a brief in Yolen's behalf, the law bit the dust. The one to keep horses calm was ruled antiquated and useless, and the one prohibiting kites with a message was judged a clear violation of free speech. Once in office, Lindsay proclaimed special kiteflying days in the park which are still observed. On a less formal level, in the decade since the laws were overturned Central Park has emerged as one of the leading sites in the nation for year-round kiting.

Continuing the trend, the FAA in 1968 softened its harsh package of antikite rules. In this case relaxation came without outside pressure. As *Kite Tales* reported in its Winter 1968 issue, the laws were modified—for the simple reason that the original package was impractical and unenforceable—to a

Lords of the Sheep Meadow: Surendra Bahadur on the left with Will Yolen and former New York City Parks Commissioner Thomas Hoving. Together, these three deserve the lion's share of credit for bringing kites back to New York City and its parks. (Courtesy of Go Fly a Kite Store, Inc.)

more reasonable permission to fly anywhere, at any time, at any height unless the kite weighed over five pounds, a weight judged truly dangerous to aircraft. Rulings by Federal authority other than the FAA still prohibit kites over military installations, over Federal buildings, and near radio and television transmitters.*

Important Digression

Before moving on to the most dramatic and telling episode in the annals of kite liberation, it is important to stop for a moment to note that kiting is not without some legitimate perils which make certain specific laws and cautions more than reasonable and quite apart from the silly repressive rules. Consider the following which is but a sampling from the extensive list of kite mishaps in recent years:

● In 1973 a kite that had become tethered to a tree was keeping planes from landing at the Norfolk Naval Air Station in Virginia. A helicopter was dispatched to fly into the kite's line to sever it. The line tangled in the craft's blades, and the plane was forced to make an emergency landing.

● In 1970 a fourteen-year-old with a homemade kite almost brought down a commercial jet at London's Heathrow Airport and a similar incident took place at the Augusta State Airport in Maine in the summer of 1975. The Augusta manager termed the incident "almost a fatal accident" because the twenty-pound-test monofilament fishing line which had gotten wrapped around the plane's wings could have gotten caught in the props and bound its engines.

● Kites knocking out lines have become all too common an occurrence. Two incidents in California in 1975 illustrate the point quite nicely. In April a San Francisco youth cut off power to 3800 homes with his kite, and in August another lad rendered the community of Solvana electricity-less for a full three hours

* *Kite Tales*, it should be noted, shies away from civil disobedience in kite matters. It takes a strong stance for coexistence. An editorial just before the FAA package was modified said, "Remember one thing: you have just as much right to fly your kite in the sky as a pilot has to fly his airplane. Just observe the rules the same as he does."

when his kite hit a key power line. A record of sorts may have been established in 1971 when a kite hit a Texarkana high-tension line robbing more than 10,000 homes of electricity and putting two radio stations off the air.

● Periodic reports from the Eastern Hemisphere tell us that kite passion without caution can be a very dangerous thing. In January 1968 in the town of Ahmadabab, India, alone, twenty people were injured falling from rooftops where they were flying kites. More dramatically the month of January 1959 saw fourteen kitefliers killed in Karachi, Pakistan, which led to the temporary banning of kites in that city. (The ban was lifted because of the loud protests of the many kitemakers in the area.) A particularly grisly development has come to light in Kuala Lumpur, Malaysia, where the police have been forced to ban kiting near highways. Malaysian fighting kites with their sharp, glass-embedded cutting strings have floundered onto highways where on several occasions they have cut the throats of those on motorcycles and motorbikes.

These incidents not only underscore the need for certain laws but also demonstrate the need for certain extralegal precautions. The most obvious, of course, is to stay clear of airports and approaches to them lest one become the first to bring down a loaded 747 with a kite string. In addition, here are three well-considered "nevers" which have been put together by the Maryland Kite Society:

1. Never fly a kite in any form of precipitation or storm.
2. Never fly a kite near wires or antennas.
3. Never fly a kite with wires or metal in its string; static electricity, even on a clear day, can deal a severe or lethal blow.

It must also be mentioned that there are specific kites which appear to be especially dangerous to the kiter's life and the electrical juices of his or her community. The Consumer Product Safety Commission (which is augustly engaged in a long-range study of the kite problem) has issued a preliminary warning against foil and mylar kites with tails of twenty-five to forty-five feet in length as particularly dangerous.

With this serious piece of business out of the way, let us return to the political saga of the kite. The most important kite confrontation yet to be acted out and resolved took place in the late 1960s in the nation's capital. What with all of the political upheaval of those war-troubled years, the tale was lost in the shuffle and is today little remembered outside of local kite circles, but is herewith recalled in some detail.

The Abode of Bliss Comes to Washington

It began with a small incident, lasted for almost a year, and ended in a phantasmagoric melange of national media coverage, Congressional oratory, high-level lobbying, arrests, legislative high jinks, memoing, and finally, victory and a victory celebration.

The original antikite law was enacted by the fifty-second Congress in 1892 as part of a broad package of civic prohibitions against such specifics as cursing, throwing missiles, rude talk, indecent exposure, boisterous assemblies, setting dogs on people, disturbing church services, "playing football, bandy, shandy or other games with balls or stones in the streets," and "fast riding or driving in excess of eight miles per hour in the cities of Washington or Georgetown and 12 miles per hour outside thereof, or turning corners in excess of four miles per hour. . ." The antikite provision read:

> That it shall not be lawful for any person to set up or fly any kite, or set up or fly any fire balloon or parachute in or upon or over any street, avenue or alley, open space, public enclosure, or square within the limits of the cities of Washington and Georgetown under a penalty of not more than ten dollars for each and every offense.

Paul Garber explained at the time the matter came to a head that there was certain justification for the ruling when it was orginally enacted. First, kites presented a real hazard in terms of electric shock and fire

that could be generated by the primitive utility lines of the time and, second, fire balloons and kites with Japanese lanterns attached to them, popular at the time, presented a real fire hazard. Garber recalled that when he was a lad back in 1904 or 1905 he launched a fire balloon of his own design—it was essentially a paper balloon that rose because of the heat from a kerosene-dipped wick—which landed in a haystack and set it afire.

However justified it may have been for its time, since 1892 the law had only been applied very occasionally. In fact, Alexander Graham Bell himself used to experiment with kites in front of his home on Connecticut Avenue in Washington without once forfeiting ten dollars. By 1967 the law had fallen into such disuse the Smithsonian felt free, after checking with the local authorities, to sponsor its first spring Kite Festival on the Washington Monument grounds. The event was repeated without incident in 1968 and 1969. Also in 1967, the now-defunct *Washington Free Press* called for a massive kite-in to protest the ancient law by blatant flying on a broad expanse of grass on the edge of Georgetown known to sunbathers and street people alike as the "P Street Beach." Law and order did not prevail as nobody enforced the ban.

In late May 1969 the law was tested more directly. A District of Columbia kite enthusiast named Joseph Boyd, who was eighteen at the time, applied to the U.S. Park Police for a permit to fly his kite on the P Street Beach and was flatly turned down. He flew it anyway to a crowd of cheering onlookers and was booked on May 31 for violation of Section 1117, Title 22 of the District Code, the kite law. Boyd's challenge, though hardly noticed at the time, had forced local officialdom to face the fact that it was responsible for enforcing the ban. Each year since the early 1960s the District of Columbia had asked its overseers at the House District Committee to repeal the ban, and every year the Committee had chosen not to act. As the drama unfolded, it became obvious that Boyd's action was the catalyst in overturning the ban.

Folding Kites.

A kite 54 inches high and 46 inches wide will instantly fold like an umbrella, to a roll only three feet long and 2 inches diameter, not as large as an ordinary umbrella. The UMBRELLA and FOLDING HIGH FLYER are constructed as above, while the HIGH FLYER and DIAMOND are made and shipped "Knocked Down," but so arranged that they may be readily put together by the boys without the use of any tools whatever.

(Courtesy of Milton Bradley Co.)

Garber, who had organized the Smithsonian kite festivals, explains what happened next: "It was decided by the National Park Service and the Smithsonian that because the boy who had been arrested used as his defense, 'If the Smithsonian can do it, why can't I?' the law could no longer be disregarded and the Smithsonian could not be its most flagrant violator. For that reason it was decided to move the festival."

The March 1970 festival was held at Fort Washington on the Maryland side of the Potomac far from the District of Columbia. It was a fine spring day with perfect breezes, but the odd location made for poor attendance. Meanwhile, back at the festival's rightful home, the replacement performance was fundamentalist-activist preacher Dr. Carl McIntyre and members of his radio congregation participating in their March for Victory in Vietnam. Regarding the war, McIntyre promised, "We're going to turn it around for God!"

In a somewhat different spirit, the prokite forces were about to take to the parks to turn it around for the District's kitefliers. On April 11 the U.S. Park Police arrested four of about thirty kitefliers who were kiting-in on the Mall (included in the blotter record of arrestees was the persistent Boyd who had lofted a box kite in full view of the officers). The following Saturday the Park Police, anticipating more disobedience, came to the Mall armed with memos which they handed to the growing crowd of fliers and observers. The memo was from the General Superintendent of the National Capital Parks, and it warned of arrest but politely concluded, "We cordially invite you to go fly a kite outside the city of Washington." The memo did little, if any, good. The dissidents flew, and justice was served as another eleven arrests were made. In all, the two Saturday dragnets had yielded fifteen violators.

After these arrests, pressure began to mount. Both the Smithsonian and the D.C. government lobbied to get Congress to address itself to repealing the ban, and Secretary of the Interior Walter Hickel dropped the first of two famous spring 1970 memos over the fence. (You may recall that the second was the one in which he chastised President Nixon for not communicating, an accusation that got him fired.) In the first he appealed to the heads of both the House and Senate District Committees urging, "immediate and favorable consideration of legislation removing existing restrictions on kite flying in the District of Columbia." The city of Philadelphia, meanwhile, extended an embarrassing offer to all District kitefliers to come to that city, where no repressive rules were in force. An idealistic lawyer working for the Department of Transportation named Fred Schwartz went to the U.S. District Court to have the law overturned, but his petition was denied as the judge pointed out that the repeal was entirely up to Congress.

For its part, the news media were of a single mind in calling for repeal. One balmy afternoon the *Washington Daily News* outdid its competitors with a lead editorial which, among other things, contained a long poetic call to the skies. Sample: "Just as man can go back to his ancestral home, the sea, with nothing more in the way of sophisticated equipment than a wet bathing suit . . . so can he reach towards heaven with a couple of sticks, some paper, some glue and a ball of string." *Life* magazine brought the situation to national prominence by reporting, "U.S. Park Police recently were set upon by determined kite lovers who, learning of a silly ancient statute prohibiting kiteflying, purposely defied the law in hopes of changing it. Eleven [actually fifteen] of them were busted and no doubt deserved it."

Each half of Congress had its own response to the pressure. The Senate spliced its repeal provision onto a very controversial D.C. Crime Bill which, among other things, allowed for police to enter without knocking. This bill suggested an odd trade: full freedom to fly a kite in exchange for a package that would deprive the capital's residents of other freedoms.

On the House side, there were no such complications. A Bill (H.R. 16476) was drafted, reported out of committee, and passed by unanimous consent on May 11, 1970. However, it was not passed without a price: the subject unleashed the disastrous pun-laden wit of the House. One Representative said, for instance, "If one citizen were to tell another to go out and fly a kite, he would be advocating the commission of a crime in the District of Columbia. I doubt that this ever happens in the District of Columbia, but just in case any citizen ever got high as a kite he would be in double jeopardy." Representative William Hungate of Missouri acidly suggested the affair was "eloquent testimony to the wisdom of our retaining home rule right here in this Chamber so we can pass on kiteflying."

Celebration of the repeal came formally on May 24 when an officially sanctioned fly-in took place on the Washington Monument grounds, the very place where the "Mall 15" had been busted. The National Park Service, atoning for vigorous enforcement, gave away 2500 standard-shaped, two-stick kites at taxpayer expense. Hundreds of kites filled the sky—not only the commercial Cloudbusters, Redmen, and Hi-Fliers, but homemade ones: well-crafted oriental kites, another in the shape of a pumpkin, one with a tail made of small American flags and, ponderously rising through all of these lesser entities, a mammoth fourteen-foot box kite. There were rock bands, a supercharged disc jockey M.C., lots of kids, laughter, bathing suits, skin, hair, kite corpses littering the Mall, and a kite-puncturing hail storm to round out an effortless afternoon of liberation.

(Also in May and many times since, the Smithsonian has scheduled boomerang-flinging fetes on the Mall. "Throwing Missiles" is still quite illegal under the remaining portions of the 1892 law but nobody chooses to enforce the ban. It's a good bet that one could probably get away with the still illegal games of bandy or shandy, if anyone could remember how to play them.)

Since the ban was lifted the Smithsonian's annual kite festival has become bigger, better, and more important. Even in 1973 when there was hardly any wind at all on the appointed day, 3000 kitefliers showed up. A good wind, like the one in 1972, will bring out 5000.

Moral

Unlike so many modern tales which have no moral to them, this seems to have at least two: one for kite-flying and a second for the general state of things.

I. Kite Moral. Over the long term, kites are irrepressible.

II. General Moral. If, as we are told, a journey of a thousand miles starts with one small step and there is something better to do than curse the darkness, then, when a candle is lit and a step taken, it is time for rejoicing even though it gives Congress or whatever deliberative body the power to tell its constituents to go fly a kite. Moreover, for each of us there is this: if we are to go out with a whimper instead of a bang and if, as the cliché has it, we are to be pecked to death by ducks—absurd laws, rules, insensitive computers, indifferent bureaucracies, attacks on our privacy, the banal, the venal, and the like—then is it not better to enjoy our small successes before the cosmic whimper and to outwit a few of those pecking ducks before we go down?

Kite-on.

Chapter 4

Joy of Flying

On the design, construction, care, feeding, and flying of kites.

I amused myself . . . with flying a paper kite; and approaching the bank of a pond. . . . I tied the string to a stake. . . . Being desirous of amusing myself with my kite and enjoying at the same time the pleasure of swimming . . . I found that, lying on my back and holding the stick in my hands, I was drawn along the surface of the water in a very agreeable manner. . . .
—From Ben Franklin's Autobiography

The first step in getting into kiting is to get hold of a kite (or kites) and some line and start flying. While many intermediate and advanced kitefliers are into designing and/or making their own kites, it is a good idea for one with limited experience to start flying with store-bought kites. This way you're in on the joy of flying right from the beginning, and you can start acquiring a sense of what flies and what doesn't for that day when you start making your own. For obvious reasons it is a good idea to steer clear of the more expensive and more exotic kites for your first few outings.

Here are the basic types of kite that you will have to choose from:

Diamond and Other Flat Kites. The "diamond" is the most popular name for the flat two-sticker from the dimestore that for many years was the commonest kite in American skies, but which is losing favor as rapidly as an errant kite can nose dive. The reason: it is not a very good kite. Many experienced kitefliers actually get mad when they talk about the unreliable diamond and the number of people who have been turned off because of it. Here is Ingraham's reasoned assessment of why it's a lousy kite: "It has to have a long tail, has a poor lift-to-drag ratio and seldom flies above a 30-degree angle." Its only good points are that it is cheap and very easy to make. Ironically, two- and three-stick flat kites like the "barn door" are much more versatile and air worthy than the "diamond."

Eddy (or Maylay). Not to be confused with the "diamond," which it somewhat resembles, it is a bowed two-sticker in which the horizontal spar is curved. It can normally be flown without a tail. The two sticks fall closer to forming a T than a +. It is a fine flier, easy to make (when you get into making them), and stable. It is one of the easiest of all kites for the novice to fly. Unfortunately, no company now

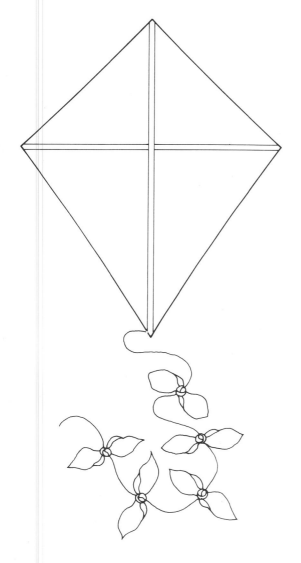

Diamond Kite.

makes an Eddy on a large scale and the only time one will find them in a store is on the rare occasion when a local kitemaker makes a few extra for sale. The Kite Shop in Honolulu sells one by mail which it oddly calls the Diamond Kite.

Box. The common rectangular box is a reliable, tailless workhorse kite that generally flies well. Its only drawbacks are that large ones are hard to transport, and they are generally difficult to bridle. (The bridle is the string or arrangement of strings which holds the kite in place to face the wind.) There are many variations on the simple box kite including the winged box, hexagonal box, barrel, and triangular box. A version of the box that is attracting a lot of attention and converts is the MTA or Maneuverable Tethered Airframe, which was originally invented in 1933 to simulate the movement of a real airplane in order to weed out prospective student pilots without aptitude. The Kite Factory produces a version of orange and blue nylon that can loop, spin (and recover), hedge hop, stall, and land just like a biplane from the barnstorming era.

Delta Wings and Other Soaring Kites. Triangular, often bird-shaped, single-plane kites which are tailless and have a keel instead of a conventional string bridle. These kites are becoming more popular all the time, and for good reason: they are easy to fly, soar well (even in a dying wind), work well in moderate breezes, and are usually easy to fold up for transportation. Kites of this type are offered in great variety and include the Blackhawk and Kitty Hawk from the Airplane Kite Company, all of the kites from the Nantucket Kiteman, a number of the inexpensive Gayla kites, and the Hi-Flier Keelkite.

Soft or Nonrigid Kites. Jalbert, Rogallo, and other kites without spars. These are spectacular kites, especially the Para-foil, which is great sport to fly. Parafoils are not for your rookie outings, if for no other reason than their price. When this was written, the prices for Para-foils at the Go Fly a Kite Store ranged from $25 for the small "Kytfoil" version to $250 for the sensational "Eagle," which measures 82 by 15 by 10 inches. These soft kites are expensive because they are especially well suited to carrying things, like cameras for aerial photography.

Scott Sled. The semirigid kite that is becoming so popular. It flies well in winds from gentle to fairly heavy, is relatively inexpensive, very reliable and hard to damage. It is a fine beginner's kite that has many fans among the experts. Also, while many kites don't adapt well to gigantic and miniature sizes, the Sled seems to do well no matter what its size.

The Tetra Kite. The cellular kite originally designed by Alexander Graham Bell which is a good climber, easily controlled, and does not need a tail. A California manufacturer, Synestructics, Inc., has done much to bring back this fine kite (the company advertises it as Alexander Graham Bell's 2nd Great Idea!).

Proprietary Kites. For lack of a better term a designation intended to cover many of the new kites now appearing on the market which don't fit into the established categories. Examples here would be the airplane-type kites being made by Stratton Air Engineering and the Skylinks "kite system" from Synestructics. The latter is a set of ten kite modules that can be linked together to form different super kites or which can be flown independently.

Specialty Kites. Indian fighter kites, miniatures, centipedes, figurals, Japanese fish kites, bird and insect kites, kites for fishing with, and the like. These are generally showy kites which are not for the beginner. Some, like the fighting kites, are bought for specific applications, while many of the others are bought more for their good looks than for their ability to fly. In fact, the Go Fly a Kite Store reports that the biggest buyers of their beautiful silk bird and insect kites from the Orient are interior decorators.

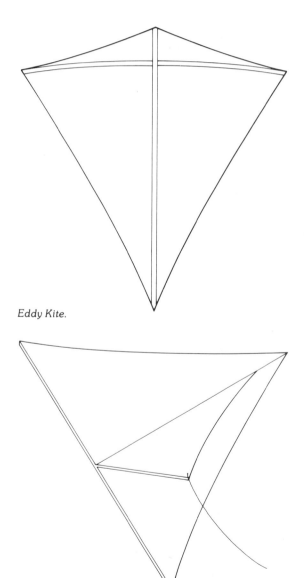

Eddy Kite.

Delta Winged Kite.

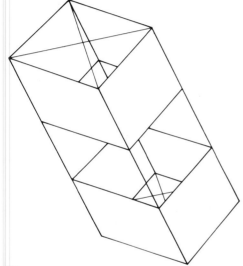

Box Kite.

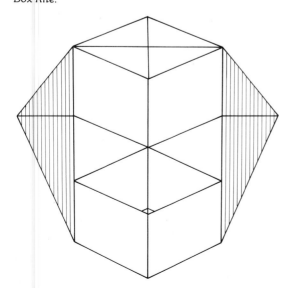

Winged Box Kite.

"Junk" or "Found Object" Kites. Kites made from the discards of a throw-away society—old shower curtains, plastic garbage bags, patchwork, coat hangers, window shades, trousers, corsets, canceled checks (for lofty puns about financial kiting), mailing tubes, and whatever else is handy. This form of recycling is very popular these days, especially at kite events where there are prizes for the most creative kites. Junk kites are great fun to move onto once the rudiments of flying and design are mastered.

The question of where to buy a kite is getting easier and easier to answer all the time as more retail outlets open. A listing of more than forty kite shops and mail-order operations appears at the back of the book. New outlets are appearing all the time, and the best place to keep abreast of this is in *Kite Tales*.

In order to begin flying, you will also need kite line, normally sold with kites, and you may also want to have a simple repair kit (Scotch tape, extra string, and a knife) and a reel or spool for bringing your kite in. A number of kitefliers use old fishing reels for this purpose. A variety of reels and spools are now for sale in the kite shops, and back issues of *Kite Tales* contain a number of plans for do-it-yourselfers.

Launching, Flying, and Landing

While many people are able to fly a well-made kite under good circumstances, there is still a body of information which is needed if one hopes to move up from the novice class without having to travel the long trail of trial and error—error commonly translating into smashed kites and frustrating afternoons. Here are some pieces of tested advice and information which have been gathered from diverse sources and add up to the conventional wisdom of kiteflying.

1. Read the instructions.
2. Pick a clear, open site away from power lines, kite-hungry trees, and buildings. Buildings and other large obstructions create strong currents that can cause the kite to veer when it comes parallel to their

highest point. Many kites have been lost or broken from such veering.

3. Judge the wind, using the Beaufort Wind Scale, which is as follows:
- A wind of 4-7 mph. will rustle tree leaves and can be felt lightly on your face.
- A wind of 8-12 mph. will keep the tree leaves in constant motion and extend a light flag.
- A wind of 13-18 mph. tosses the tops of trees, raises dust, and blows loose paper and other light debris.
- A wind of 19-24 mph. makes small trees sway.

4. With approximate wind speed determined, one should know the following and act accordingly:
- Most kites fly *best* in 8-12 mph. of wind, but most lighter kites will rise on a breeze of 4-6 mph.
- Wind speeds of 15-25 mph. are too stiff for most kites and most line. Winds above 25 mph. are a sure disaster for the amateur.

5. If there are two of you, the best way to launch a kite is for one person to hold the line while the other walks the kite out 100 or so feet. When the breeze feels right the kite should be fed into it by hand. Properly executed, the kite should arc up into the air with ease.

6. If you are alone, "feed" the kite into the breeze and work to get it up as fast as you can. Most kites will oscillate on the short line they have just after launch. Quick feeding of your line at this point helps give it balance.

7. "Pumping" or "pulling down" is a good way to get a kite up to a smooth sailing altitude. One pulls back on the kite line about a foot, lets up a little, pulls again, and so forth until it is safely airborne. The effect of pumping will be enhanced if you walk backwards as you are doing it.

8. Except for a near windless day, if you have to run a lot with your kite to get it up, chances are something is wrong with the kite or the way it is rigged.

9. When your kite is up 25 feet or so, it is a good idea to slowly stop or "snub" it. If it flies well in place, it is ready for higher altitudes. If not, bring it back for adjustments.

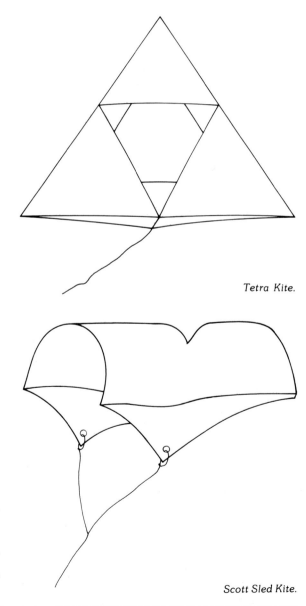

Tetra Kite.

Scott Sled Kite.

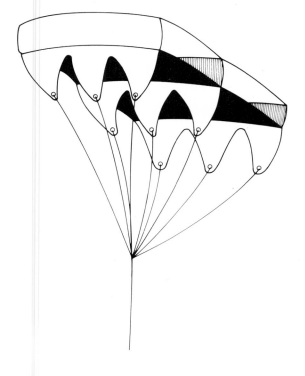

Parafoil Kite.

10. You have too much tail if the kite sags and is generally sluggish.

11. A diving kite is usually the result of (a) poor design, (b) a lopsided bridle, or (c) too short a tail.

12. To make your kite fly higher when it won't go higher, bring it back to earth and shorten the upper leg of the bridle.

13. To save a kite that is diving or looping out of control, let it get near the ground and then suddenly let out as much line as you can. This should let it float to a safe landing.

14. To bring a kite down under normal circumstances, reel it in slowly until it comes to the ground. Once a kite has landed, hold tight to the line to prevent it from bouncing along the ground, but rather have your partner go out and fetch it or peg the line to the ground and walk out and get it. *Never* pull the kite along the ground to you.

15. When you have become skilled enough, it is a mark of the pro to be able to catch your kite in your hand.

As these basics become second nature, you will learn about your kites, gather insights, and begin moving up to higher elements of style. You may, for instance, discover as Dinesh Bahadur and other pros have that you get especially good results when you talk with your kites . . . just as plant lovers have discovered after talking with their coleuses. "No two kites are alike," says Al Hartig, who even sees personality differences between individual copies of his own kites. He is one of many who believe you must get to know and gain rapport with each new kite that comes into your hands.

You will also probably develop your own preferences rather quickly. A number of advanced kitefliers not only look down their noses at kites with tails but won't fly them because they see them as a caste below kites without tails. Paul Garber, for one, thinks this is nonsense. "It is often extremely satisfying to work a playful kite with a long, colorful tail. It decorates the sky." So too there are those who instinctively put their kites as high in the air as they can, while others, who prefer to admire their kites, never go above a few hundred feet. Then there are those who love giant kites that block out the sun, just as there are men and women who love the challenge of miniature kites flown on the slenderest of threads. Stories about tiny kites abound. One legend has it that two Oriental masters kept fighting normal-sized kites to a draw, so they moved on to a "sudden death" situation in which they fought with postage-stamp-sized kites over a lit hibachi to guarantee sudden death to the loser. A few people have even developed the skill of very low flying—the late Surendra Bahadur was able to fly one of his kites a mere six inches off the ground.

The list goes on and on . . . those who love richly decorated kites versus those who couldn't care less, the kite fighters and those who see this as an inappropriate activity for the peaceful kite, the World War I flying-ace types who stall, dive, and loop the loop and those who are as straight in their flying as a TWA pilot . . . amply making the point that there is more than one way to fly a kite.

Making Your Own

A number of top kitefliers have never flown anything but kites made by others and who, like Will Yolen, rhetorically ask, "Did Babe Ruth make his own bats?" Others insist that the full thrill of kiting comes in making and flying your own kites. This brief section is intended for those who would like to try the latter.

Because of his long experience making kites and teaching others how, I turned to Paul Garber for advice in this area and what follows is in large part taken from conversations with him on the subject.

Like just about everyone else in the field, he believes that one should begin with a good store-bought kite (his pick for the best starting kite would be a Hartig Valkyrie) to learn to fly with. He goes one step further to suggest that one begin making kites by duplicating that first kite to get a feel for what it's all about.

Meanwhile, you are going to need certain supplies and tools to get started, specifically:

Sticks. Various lengths of such light woods as

Three Stick Barndoor Kite.

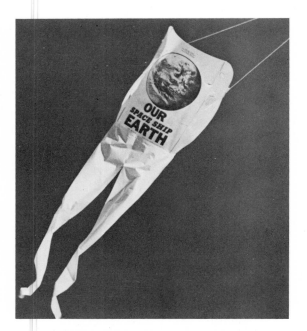

Just two of the hundreds of kite models now on the market. These are part of the line of the Airplane Kite Company of Roswell, New Mexico, and are the Giant Skyscraper and "Our Space Ship Earth." (Courtesy of Airplane Kite Company.)

cedar, straight-grained spruce, and cypress are good to have on hand for kites in which the goal is lightness and strength. Balsa is fine for small, very light kites. These can generally be purchased precut at hobby shops or made much more cheaply at home by cutting a large piece of wood into strips with a table saw. Well-dried split bamboo is a good, inexpensive, and versatile material for all but the largest kites and one will never want to pass up a good source of this wood. Bamboo poles used to roll rugs around or bamboo porch shades are often discarded and worth keeping an eye out for. Short of finding free bamboo it often makes sense to buy a new porch shade to take apart and transform into kite frames. In his book *Chinese Kites: How to Make and Fly Them*, David F. Jue points out that he made 200 kites from a shade that cost him $3.50 at Sears.

Covering. For paper kites you will want to use light but tough papers, such as light wrapping paper or, better yet, some of the special papers sold in hobby shops for model airplanes. Rice paper from an art supply store is also light and strong and especially appropriate for Oriental kites and other kites you plan to decorate with watercolors or poster paints. Tissue paper and newspaper are pretty much worthless except for small kites you only plan to use once or twice, and crepe paper should never be used, as it stretches in the wind. For more durable kites one will want to begin collecting light, tough fabric remnants. You will also want to have plastic sheeting to experiment with and perhaps try to get hold of a few yards of Du Pont Tyvek, a synthetic which is very popular among kitemakers these days. Since paper is the cheapest and easiest to work with, you will probably want to work your way up to the better materials with experience.

Adhesives and Joining Materials. You will want Elmer's Glue-All for paper kites, needle and thread or a sewing machine for cloth kites, and strong cellophane tape for joining plastic and making repairs to all kites.

Line. A selection of cotton and nylon cord of various test strength. Garber says it is a good idea to

This giant is the "Dilta," a delta-wing with a 40-foot wingspan made plans marketed by Dan Lirot of the Butterfield Studios of Elmhurst, Illinois. (Courtesy of Kite Tales *magazine.)*

do your line shopping at a place that sells fishing tackle rather than at a toy store. Some of the so-called kite twine sold in toy stores is lucky to last for more than an afternoon even with a fairly light kite in a light wind.

Tail Material. Rag strips and crepe-paper streamers are all you'll need here.

Tools. Penknife, short-bladed hobby knife for working with bamboo, scissors, a ruler, and pencils are essentials, but one may also want to have an awl, a small saw with fine teeth, paintbrushes, and paint.

Garber suggests that once you have made and flown a copy of your store-bought kite, that three good kites to move on to are the Eddy, box, and barn-door kites. Incidentally, Garber feels that the three-stick barn-door is a "tremendously underrated kite" that is overdue for a popular comeback. He points out that it is vastly superior to its flat two-stick cousin, is very easy to fly, fun to do tricks with, and one of the most suitable of all kites for decoration. Detailed plans for each of these three kites appear as Appendix IA of this book (beginning on page 178) along with plans for several miniature kites, including a tiny Thai "Chiringa" kite that can be cut right out of the book and flown with a little thread.

Of course, making a few basic kites is just the beginning if you get into kitemaking. You may wish to plough through *Kite Tales* (past, present, and future) for tips, plans, and ideas and start a small library of kite-design books like David Jue's *Chinese Kites*, L. L. Hunt's *Getting Started in Kitemaking*, and *Kite Crafts* by L. and J. Newman. Eventually you may wish to move on to designing your own kites, which many feel is the highest, most challenging, and most rewarding level of kiting.

Solicited Testimonial

Kitefliers must be prepared for little frustrations here and there, which can either be entirely your own fault (finding that you have forgotten to pack extra string when you run out of it on the perfect kite day), out of your hands (a windless day when the urge to fly is at its peak), or a combination of both (a gust of wind that catches you unprepared, resulting in a kite fatality). For such times this chapter—and the section on kites—closes with a small collection of quotes the author has gathered from various sources to help get you over frustrating hurdles. Each entry is an unabashed verbatim testimonial for kiteflying.

"Every day I learn something new from my kites, a lesson in patience, in strength, in how to relax and play. And I meet so many happy people. Everybody loves kites." (*Dinesh Bahadur*)

"Kite flying is a kind of game between man and nature. Often it's an exhilarating ramble in the wind, sometimes a challenge. . . . It's a clean activity totally in harmony with nature." (*Sergei Condrashoff*)

"But there are a few mystics left, men who sow bright papers into the wind and reap a contract of glory, men who can still link the visions of childhood with the ticking of those relentless clocks. Kite fliers are such men. (*Jane Yolen*)

"I firmly believe every male in society has an unfulfilled desire to complete those kite flights he began when he was eight or nine years old." (*Edward A. Aff*)

"I never see a child's kite in the air, but it seems to pull at my heart. It is to me a 'thing of life.' I feel a twinge at my elbow, the flutter and palpitation, with which I used to let go the string of my own, as it rose in the air and towered among the clouds. My little cargo of hopes and fears ascended with it. . . . " (*William Hazlitt, 1821*)

"Of course kite flying is ridiculous, useless, frivolous. This is what kites are for, to lift the mind and the soul above the monotony of the world. We need moments to sail with the winds, to rise with the clouds, to overcome earthly inertia and find freedom.

"If you would fly a kite, forget about any other purpose or supposed value in flying. Kite flying is an art in itself, not merely a means to some other achievement. It is as much an art as creating a painting or making love." (*Christopher Raible in Kite Tales*)

"Kite flying is a little like fly fishing and sailing. It's a chance to match your wits against the elements — to get a kite up with almost no wind is a real challenge. It's also a very peaceful pastime." (*David Checkley*)

"It is a hell of a lot of fun." (*Paul E. Garber*)

"Kites are important to me basically because they have fulfilled my interest in the flight of objects heavier-than-air and are a challenge to my ingenuity in creating aerodynamic forms. Aesthetically they are an adornment of the sky and a peaceful pastime with great therapeutic value — calming the most turbulent mind." (*Robert Ingraham*)

Occasionally a kite quote comes along that actually transcends kiting and is useful to other pursuits as well. Here are two versions of one such thought:

"Don't be afraid of opposition. Remember, a kite rises against, not with the wind." (*Domina Jalbert*)

"Kites rise highest against the wind, not with it." (*Winston Churchill*)

Chapter 5

Yo-Yoing: The Fad that Keeps Coming Back

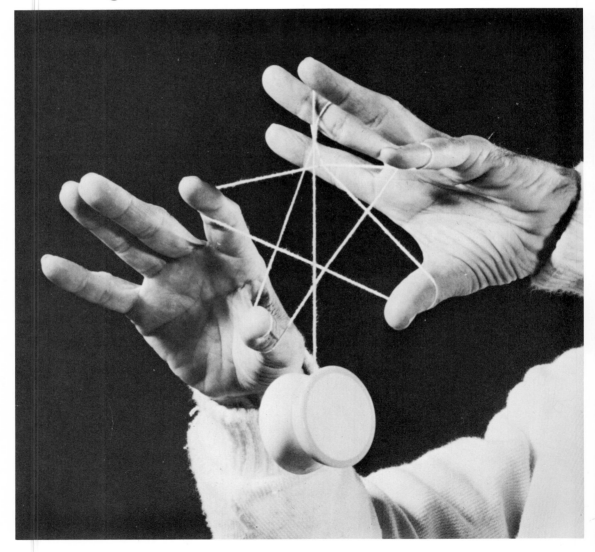

. . . A toy for the seventies—it bombed in the sixties, was the big street-corner sensation of the fifties, and has been known to sleep for centuries, only to snap back, just like a yo-yo should.

Anyway those were good times, working out in front of Carl's Spa until my yo-yo finger turned blue and I had to quit. I'm not as good as I was then but I'm still a yo-yo freak. Two years ago I did some neat tricks on a flashy electric job that lights up all red, white and blue for the International Socialists Conference at Columbia University. At the House Un-American Activities Committee in the Fall of 1968 I did a 'walk the dog' the length of the hearing room for which they sent me to bed without any supper.
—Abbie Hoffman on "Yo-Yo Power" from Esquire.

Compared to the kite, the yo-yo is a humble device inviting such comparisons as that between filet and chili, chess and checkers, and Russell Stover and O'Henry. This is not meant to degrade the yo-yo in any way but to put it in the proper scheme of things.

Indeed, much of the yo-yo appeal rests in its lack of pretension and outward humility. One sees a kite and gently smiles, thinking of lofty things; but when one looks at a yo-yo, the tendency is to break out in a broad grin as earthly images return of candy-store yo-yo contests where beanied perfect masters vied for the chance to take home a cloth Duncan "champean" patch. . .of itinerant Filipino demonstrators who were as much a sign of spring as the robin or Good Humor man and who not only seemed to know *every* yo-yo trick in the book but could carve your name and a palm tree into the side of your maple "Imperial" in a matter of seconds . . . of fingers rendered just sore enough that it was impossible to wield a pencil in school but that came back in the late afternoon for "walking the dog" and "rocking the baby in the cradle" . . . and of frustrated educators who, often for good reason, gave it the nickname "the truant's delight." To the children of the Thirties, Forties, and Fifties, few items are as truly nostalgia-laden as the yo-yo. (Given current yo-yo sales, one can predict confidently that this nostalgia will someday also accrue to the yo-yo of the Seventies.)

Another important facet of the yo-yo in America is its near universality. Sources within the industry estimate that roughly a half-billion of them have been sold since 1930, which would mean that even if half of those rolled down sewers, were thrown away by distraught parents, had their axles cut from overuse (in the case of wooden models), or were otherwise lost or destroyed that there are still a good many more yo-yos than there are people in America.

The business of universality goes beyond mere numbers. Any object that links such faded luminaries as Abbie Hoffman (who was indeed cited for contempt of Congress for "walking the dog" in an effort to entertain the committee that was investigating him) and Richard Nixon (who it will be recalled made headlines when he yo-yoed on stage at the opening of the new Grand Ole Opry in 1974) must be considered truly universal.*

Its universality is also underscored by the rich collection of metaphors and similes which have attached themselves to its name. On the negative side, there is the person who is called a yo-yo, which depending on the context means that he or she is being called a (1) garden-variety fool (general context), (2) person whose political principles change for personal gain (political context), or (3) freeloader (when used by older people who still intend this somewhat archaic meaning).† "Like a yo-yo" has become an important simile for describing rapid fluctuation in areas ranging from Wall Street and its occasional "yo-yo markets" to sports announcers who talk of "yo-yo" crowds whose moods vacillate during the course of a game.

A strong contributing factor in this universality has been the economics of yo-yoing. The price of a decent yo-yo which has gone from a dime in the twenties to a buck-plus in the seventies has kept it within the reach of the most miserly weekly allowances. But the strongest factor of all is the simple, undeniable appeal of the thing.

It is ever so simple in principle — two hemispheres on a string, joined by an axle, which fall by the force of gravity and return by momentum — yet so much more complex and enticing in practice. Perhaps the best testimonial to the yo-yo ever published are these words which appear in Frank Conroy's rich memoir of youth, *Stop Time*;

> The greatest pleasure in yo-yoing was an abstract pleasure — watching the dramatization of simple physical laws, and realizing they would never fail if a trick was done correctly. The geometric purity of it! The string wasn't just a string, it was a tool in the enactment of theorems. It was a line, an idea.
>
> I practiced yo-yo because it pleased me to do so, without the slightest application of will power. It wasn't ambition that drove me, but the nature of yo-yoing. The yo-yo represented my first organized attempt to control the outside world.

Conroy's sense of control is recalled in different words by other thoughtful adults who think back to moments of pure individualistic mastery that could be achieved at a time in life when the rest of the universe seemed to be composed of know-it-all adults, closely supervised team sports, Scout troops performing in unison, and other forces that made us parts of larger wholes we had little influence over. A youngster equipped only with a beat-up Duncan or Cheerio, a few spare strings of two-ply Egyptian cotton and a carefully collected headful of tricks was a whole unto him- or herself (boys dominated overall, but in many neighborhoods the champ to beat was a girl). There was also a small dose of rebellion locked up in the yo-yo (perhaps at the root of the Hoffman case), because the more teachers and parents called it names like "the idiot's pastime," the more important it became. Outside of the demonstrators who were in a special class of adults along with the likes of Captain Video, George "Gabby" Hayes, and Buster Crabbe, how many of our elders knew what a "spider's web" or "loop-the-loop" was, let alone had the skill to perform them? Finally, the formula included just a whiff of danger because there was always the chance of a "jawbreaker" (in which the jaw was seldom broken, only bruised) if we let power exceed control or the anarchy which ensued when the pent-up power of the yo-yo was unleashed as your string broke. Rumors were often rife during yo-yo season of plate-glass can-

---

* Like so many other "spontaneous" human gestures of the Nixon years, this too was a carefully planned and packaged act which a White House advance man told columnist Bill Anderson was an example of "political subtlety." The yo-yo, an onstage gimmick of long-standing at the Opry, was used by the President's handlers to show that he was in touch with all of those to whom Nashville is Mecca.

† Nasty references are not unusual in the world of simple pastimes as even the good name of the kite is invoked to describe intoxication ("high as a kite"), financial irresponsibility ("kiting a check"), and disrespect ("go fly a kite").

Back in the early 1960s when this picture was taken, Duncan yo-yos were selling at amazing rates. Here are 24 of the 25 Duncan demonstrators on the road in 1962, who taken together represented some 338 years of professional demonstrating. Pictured are (front row) Fortunato Anunciacion, Timothy Kelley, Bud Lutz, Charles Sears, Kenneth Filary (now Flambeau sales manager), David Emerson, Robert Baab, ''Skeeter'' Beebe, Bill Oliver, and Carl Bates; (second row) Joseph Reyes, Joe Melendez, Bob Rola, Alfredo Mendoza, Larry Lewis, Barney Akers, Gus Somera, George Somera, Robert Rule, and Wayne Lundberg; (third row) Charles Carrano, Fred Mills, Frank Young, Fred Charlton, James Flanagan, and Donald Winters. (Courtesy of Flambeau Products Corp.)

dy-store windows being destroyed in the name of the sport.

All in all, a marvelous instrument!

Yo-Yos From the Top

Historically, the yo-yo is an offshoot of one of the most ancient of toys, the spinning top, which explains why its scholarly name is the "recuperative top." However, despite the top's antiquity the yo-yo is hardly a late-blooming spin-off. It has been discovered, lost, and rediscovered at various times in various places dating back to ancient times.

There were yo-yos in ancient Greece. A vase dating from about 500 BC now on display in the Berlin Museum shows a boy playing with a yo-yo. D. W. Gould, *the* historian of the top, insists in his definitive book *The Top: Universal Toy, Enduring Pastime* that two sets of decorated, joined, ceramic discs (one at the Metropolitan Museum in New York and the other in the National Museum in Athens) are not only yo-yos but workable ones. Claims have been made by several toy historians, such as Antonia Fraser in her *A History of Toys,* that there were yo-yos in ancient China, but very little hard evidence has been presented with these claims.

While some have been quick to insist that the Greeks or Chinese were the first to yo-yo, the issue is not to be resolved so easily. The people of the Philippines have long insisted that the device was being used in their Islands in prehistoric days, when it was first employed as a weapon. This application continued for a number of centuries because one account from the 1500s tells of killer yo-yos fashioned of four-pound hunks of flint attached to twenty-foot-long thongs. The yo-yoer would wait in a tree for his prey (a human enemy or animal) to pass by and either knock it senseless, or dead, with a blow to the head or tangle the thong around its neck, bola-style, to capture it. If he missed with the first shot and was quick enough, he could retrieve the weapon for a second try.

As its use as a weapon declined over the years, it evolved into the nonhostile national pastime of the Islands, and on occasion yo-yo contests were staged as a nonviolent means of resolving disputes. To this day, young, rural Filipinos spend weeks creating their own custom yo-yos out of rare wood or a piece of buffalo horn.

Yo-yos had become popular in Europe by 1791, when Larousse's *Grand Dictionnaire* incorrectly states that it was "invented" in Paris and when a painting was painted, now hanging in the British Museum, which shows a young George IV, then the Prince of Wales, playing with one. The European origin of the yo-yo is unclear (one report, among others, was that it was brought back from China by French missionaries), but from the beginning it was a favorite diversion of the royal courts of France, Spain, and England. In addition to the George IV canvas, there is a painting in the Louvre of a French nobleman similarly engaged. One contemporary account of the French Revolution notes that several noble Frenchmen were seen yo-yoing in the carts hauling them off to the guillotine—presumably their way of exhibiting disdain for the bloody business at hand. Significantly, the early French name for the yo-yo was *émigrette* (sometimes *émigrant* or *émigré*) which dates from the emigration of French nobility with their voguish toy during that period of upheaval. Adult infatuation with the yo-yo during the nineteenth century was such that at times clubs were formed to compete with one another in the art.

The yo-yo assumed many names in Europe: *disc* in Greece; *incroyable, bandolore,* and *quiz* in England and, besides *émigrette, joujou* in France—one of several possible roots for the modern American name. Some of the yo-yos of the eighteenth and nineteenth centuries were true works of art—for instance, one from the Napoleonic Era that has survived to the present day consists of two beautifully decorated ivory discs joined by a brass axle.

The modern incarnation of the device can be traced to a wily gent with a flair for promotion named Donald F. Duncan. He was a man of diverse interests whose lists of accomplishments included having invented the reflectorized motion-picture screen, having been the first to promote the four-wheeled hydraulic brake (he was in partnership with the man who invented it), and having been one of the originators of the parking meter. The company he created to exploit the parking meter has at times controlled as much as eighty percent of the market. In 1928 Duncan was in California on business, saw his first yo-yo, and immediately concluded that it would be an easy item to promote throughout America during that decade of fads.* A small company was making yo-yos and meeting with some success in selling them locally in California. George Somera, a Filipino who went to work for Duncan in 1931, recalls, "The name of the man with the yo-yo company was Pedro Flores. The reason Duncan knew it would sell was that Flores was able to attract large crowds with just a few tricks. Mr. Duncan was a good man because he could have just taken the idea but instead offered Flores $25,000 for it which he took." He adds, "[that] was a lot of money back then."

Yo-yos had predated Duncan in North America. In 1866 two Ohio men patented a yo-yo called "an improved bandolore" and a year later a German immigrant named Charles Kirchof patented and produced a "return wheel" which met with moderate success for a few years.*

However, two things set Duncan apart from these pioneers. First, the yo-yo which he had bought from Flores contained an improvement which was as important as the invention of the yo-yo itself: instead of using string that was anchored to the yo-yo and would only permit the yo-yo to go up and down, this yo-yo's string was looped around the axle enabling it to spin (or freewheel) at the end of the string. This improvement, which originated in the Philippines, was the basis for all the major yo-yo tricks and turned a

The late Donald Duncan, the man who made the yo-yo an American rite of spring. (Courtesy of Donald F. Duncan, Jr.)

* A story that refuses to die and that has appeared in print in places ranging from The *Philadelphia Inquirer* to the *Guinness Book of World Records* is that it was toy magnate Louis Marx, not Duncan, who first saw its potential. The author has been unable to find one shred of evidence to support this Marxist revision of history.

* For what it's worth: a few years later Kirchof invented the pop gun.

The "Our Gang" comedy troupe takes a break with its trusty Duncan yo-yos back in 1932.
(Courtesy of Donald F. Duncan, Jr.)

thoughtless amusement into a skill toy of imagination and dexterity.

Duncan's second distinction was his great ability as a promoter and exploiter of the yo-yo. He got the yo-yo into production, registered the name "Yo-Yo" with the U.S. Patent Office (No. 330,914) and coined the motto, "If it's not a Duncan, it's not a Yo-Yo."* One of his early partners in all of this was William Randolph Hearst, who was convinced by Duncan that yo-yo contests were just what was needed to spur lagging newspaper sales (especially since the competitors in these contests had to sell three subscriptions to a Hearst paper before they could enter). One Duncan-Hearst thirty-day promotion in Philadelphia in 1931 was responsible for the sale of three million yo-yos.

Meanwhile, Duncan began hiring Filipinos who had yo-yoed since childhood and ex-vaudevillians with quick hands to demonstrate the device. He soon had one of his "pros" (who have always been identified as "champions" no matter how many were on the road) at work for every 100,000 Americans. Duncan's flair for publicity came into play in the early days and just about every actor, actress, home-run king, and big-city mayor got photographed playing with a Duncan. At one point Duncan got a young singer named Bing Crosby to croon promotional ditties for the toy including one long-forgotten offering which contained these far from immortal lines:

What is the dearest thing on earth, that fills my soul with joy and mirth?
    My Yo-Yo.
    What keeps my sense in a whirl, and makes me break dates with my best girl?
    My Yo-Yo.

Duncan was also quick to spot the possibilities of competition on a national scale (as opposed to the

* There are two conflicting versions of how the name yo-yo came into being. The first is that it is a derivation of the aforementioned French term joujou and the second is that it comes from a Philippine dialect word meaning "to return." This notwithstanding, until the rights to the name were lost in court (after many assaults by competitors), the Duncan organization owned it, and competitors were forced to use terms like "returning top" to describe their products.

special, localized newspaper contests), and his demonstrators were soon running contests with, as the fliers promised, "Thousands of Prizes Given Away!" One of the most coveted of these early prizes was the All-American Yo-Yo Sweater given to neighborhood champs. In short order the original Duncans (the No. 33 Genuine O-Boy Junior Duncan which sold for a nickel, the dime No. 44 Beginner's Duncan and the quarter No. 77 Original Tournament model made of "selected northern hard maple, in assorted lacquered colors") were to be found everywhere along with the only other supply you really needed, "Genuine Duncan Egyptian Fibre Yo-Yo Strings" at two for a nickel.

Nor did the initial late twenties and early thirties fad created by Duncan confine itself to the United States, but traveled through Europe, South America, and beyond, where it was sometimes less than welcome. In far-off Persia one newspaper said in an editorial on the dangers of the yo-yo, "This game, like the deadly plagues which used to come from India or Arabia, has come from Europe . . . even mothers who formerly attended to the care of children and households, now spend all their time playing yo-yo." Even in France where yo-yos had had their day earlier and where the new fad had been enough to pull the wood-turning industry out of the doldrums, there were a few spoilsports including one newspaper editorialist who termed it "a time-consuming and immoral novelty." Interestingly, the toy became extremely popular at Biarritz, Deauville, and the haunts of the rich along the Riviera.

It is also interesting to note that from Duncan's initial success there came a parade of inventors with patentable yo-yos of their own design attempting to come up with their own Duncan-like version of the success story. Such American dreamers whose names as yo-yo innovators live on only in the drawers of the U.S. Patent Office include Irving Brown of Baltimore and his hybrid yo-yo sparklers which gave off sparks as it went up and down; Patrick Amell of Honolulu and his reeded yo-yo that sounded like a harmonica; and the musical offering of one Alfonso Murafuentes

One of the many photographs which have been used over the years to get yo-yos into the paper in the spring. (Courtesy of Donald F. Duncan, Jr.)

These unconventional models are part of the extensive Festival line. (Courtesy of Union Wadding Co.)

The world's most successful yo-yo line rolls on in trucks like these which each carry some 100,000 plastic Duncans manufactured by the Flambeau Products Corp. (Courtesy of Flambeau Products Corp.)

whose instrument could be tuned in different keys. However, one is hard pressed to come up with a more imaginative variation than the edible yo-yo invented by Hubert Meyers of Toledo which could be made of "paraffin gum, candy or other confection." And the quest goes on: a few years ago a hollow yo-yo was marketed that could be filled with ice and liquid for making martinis. Yet with all of this, it would appear that the person with the best chance of coming up with something on the order of the original Duncan is son Donald F. Duncan, Jr., who in 1974 patented a yo-yo that he reports will spin two or three times as long as any existing yo-yo (it gets its extra spin by having most of its weight on the outer edge of the yo-yo body). Duncan, who is not in the yo-yo business anymore, is considering marketing this "Cadillac of yo-yos" in the near future.

Meanwhile, the initial yo-yo fad that Duncan had touched off kept going through the Depression with especially good years in 1935 and 1938. They held onto their popularity during the war years, although sales were curtailed by shortages, and 1946 was another boom year. It was also the year in which the company started a large plant in Luck, Wisconsin, capable of turning out tens of thousands of maple yo-yos a day. Things would be busy at the Luck plant because the years between 1950 and 1962 were to be the best of times for the yo-yo business. At times during the 1950s the factory was turning out 60,000 of them a day, and at times there were fifty or more Duncan demonstrators deployed across America. It was a time for major contests—in one which attracted entrants from thirty-five nations a man named Nemo Concepcion broke the final tie by flipping his yo-yo high into the air and catching it in his inside coat pocket. In one astounding two-month period in Nashville, to cite one of many such statistics, more yo-yos (350,000) were sold than there were people (320,000), and that total just includes Duncan models.

The Duncan Imperial (the postwar equivalent of the old No. 77) was, of course, the classic workhorse of the period but there were other brands and other

Two of the nation's most famous yo-yo demonstrators. Barney Akers is shown instructing a youngster and "Skeeter" Beebe is captured doing an intricate string trick. (Courtesy of Flambeau Products Corp.)

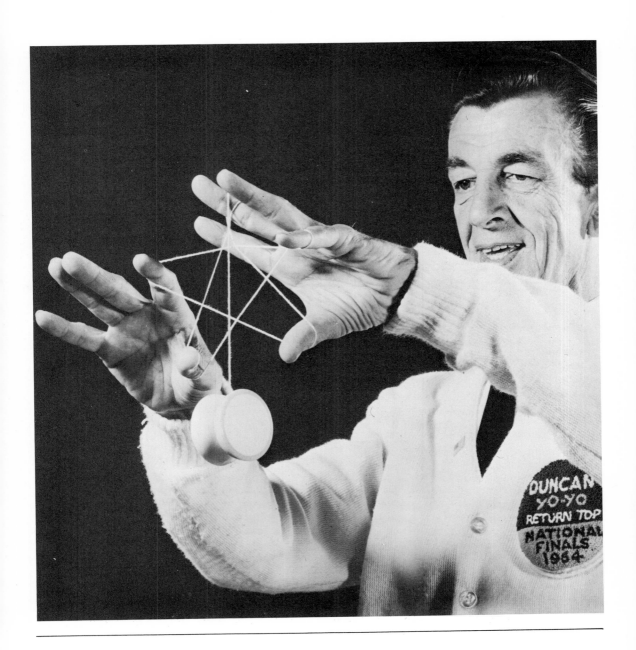

models; Cheerios, Russells, Chicos, Royal Tops, Goody Filipino Twirlers, and Dell Big "D"'s, to name just a few trade-marks; yo-yos covered in suede, emblazoned with the red-and-white Coca-Cola logo, and designated the official Mickey Mouse Club top; a Gargantuan hand-rubbed walnut "executive" Duncan which could be ordered with a sterling monogram; the rhinestone-studded "Black Beauty," and more.

There was also the fabled mystery yo-yo of the period, which came to light in 1955 in, of all places, a meeting of the Senate Internal Security Subcommittee looking into the financial affairs of Senator Joseph McCarthy of Wisconsin. A witness, whose wife had been a heavy McCarthy contributor, said that he had invented "a stringless yo-yo," but under further questioning from fascinated members of the panel he refused to tell how it would work or when he planned to market it. For the adult world the incident produced a quickly forgotten moment of levity in an era when politics were not very funny, but to thousands of kids the "stringless yo-yo" was fodder for months of speculation and talk. As of this writing, there has still been no further news of this mystery device.

In 1962 yo-yoing reached a new peak for the Duncan company, which by then was commanding ninety percent of the market. In that year it produced a record twenty-five million of them which translated into sales of $6.8 million, up from $1.7 million in 1961. What's more, Donald F. Duncan, Jr., who had taken over the company reins in 1958, estimates that even at that volume it was supplying only about *half the demand*. One major aid in creating the boom was television advertising which, as we shall soon see, was effective to a fault.

Save for an occasional minor boomlet here and there, the rest of the 1960s were as bad for the yo-yo as the years leading up to the crest of 1962 had been good for them. Part of the problem was the inexplicable ebb and flow of popular taste. Hula hoops, skateboards, and Frisbees were consuming the loose change that had once gone to buy a yo-yo. Another factor was the 1962 boom itself. Let Donald Duncan, Jr., explain:

We created an unbelievable demand for yo-yos . . . We were not ready for it. For years it was hard to get sales and then suddenly we couldn't fill orders. And unfilled orders were canceled after a few weeks because of the nature of the product. Our big mistake was in overextending ourselves to increase production because with growth, more capital is needed; and without outside capital you begin to borrow—first on the plant, then on accounts receivable. Our sudden unplanned spurt awakened our competitors to challenge again our trademark Yo-Yo, because they could see that if they could call their product a Yo-Yo instead of a Royal Top, or Dell Big "D" or Whirl-A-Gig, they could also sell more.

Besides the dangerous mix of undercapitalization and boom, there were other problems: high air freight bills to move yo-yos from Luck; a new product, called the "Bang-A-Ball," which was a major failure, and the need to pay premium prices to get hard maple needed for the yo-yos.* Each problem cost money—over $200,000 alone in the unsuccessful attempt to defend the trademark—and the company was getting into deeper and deeper trouble. As things got worse, the old tricks (booklets explaining tricks, demonstrators, more contests) were tried along with new ones (multicolored models like the Mardi Gras, which broke with the two-tone tradition, a whistling "Sonic Satellite" model), but to no avail.

In early 1965, the string broke for the Duncan Co., and it declared bankruptcy with assets of $750,000 and liabilities of over a million. Outside of the town of Luck, Wisconsin, the self-proclaimed Yo-Yo Capital of the World, and the dwindling corps of demonstrators, the demise was little noticed.

At this point it looked like the yo-yo might have gone into a sleep that it would never come out of, but two fortunate developments prevented this. First, a Duncan vice-president named Wilfred H. Schlee with strong yo-yoing ties (his father had introduced Ameri-

---

* Even the wood itself became part of the problem as it took as long as six months to get it properly dried for the lathes. This not only meant that a lot of money got tied up in wood, but that there could be little flexibility for meeting sudden increases in demand.

can style yo-yos in Canada and England in the twenties, and he had been in charge of the Cheerio yo-yo line before it was bought out by Duncan in 1954) created a small yo-yo company of his own before the demise of Duncan called Festival Products Inc. Second, after some hunting for an interested party, the Duncan family sold the name and its good will to the Flambeau Plastics Corp. of Baraboo, Wisconsin, in 1968. Flambeau with its line of plastic Duncans, and Festival, which was made part of the Union Wadding Co. of Pawtucket, R.I., in 1966 were soon to provide the raw material for the Great Yo-Yo Revival of the seventies. As before, the Duncan line would be the dominant one, but Festival would fill a strong second place.

Although there were some good signs before the big comeback year of 1971—for one, a tremendous revival in the fall of 1970 in Philadelphia, where Flambeau conducted a campaign to sell $80,000 worth of yo-yos and ended up netting $500,000—it was not until April 19, 1971, there could be no questioning the fact that the yo-yo had returned. On that day the trade publication *Toy and Hobby World* published its weekly "Toy Hit Parade," which read as follows:

> Kenner's SSP Racers
> Kites, all makes
> Parker's Nerf Ball
> Wham-O's Frisbees
> Play Balls, all makes
> Silly Putty's Silly Putty
> Kenner's Screecher
> Flambeau's Yo-Yos
> Topper's Dawn Dolls and Clothes
> Athol's Fidget
> "Clackers," all makes
> Mattel's Rock Flowers*

The toy world was quickly abuzz with the prediction that yo-yo-wise the seventies would be another fifties and shortly the news media, which had paid scant attention to the demise of the original Duncan company, was treating its return as big news (who says the media only reports bad news?). "It's the year of the Yo-Yo. The biggest in history," screamed the normally restrained *Christian Science Monitor* in the lead to an article on the revival, and *Sports Illustrated* took editorial time out from major sports to wax poetic about the turn in public taste. Such notices continue to come in as the boom continues.* In early 1975, for instance, *Newsweek* announced somewhat belatedly that the yo-yo fad had returned in full bloom. However, as late 1974 and early 1975 was a particularly good time for yo-yo sales (running about ten percent above projection) *Newsweek* had apparently waited for a boom on top of a boom before sticking its neck out on the issue. (As 1974-75 was a period of recession, this would seem to bolster the old Depression Era contention that yo-yos do well in hard economic times. No less a personage than Flambeau's comptroller, William Reck, says, "In relation to the economic statistics of the country, we do know that when the economy is on the decline, sales increase.")

Moreover, the seventies revival was more than a carbon copy of the fifties golden age. For one, yo-yos have become a big thing on campus this time around, with some colleges actually getting involved in intercollegiate yo-yo competition. A number of explanations have been tendered for this—ranging from the fact that the era of protest is over and it is time again for less important things, to the nostalgia boom—but one quite simple reason seems to dominate: the collegians of the 1970s were growing up in the yo-yo-bleak 1960s and were catching up on something that they missed.

---

* You will note that the list includes both the yo-yo and the Frisbee in eighth and fourth places respectively. This is significant because the conventional wisdom in the toy industry in the sixties was that only one of these descendants of the top could be popular at one time.

* Amid all the hoopla of the revival, on May 15, 1971, to be precise, there was one sad note as the greatest force in modern yo-yoing died at the age of 71 in Los Angeles. Donald F. Duncan, Sr., had lived long enough, however, to see yo-yos with the Duncan name return to the American scene.

The new college infatuation is producing its share of confusion, fun, and derring-do. As many as a half-dozen schools—ranging from giant Ohio State to tiny Antioch—have proclaimed themselves "national champion" at the same time, top demonstrators are now big on the campus lecture circuit vying for podium space with Ralph Nader and Watergate alumni, and the push is on to set new records and accomplish big stunts. For instance, on February 4, 1973, a group of ten Massachusetts Institute of Technology students under the direction of Dr. James H. Williams, an assistant professor of mechanical engineering, created what is unquestionably the world's biggest yo-yo. The yo-yo itself was made of two twenty-six-inch bicycle wheels connected to a steel shaft and kept going by a mechanical finger (an aluminum beam controlled by a 1.5 horsepower motor) attached to its braided nylon string from the roof of a twenty-one-story building. It worked, and the technically minded students determined that when the yo-yo hit bottom on each spin it was whizzing at an amazing 1000 rpm. and that the rims of its wheels were rolling at eighty miles an hour.

By 1975 there seemed to be nothing but bright horizons ahead for yo-yos, which were consistently selling in numbers high above the twenty-five-million mark set in 1961. There were fifteen Duncan demonstrators on the road, and it was hard to find a nook or cranny of the nation where Duncans, Festivals, and lesser brands were not for sale on a year-round basis.

Given this and the up-and-down history of the yo-yo, one question begs to be asked: Who are these people now in charge of the industry and how can they prevent another 1965?

For one thing, the General Motors and Ford of yo-yoing are both diversified companies. Flambeau makes all sorts of plastic goods in three factories, only one of which is dominated by the yo-yo, and Union Wadding, which controls Festival, makes wadding, batting, Christmas tree ornaments, and other toys. This stands in vivid contrast to the old Duncan operation, which in its total dependence on yo-yos was un-

able to ride hard times by relying on other products for profits.

Festival is willing to ride up and down with the yo-yo as its popularity crests and recedes, apparently figuring that if the yo-yo has a bad year it can be carried by a good year in wadding or whatever. This company also counts on other interests and fads to help sell yo-yos, such as its hockey-puck-shaped yo-yos bearing the emblems of the various NHL teams.

However, the most important single factor in today's yo-yo world is the determined marketing plan which is proving to be so successful for the leader, which sold eighteen million yo-yos in 1975 alone. Borrowing the best from the old Duncan operation and adding elements of its own to keep the boom on an even keel (rather than let a big year come along followed by a fallow one), Flambeau's plan of attack is keyed to eight-week-long saturation promotions in local markets staged every three years on a staggered basis, with the result that local booms are going on all the time. The way Flambeau has it figured, if you go all out in, say, the Cincinnati area in the fall of 1974 and sell a couple million yo-yos (as was actually done), it will take until the fall of 1977 before the same controlled frenzy can be produced again. It is further reasoned that in between these locust-like returns that remembrance of things past and anticipation of the future will produce a fairly steady market for yo-yos in the area.

Each of these eight-week saturations combines a variety of promotional techniques: TV spots on local kids' shows, posters, publicity drives to get yo-yos into the news, ads, and the like. But the key to each promotion is the demonstrators who sweep into the area for the eight weeks and "follow the sun" in accordance with the marketing plan, which may put a man in Minneapolis in September-October, Miami before Christmas, Phoenix after Christmas, and so forth. Quoting from the "Promotion Manual" I was given on a visit to Duncan headquarters in Wisconsin, here is how the demonstrators work an area:

Our Duncan champions . . . have a large contest poster,

60″ x 40″ announcing contest locations and times that they place in stores. They request contest locations from the distributors in a city. They then "case" the town to determine the best way of working the city. They will start contests after school hours in the afternoon, working 3 or 4 contests. On Saturday they will work from 8 to 12 contests, depending on how close they are together. Where there are no "blue laws" they will also work Sunday. . . . They try and concentrate on a certain area of town until it is going well, and then move to another section. The usual technique is to post a sign stating that a contest will be held at, let's say, Monday at 4:00 PM. This is done a week to ten days prior to the date the champion will award patches. These winners are eligible for city or area contests. A demonstrator can effectively work up to a million people, and can do a fair job up to a million and a half people. . . .*

As the "Manual" shows so clearly, the demonstrators are still critical linch-pins of the industry and worthy of some attention before moving on to the critical how-to portion of this presentation.

The Pros

"Folk hero" is not a term to be bandied about with abandon, but it would take a cold heart indeed to bar the yo-yo pro from that American folk Olympus which includes the lumberjack, cowboy, soda jerk, and Fuller Brush man.

Consider the evidence. He (and the term is used advisedly because, unfortunately, there has never been a female Duncan demonstrator or freelance yo-yo pro) has been a dispenser of knowledge, athletic prowess, and highly coveted prizes for some fifty years now. He alone can bestow neighborhood royalty with his fuzzy championship arm patches and tinny little pins which always seem larger than they really are. Unlike lesser demonstrators — the Vegamatic man for one — he is a true athlete in his

own right often capable of such stringed sorcery as the "Atom Bomb," "Eiffel Tower," and "Apollo," which perhaps only a dozen other humans have ever mastered.

What is more, they are a breed apart, yet a breed that encompasses so many types. . . . There is the venerable Barney Akers who has been at it for more than forty-five years, having started just out of high school when his uncle, Donald Duncan, got him hooked. Over the years Akers has mastered nearly a hundred tricks (some of which are of his own invention), demonstrated as far away as Hong Kong and Australia, and is still on the road — in fact, a check with Flambeau HQ on the day this was written revealed that the tireless Akers was on his way to Syracuse to mount a promotion. . . . Prodigies like Don Cutright, who jumped right out of the city championship in Detroit in 1955 onto the Duncan team, and Tom McCoy, still in his twenties, who can nonetheless use a yo-yo to pluck a quarter from the back of a child's ear without mussing said child's hair and can already recall his share of fluke yo-yo mishaps including an errant "Shoot the Moon" that cracked his nose and a "Ferris Wheel" that broke his glasses . . . Lupe Villarreal, the Somera cousins, Elfredo Mendoza and the other Philippine wizards past and present . . . master tricksters like ex-prizefighter Tom Hatcher whose mastery includes being able to keep two yo-yos going while lying on his back . . .

. . . And the now-retired man whom yo-yoing will never forget — Irwin "Skeeter" Beebe, whose mix of tricks, flamboyant style, past experiences, and ability to generate publicity set him apart as the most colorful of a colorful crowd. Before he got into yo-yos he had been a singing waiter, a vocalist with Jack Teagarden's band, and Ernest Hemingway's valet. He once recalled in an interview that Hemingway had slugged him in the mouth for dropping a pet fishing reel overboard on a fishing trip and was then near tears for what he had done. During World War II he had learned to yo-yo and after the War took to using the device as an adjunct to his act as a nightclub singer. One fateful night in Chicago Duncan himself

* The rest of the manual is as precise as this portion and even includes a series of charts and maps worthy of a West Point class in tactics which show how a city is taken, working from the center to the outermost suburbs.

took in the act and immediately offered him a job as a demonstrator, which he took. Before his long career was over he had yo-yoed with Presidents (he told an interviewer in 1971 that John F. Kennedy was good, but that LBJ could just barely get it to go up and down), celebrities galore, and about five million kids. What's more, he seemed to be able to generate news wherever he went. He was once banned from a Shreveport, Louisiana, television station when he showed up with an integrated group of children for a yo-yo contest he was scheduled to run on the air. New York City gave him a commendation for cooling tensions with yo-yo demonstrations during a particularly uneasy period in Harlem. But perhaps the most interesting story attached to his career was an intensely personal one. It began when a newspaper in his native southern New Jersey did a feature story on him which led to his reunion with his son and daughter after a twenty-four-year separation. Beebe's first wife had died when his two children were infants. Shortly thereafter in order to make some money he went on the road for a paint company as a salesman and left the children with a relative. He returned and they had moved on without leaving a forwarding address and contact was broken. Years later his daughter, by now married and living in Florida with children of her own, gave her father's picture to a friend in Millville, New Jersey, on the off chance that she might someday run into him if he returned to that part of the state. The friend saw the picture and reunion followed.

Aside from Beebe and the other Duncan men past and present, there are the freelance pros. There is Tom Parks, now a teacher in Massapequa, Long Island, who turned pro at thirteen for the old Cheerio company, who still puts on pro exhibitions on occasion and who possesses what may well be the world's top yo-yo collection—over three hundred different models. Bob Rule, the self-proclaimed "Mr. Yo-Yo," does business using his yo-yo for promotional attractions (trade fairs, sales meetings, store openings, and the like) as well as at state fairs and during half-time breaks at athletic events. He is also the author of the "Yo-Yo Secrets" booklet offered for sale by Festival on the back of their yo-yo packages.* And there is Everett (Bunny) Martin of Belton, Texas, who left his post as a college administrator in 1972 to put on yo-yo shows for audiences looking for "good, clean fun." Martin may well be the top-paid pro in America today as he told The National Observer that he would take in $40,000 in 1975 (compared with the $18,000-$20,000 that Duncan demonstrators make). One of Martin's show-stoppers is to light a match clenched in another person's teeth with a yo-yo covered with sandpaper.

In a different class from these gentlemen but worthy of mention are the handful of itinerant yo-yo men who work bars, pool halls, and amusement arcades either as demonstrators who pass the hat after their impromptu show is over or as hustlers who involve others in wagered contests they can't hope to win.

For the true pros, however, there seems to be something about it which gets in the blood—the kind of thing that made the Duncan pros keep working (some as far away as South America) during the dark seasons after the Duncan company went under and that made them so eager to return when Flambeau started putting the pieces together again. A good case in point are the Somera cousins, Gus and George, who have put in a collective total of more than eighty years of demonstrating. Gus, who began in the late 1920s, is still working and brags, "I know the country like a service station attendant knows a city." George is retired, but not completely. When I tried to call Gus at his motel during a big 1975 campaign in New Jersey, I got George instead. I told him I'd been led to believe that he had retired, and he replied, "That's true, but I still love it and still go on the road with Gus for a few weeks each year." The Someras have lost count of the number of demonstrations they've staged

* Rule, by the way, comes from Detroit, where he was once city champ. For some reason this city has for a number of years been a top yo-yo town that has produced more than its share of pros. Besides Rule and the aforementioned Cutright, there is Ken Filary, who is now director of sales for the Duncan line, but before that was a top demonstrator who put on close to 20,000 demonstrations in the field.

Yo-yo photos. (Courtesy of Union Wadding Co. and Flambeau Products Corp.)

and the millions of kids they've wowed. "Figure it out yourself," says George, "up to ten demonstrations a day apiece, six days a week for about forty years apiece—it's a lot."

George Somera is one of those who still remembers Duncan and the early days. During 1933 he and Duncan swept through Europe on a grand demonstration and promotion tour, and they became good friends at that point. He recalls that for all of Duncan's promotional zeal he was an easygoing, friendly man who never once got mad at any of his champions for any reason.

Yo-Yo Fundamentals

The first order of business is selecting a yo-yo. In this regard you should not overlook attics, basements, footlockers, and closet bottoms, as great numbers of them have been put away and forgotten in such places. Your reward for such a hunt may not only be a serviceable yo-yo but a classic which is now a collector's item, such as one of the earliest Duncans, a short-lived novelty yo-yo like the Kozmic Electric Yo-Yo which lit up when it spun, or a sterling-silver-clad offering by Gorham which sold up until a few years ago for $10.

If the yo-yo you find was tucked away prior to the demise of the original Duncan company, the odds are good that it will be wooden and probably a pretty good yo-yo, especially if it is one of the old "Imperials" with its bright two-tone spray job. (Beware, however, if your find is a wooden black-and-red Duncan "Jr.," as this model had an anchored string which will not allow it to sleep.)

However, too much has been made of the fact that the older yo-yos were made of wood and most of the newer ones are of plastic. For one thing, the wooden axles went pretty fast and were known to burn through inside a month in the hands of a determined yo-yoer. They are no match for the modern models with their metal axles that can take all the friction you could ever give them. And while a wood yo-yo in fine condition is a pleasure to use, one that has seen a lot of former glory may be just enough off-balance to prevent you from doing some of the better tricks.

Still, there are those whose sense of the past dictates wood, and for this group there are the Festival Zapper and Big Zapper models with the latter being the closest to the old Duncan wood Imperial.

You will also find that there is a broad variety of plastic yo-yos on the market today. Anchored string models like the Duncan Junior should not be considered by anyone who wants more than a yo-yo that simply goes up and down. So too, there are a number of gimmick yo-yos that come in handy for special effects but are hardly suited for workhorse application. Yo-yos in this category would include the Festival Screamer with its built-in whistle and the Duncan battery-operated Satellite, which lights up when in use. But even by eliminating these types, you are still faced with the Tournament, Imperial, Butterfly, Gold Award, Velvet, and Professional from Duncan; and the Dragonfly, All-Star Champion, and Be-a-Sport line from Festival. (To further confuse, Festival is big on such things as Joe Namath Yo-Yos, National Hockey League "Puck" Yo-Yos with team emblems on them, Walt Disney character models, and more, but in most cases these are just embellished versions of their regular line.)

A real problem facing the modern yo-yo consumer is that both companies are big users of that miracle of modern packaging known as the blister-pack (i.e., they are enclosed in a plastic bubble so well riveted to a piece of stiff cardboard that one normally has to destroy the package to open it) which makes it impossible to "try on" a yo-yo before buying it. This factor and the fact that *Consumer's Report* has yet to enter the realm of the returning top, means one is forced to rely on those old standbys trial and error and word of mouth, in selecting a yo-yo. For what it is worth, the author feels it is hard to go wrong with the Festival All-Star Champion, new Duncan Imperial or, his favorite, the Duncan top-of-the-line Professional, a rugged hunk of Tenite acetate with a steel axle, which at $2 a throw makes it the Rolls-Royce of yo-yos.

Once your selection has been made, there are some preliminary bits of information and instruction

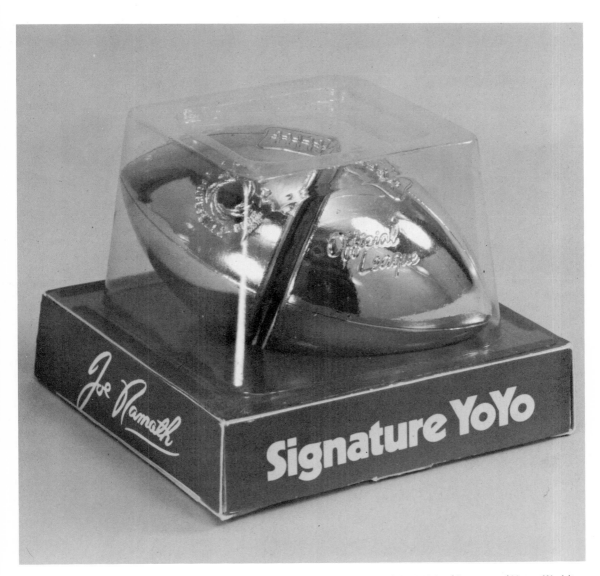

A modern prestige yo-yo sure to be worth a small fortune at the flea markets of the 1990s. (Courtesy of Union Wadding Co.)

The top-of-line Duncan Pro. (Courtesy of Flambeau Products Corp.)

that are important, to wit:

The String. The length of the string should depend on your height. The tried-and-true method of getting the proper length is to lay the yo-yo on the ground between your feet and cut the string at your waistline or just above it (but not more than a few inches). Tie a small loop at the end of the string and make a slipknot by pulling part of the long end of the string through the loop.

Extra Performance. Strings last longer and yo-yos spin longer with the application of a little string wax. A dab of candle wax or the special Duncan wax sold in toy and novelty shops should be rubbed sparingly along the top six to eight inches of the string. Be careful as too much wax will cause the yo-yo to slip.

Major Precaution. The only truly delicate element of the instrument is its axle. Countlesss thousands have been permanently ruined by being scratched by someone with a knife or pair of scissors trying to remove a broken string or cut a knot. The small burr produced by the scratch acts like a buzzsaw against new strings, and they seldom last for more than a few spins. The instrument best suited to such surgery is a dull crochet needle.

Unwinding. An overtwisted string won't spin. Watch for this and let out the yo-yo and let it untwist by its own weight as often as necessary.

Cleanliness. For inexplicable reasons, a dirty string tends to inhibit the performance of a yo-yo, and it is a good idea to change it when it turns gray.

Now you are ready to begin. Place the slipknot around the first joint of the middle finger. Palm upward and the string leading off from the top, flip the yo-yo over the top of the finger. When it comes to the end of the string, a slight jerk will bring it back to your hand, which you should turn over to catch the yo-yo.

Once you have gotten a feel for the up-and-down movement of the yo-yo, the next item on the agenda is to get it to "spin," or "sleep." This time flick the yo-yo rather vigorously at arm's length and don't move at all, and it should spin at the end of the string. After it has spun for a moment, give it a jerk and it should come back. As sleeping is the key to most other tricks, you will want to learn to do this well, adding to the number of seconds you can get it to spin while still being able to get it to return. If it does not sleep, the odds are either that you are not flicking it hard enough or the string is too tight at the yo-yo end, which can be corrected by letting it unwind.

If you can get the yo-yo to sleep for four or five seconds, you are getting the knack of it. Even the most difficult tricks only require a six- to eight-second spin. Expert Bob Rule has come up with a rule of thumb with which to judge yourself: two to four seconds is a good beginning spin, five to ten seconds puts you in the intermediate class, anything over ten is truly good, and fifteen is excellent. The reputed world's record spin is over 25 seconds.

Despite the apparent ease with which experts get their yo-yos to spin for long periods of time, they are putting considerable wrist power into their flicks, and the key to getting long spins is to build more and more power into your flick without losing control.

With a basic mastery of sleeping, you are ready for a basic repertoire of tricks.

Walking the Dog. Simply, getting a good spin and letting it roll along the ground for a short distance before bringing it back. Your key to success here lies in not letting any slack get in your string while the yo-yo is walking.

The Buzz Saw. A variation on walking the dog in which the yo-yo walks across a piece of newspaper, which produces a buzzing sound.

The Forward Pass. Drop your yo-yo hand to your side, swing it back just a little, and then throw it out fast, letting go of the yo-yo at the same time. The yo-yo will go straight out and you open your hand to catch it on its return.

Over the Falls. Start with a forward pass, but rather than catching the yo-yo on its return bend your hand to allow the yo-yo to drop down by your feet. When it comes to the end of the string, bring it back up into your hand.

Around the World. Again, start with a forward pass but this time keep your arm moving upward to get the yo-yo to sleep out in front of you. The motion of your arm will put the yo-yo in full circular orbit behind you. As it comes back into view at about knee-level give it a tug to bring it back to your open hand. Being able to send the yo-yo out for more than one orbit before getting it back in hand is one mark of an expert.

Caution: This trick requires plenty of room and is best practiced outdoors.

The Break Away. Put your yo-yo arm up in the position used to make a muscle and then snap the yo-yo down and sideways across the front of your body. What happens next is described most enthusiastically in the old Duncan "Tricks" booklet; "When the yo-yo reaches the end of the string, it'll hang in the air for a moment, defying the law of gravity before returning to your hand!"

The Creeper. This is done by first throwing the yo-yo into a fast spin and then letting it creep across the floor as you lower your yo-yo hand almost to the floor. Give it a sharp jerk when it reaches the end of the string, and it should come right back along the floor into your hand.

Loop-the-Loop. Start with a forward pass, but instead of catching it on its return, snap your wrist sharply to cause it to shoot out in front of you again. With a little practice this can be repeated many times without stopping.

Three-Leaf Clover. A variant loop-the-loop in which the first pass is high, the second goes straight out in front of you, and the third is low.

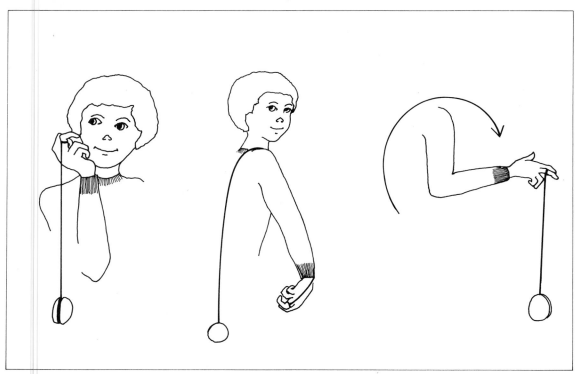

"Around the Corner."

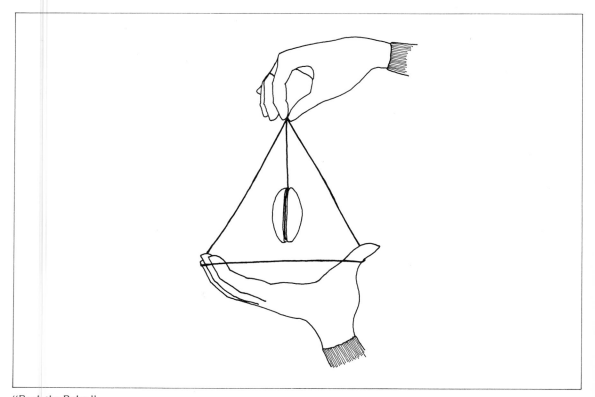

"Rock the Baby."

Around the Corner. Get a fast spin going and while it is spinning move your hand up and work the yo-yo around behind your arm so that it is literally spinning over your shoulder. Now start bending your arm so that the string hangs over it and with your hand jerk the string about three or four inches from the yo-yo which should make it come up the string, over your arm, down to the end of the string, and finally up into your waiting hand.

Rock-the-Baby. A classic that requires practice. First, throw a spinner. Begin forming a triangle of string by making its base by looping the string around your left thumb and pinkie about half way down the string. This forms the base of the triangle. Complete the triangle by grabbing the string about four inches up from the yo-yo. Now rock the yo-yo back and forth within the triangle. Bring the yo-yo back to your hand by flicking it out with your right hand and letting it come back to you.

Before attempting this fancy stringwork, it is a good idea to practice with a dead yo-yo that is not spinning.

Bite the Dog. Yo-Yoing's most risqué offering. You must be wearing slacks to try this. Standing with your legs about two feet apart, use some force to arc the yo-yo through your legs, hitting yourself squarely in the buttocks. With practice the yo-yo will stop dead, giving the illusion that you have captured it with your body in an amazing display of sphincter dexterity. But what has really happened is that the fast-spinning yo-yo has literally grabbed the fabric of your pants, jamming just enough fabric into the space between the two hemispheres of the yo-yo to make it stick. As the yo-yo stops when it makes its grab, it will not return to you but you give the trick a logical ending by spreading your legs another inch or two which stretches the fabric enough to let the yo-yo drop. (Some experimenting is in order here because some fabrics "bite" better than others.)

The Rocket. A good way to end your act. Get the yo-yo spinning and, while it is, quickly slip the string off your finger, give it a sudden jerk, and stand back. On its own the yo-yo will go up in the air, and you can casually field it as if it were a pop fly.

There are more tricks—the Sleeping Beauty, Eating Spaghetti, Lindy Loop, Taffy Pull, Y-is-for-Yo-Yo, Rattlesnake, Elephant's Trunk, Double or Nothing, Skin the Cat, Man on the Flying Trapeze, the Machine Gun, and Crazy Cradle, just to name some—but we must put some logical limit on the number described here. Besides, it is not as if they cannot be learned elsewhere—from kids, Duncan demonstrators, or the proper adults who begin recalling the most esoteric routines when handed a yo-yo.

Finally, now that you are armed with a basic set of tricks, you may want to engage in a yo-yo contest. These events take a number of forms, but here are the rules for the most common contest which was created by Duncan some years back and has been staged in thousands of playgrounds to determine who is champ of the neighborhood.

Rules
Each contestant will do any ten different tricks.
    1. If the performer misses on the first try, he is allowed a second chance for each trick.
    2. Each contestant takes a turn doing a trick. This continues until everyone has completed ten tricks.
    3. If the string breaks during a trick, a second chance is allowed the contestant without penalty.
    4. Each trick must end with the yo-yo back in the player's hand and the string wound up in the yo-yo.

Scoring
    1. Ten points given when trick is done on first try.
    2. Five points given when trick is done on second try.
    3. One hundred points is a perfect contest score.
    4. Two tries allowed each contestant per trick.
    5. In the event of a tie, the winner will be the one who can loop-the-loop the greatest number of times.

Chapter 6

The Eternal Orb

. . . A rolling stone that has gathered a lot

And above all, the game of marbles is like any other sport. In order to become a champion, you can't miss a day of practice. And this doesn't mean just shooting at the marbles—it means practicing your backspin, working on snoogers, getting your aim, and keeping your lag work going.
—Shirley "Windy" Allen, Boy's National Champion for 1951, from his manual "The Game of Marbles."

It's enough to drive my mother crazy. There's this click, click, click in the house all the time. You ought to see our living room carpet. Covered with marbles it is.
—Alan Smith, 30, British marbles champion and son of Len Smith, founder of the Toucan Terribles

Nobody has the vaguest idea when or where the first marble was rolled across the surface of the earth in the pursuit of sport, but it was certainly very early. Small stones, deliberately chipped and rounded, have been unearthed at Stone Age digs on three continents, and the marbles of ancient Egypt, Rome, and Greece are on view today in such august places as the British Museum and at the Metropolitan in New York. Chinese marbles date back over 5,000 years, Aztec ruins have yielded little troves of them, and in North America they were found in the mounds left by the ancient Mound Builders.

In fact, from the Stone Age forward they seemed to show up everywhere. They are mentioned in Shakespeare's plays, are depicted in Breughel's paintings, and are mentioned by such lofty thinkers as Ovid and Cato (the latter warning people to shun dice and take up marbles). Early white settlers in North America found the Indians playing marble games not too much unlike those played in England, and one authority has suggested they were played by Moses when he was a child in the Pharaoh's palace. Marbles were literally carried by the Roman legions, which left marble games all over Europe as part of their legacy.

Marbles have also worked their way into great works of fiction going all the way back to Homer's time. *The Oxford Classical Dictionary* says that the suitors of Penelope, Queen of Ithaca and wife of Odysseus, played marbles for her hand when they thought her husband was dead. Shakespeare mentions them on several occasions in his writing, and they show up in John Donne's fourth *Satire* and in the writings of Richard Addison and of Rabelais. In 1835 Alfred de Vigny wrote an early murder mystery entitled *The Military Necessity*, in which the murder weapon was loaded with a large marble. In Charles Dickens' *Pickwick Papers* Mr. Serjeant Buzfuz points out in defense of Mr. Pickwick in court, "His 'alley tors' and his 'commoneys' are alike neglected; he forgets the long familiar cry of 'knuckle down.' ''* Mark Twain's *Tom Sawyer*, who counted wealth in marbles, tadpoles, and such, picked up no less than a dozen of the former (including a fine white alley) as part of the loot he earned for letting others whitewash Aunt Polly's fence.

While most of the marble players in literature are, of course, children, the adult world is also well represented. In a less-popular novel than his famous *Robinson Crusoe*, Daniel Defoe describes the passion of one of his characters as such:

> Marbles, which he used to call children playing at bowls, yielded him a mighty diversion, and he was so dexterous an artist at shooting that little alabaster globe from between the end of his forefinger and knuckle of his thumb that he seldom missed hitting plumb, as the boys called it, the marble aimed at, though at a distance of two or three yards.

While many peoples have embraced the marble as a pastime, a few have turned it into a passion. The British are a case in point. Here marbles have been a common pub game since there were pubs and have reached such heights as a university fad that has centuries-old rules which are on the books at both Oxford and Cambridge stating where they can and cannot be played. There is even an old poem which tells of a boy who graduated from Eton who was, "A dunce at syntax / But a dab at taws." They even fit into the religious life, as years ago the British clergy saw in marbles a quiet pastime suited to reverent times and prescribed them as a proper Lenten game for children and adults. To this day, Good Friday is still considered marbles day in the British Isles.

As marbles were very popular at the time colonists were leaving England for America, the British passion arrived undiluted in the New World, where it quickly became a diversion for children as well as adults.* George Washington, Thomas Jefferson, and John Adams were all marble players. *The National Geographic Society* recently reported that Abraham Lincoln played while in the White House (although it was unable to find where his ring was—perhaps it was covered over by Harry Truman's famous horseshoe pitching pit), and Vice President Andrew Johnson was playing marbles with his son when told that Lincoln had been shot. Not all of the famous players were content just to play at marbles. As Fred Ferretti reports in his *The Great American Marble Book*, "the most notable marble collector in our history was Thomas Jefferson, who not only was an avid player but often exhibited his finest marbles to guests."

Of course, millions of lesser Americans have been taken with marbles. In earlier times they were often played at large gatherings; for instance, a nineteenth-century minister writes about 400 members of his flock gathering for a peaceful but mammoth marbles tournament. Popular interest in marbles was such as early as 1829 that a book published that year, *The Boy's Own Book*, contains an extensive section rating the various marbles on the market at the time, most of which were then being imported. The ratings ranged from the worst (clay marbles imported from Holland) to the best ("blood alleys" made of pink marble with dark red veins).

Despite their avid interest, it took awhile before Americans manufactured their own in any significant quantity, but when they did they revolutionized the industry by making them a mass production item. Romantic notions about hand craftsmanship notwithstanding, this was a boon to the sport because it significantly reduced the per-bag cost of marbles and continues to insure that a youngster can fill his pocket

---

* Translation: "alley tors" are marbles in general and the term dates back to the time when marbles were made of alabaster, which over the years got worn down to "alley tors," or "tors," and then "taw," a term that is still in use today. "Commoneys" are common marbles—cheap and easy to come by—and "knuckle down" is what one yells when another player lifts his shooting hand from the ground.

* The strength of this passion was demonstrated in 1963 when a reporter from *The National Observer* happened on the community of Blue Eye in the Ozarks where he found old men playing marbles with handmade heirloom marbles of limestone, real marble, and clay which were brought to America generations ago from England and Ireland.

Missouri Rep. Bill Burlison rolling over his Capitol Hill opponents with his brown "shooting taw" marble. (Courtesy of Wide World Photos.)

with them for less than two-bits.

American manufacturing began in Ohio in the latter part of the last century and at first marbles were primarily made of clay. The first factory for which records still exist was one owned by one C. Dyke of South Akron, which came on line in 1884 and was soon rolling out 30,000 marbles per day. But the great American marble medium was not clay but glass and when the last clays were coming out of the kilns around 1910 the national center was moving to new quarters, specifically a glassworks in West Virginia and the Peltier Glass factory of Ottawa, Illinois.

Although crude marble-making machines were made earlier in Ohio, it was not until a man named Clinton F. Israel of the Akro Agate Company of Parkersburg, West Virginia, began to come forth with a series of mechanical innovations culminating in 1926 with a fully automatic machine, that the revolution was completed. The machines in use today differ only slightly from the one invented by Israel. (Interestingly, the Peltier company came up with a similar machine at about the same time, touching off a long patent battle in the courts.)

Today there are five companies making marbles in the United States, with four of them located in West Virginia and the fifth being the long-established Peltier operation. The largest company is Marble King of Paden City, West Virginia, which produces more than 300 million per year or about a million per working day. Although the dollar volume is hardly large, the volume of marbles consumed in the United States today is huge, as outside of the half-billion or so produced domestically, millions more are imported from the Orient.*

* Marbles are used for many things besides games. Among other applications, they are used as the agitator in aerosol paint cans (the clicking you hear when you shake the can), they are rolled across lithographer's copper plates to polish them, and they act as filtering agents in sewage-treatment plants. Millions are dropped into aquariums and millions more are embedded in highway signs as reflectors. One little-known use which makes the marble a true cradle-to-grave item is as an aid to funeral directors who throw them under coffins to help slide them into crypts.

Rolling Slow

Although still a game played by millions, in recent years there have been signals indicating a lessening in the importance of marbles in the national scheme of things. Examples:

- Interest in marbles in many urban centers began to decline noticeably starting in about 1968 — following the boom year of 1967 when some of the West Virginia plants were on three shifts, with one, Vitro-Agate, pumping out three million a day. Park officials in Los Angeles and Chicago, among others, actually canceled their city tournaments and marbles programs for lack of interest.

- Hard times began to hit the national marbles tournament, which had been zipping along steadily since 1922, when the first one was held for boys and girls fourteen and under. Businesses which had backed it began pulling out, and the scholarships and prizes offered the winners began to deflate in size. In 1971 the city of Wildwood, New Jersey, where it had been held for many years, let it be known that it really didn't care much about its status as the Olympus of American marbles. A report in the *Baltimore Sun* from the scene said, "Its mayor, according to one source, would just as soon see all the marbles roll into the ocean."

- Several periodicals, *The New York Times* among them, said in so many words that marbles had pretty much had it as an American sport save, perhaps, for some rural areas and a few marble-happy urban pockets.

By 1973 (the year of the *Times* article, which amounted to an obituary) things indeed looked bleak. The only bright spot was the appearance of Fred Feretti's book on marbles, but even this homage to the sport brought bad news with it, for he talked about the decline as a matter of fact in the opening of the book. It was as if he were trying to write down all the rules and terms before it was too late, akin to an anthropologist trying to record everything he can about a tribe about to become extinct. Could it be

Kyle Rote shakes hands with the Mayor of Wildwood back in the good old days when the Nationals were really a big thing. The 1962 champions, Peggy Mullen and Mark O'Mahoney, are both from Pittsburgh, demonstrating the lock that the city has on the sport. (Courtesy of Oka Hester/National Marbles Tournament.)

The "Marbles Bowl" at the National Marbles Tournament in Wildwood, New Jersey. (Courtesy of Oka Hester/National Marbles Tournament.)

Two opponents in the 53rd National "Big Blue Marble" Marbles Tournament, sponsored by International Telephone and Telegraph. (Courtesy of the Big Blue Marble and ITT.)

that the sport of Jefferson and Tom Sawyer was about to pass into the realm of forgotten games only to live as a historical footnote?

The answer is no.

Marbles began reascending in 1974. Roger Howdeyshell, president of Marble King Inc. of Paden City, West Virginia, now the largest in the business, reports that both 1974 and 1975 were big years for his company and the industry as a whole and that 1976 looked even bigger. Marble King's sales were up thirty percent in the first year, took another thirty percent leap in 1975, and looked so good for the future that when I talked with him he was tooling up for the production of special bicentennial marbles for 1976. As with his peers in the yo-yo world, Howdyshell loves periods of recession because that is when people turn back to the simpler, less expensive things. In a statement you won't hear very often and one which will probably never get relayed to the President's Council of Economic Advisors, Howdyshell told me, "All the prosperity of the last ten or so years really hurt us. All this industry needed was a good recession and we got one when we needed it most."

The recessionary sales spurt is not the only sign showing that the pendulum is going back the other way. New support for the nationals was building. Because of a TV show it was sponsoring called *The Big Blue Marble*, International Telephone and Telegraph (ITT) thought it fitting to pick up part of the tab for the Wildwood event in 1975, and other companies have since become interested. In 1976 the tournament site was changed from Wildwood to the Great Adventure amusement area in Jackson, New Jersey, a more hospitable location. Also new for 1976 was the first Congressional marble tournament sponsored by "Big Blue Marble." The winner of the 1976 tournament was Rep. Bill Burlison of Missouri who beat such stalwart mibsters as Rep. Thomas Railsback of Illinois, Mayor Peter Flaherty of Pittsburgh and Sen. J. Glenn Beall of Maryland. The press, which had lost interest in the tournament, returned as if sensing that there was a good story there once again. One contender was actually able to complain to the *Washing-*

ton Post (in a big 1975 spread on the event) that the year before a photographer from *Sports Illustrated* had gotten too close to him while he was playing and that a lensman from the *Times* had crowded him this time. (As if in response to that newspaper's premature obituary, the lad indicated that he really didn't care if his picture appeared in the *Times*, which according to the *Post*, was a source of exasperation for the photographer who walked off muttering, "The biggest paper in the country.")

Meanwhile, the combined effect of the recession and tightening municipal budgets had park and recreation directors taking a renewed interest in one of the cheapest of all playground activities. Howdyshell, for one, was taking advantage of the situation by showing up at recreation conventions to deliver simple messages like, "All a kid needs is a 19¢ bag of marbles, a shooter and a place to play and he's set."

Perhaps the most important news of all is that new interest in the sport is being generated by a sudden turn to *international* play. This all began in 1974 when a group of American youngsters decided to take on the fabled Toucan Terribles for the international team title. For those for whom the name Toucan Terribles does not ring a bell, a bit of background information is in order.

It seems that a large portion of the adult male population of Tinsley Green, a village in Sussex, England, near East Grinstead, and surrounding towns have been playing marbles with great earnest as long as anyone can remember.* One man in his eighties was

---

* The tradition of great marbles communities is not exclusive to England. In the United States certain towns and cities mostly on the East Coast have long-standing cases of marbles-mania and have produced the lion's share of finalists in the national championships. These leading marbles centers are: Pittsburgh, Wilmington, Yonkers, N.Y., Cumberland, Md., Augusta, Ga., Canton, Ohio, Springfield, Mass., Reading, Pa., Greensboro, N.C., Niles, Ohio, Allegheny County, Pa., and a number of towns in West Virginia (Whitesville, Wharton, Mullens, Huntington, Richwood, and Beckley, among them). Often this comes as a result of a dedicated adult, such as Walt Lease of Pittsburgh, who year in and year out works to groom players of championship calibre.

recently quoted to the effect that his grandfather had played marbles in the town with tiny orbs that are now two hundred years old. Other evidence exists which seems to prove that the game was played avidly on the Green in the Elizabethan Era. One story that is still told in the town is supposed to have taken place in 1683 when two young rivals for the hand of a local maid played marbles to see who would win her hand. The maid saw this as such a trifling game to be won in, that she eloped with a soldier from another town.

Understandably, over the years Tinsley Green became the center for the sport in the British Isles, the Wimbledon of Marbles as it were, and it also became a matter of course for local teams to take on and defeat all comers. Somewhere along the way it was decided (probably in the pub adjoining the Green) that whatever team won in annual competition here would be called the world's champions. Over time some very specific rules were set up for the contest including the requirements that it must take place on Good Friday and that each team must have six members. Unlike American Ringer with its ten-foot ring and cross of thirteen marbles, the game played here takes place in a six-foot ring in which forty-nine marbles are clustered in a tight circle at the center. However, the object of both games is the same one of getting the most marbles out of the ring.

While the area has produced its share of great teams, few have come near matching the record of the Toucan Terribles, which was founded in 1950 by a local steelworker named Leonard S. Smith. The team secured its first world's championship a few years after it came into being and then held onto the title for twenty consecutive years during which time it not only vanquished strong local teams like the Acrobats, Halfmooners, and Rebels but put down its share of American teams including a strong entry of American sailors who called themselves "the Grosvenor Gobs."* Lack of success in the fifties was enough to

* While this group obviously takes its name from the Grosvenor Square location of the American Embassy in London, no hint remains to explain the inhospitable name of another American team of the period, "The Swede Bashers."

make American teams give up, and the Terribles were allowed to reign through the sixties and into the seventies.

For years there had been talk about fielding an American challenge to the Toucan Terribles, who were not getting any younger. Several including founder Smith and team captain Arthur "Hydrogen Thumb" Chamberlin were now in their fifties, and if the Americans waited too much longer they would risk being accused of waiting until the Terribles had passed their collective prime.

Then in the summer of 1974 four rather special American teenage boys—respectively 1970 national champ Ray Morgano, 1971 champ Rick Mawhinney, 1972 champ Ray Jarrell, and then-champ Larry Kokos—and their coach Walter Lease got together and, with the help of funds put up by *The National Enquirer*, set off for Tinsley Green. An exhibition match was staged in which the young Americans unceremoniously blasted the Terribles in three consecutive games (25-2, 25-13, and 25-7), and word flashed back to the United States, albeit to a somewhat limited public, that the world champs had fallen. ("Not quite as extensive as the War of 1812, but no less significant . . ." was part of the speechifying on the event from Rep. William S. Moorhead of marble-happy Pittsburgh.)

Despite the fact that the Terribles were bowed and humiliated, they still officially held the title, as the contest was only an exhibition. There was no way it could be counted since there were four, not six, Americans, and they had arrived months after Good Friday.

What had to be done next was evident: two new members had to be recruited and funds lined up for another trip to England over Good Friday 1975. The new members were lined up easily—Jerry Mages, fifteen, one of the 1974 finalists in the nationals and Susan Regan, thirteen, winner of the girls' national championship for 1974 and a member of a family with great interest in marbles (her sister, Maureen, had won the nationals in 1969). *The National Enquirer*, meanwhile, said it would back a second trip, so it seemed like everything was set.

But then at the last minute the tabloid's president,

Generoso Pope, Jr., withdrew the offer stating the state of the national economy as his reason. "I guess we should have expected something like this," said the team's coach Walter Lease at the time. "*The Enquirer* was never giving us firm dates or times for arrangements for this trip. But the kids are really disappointed. They've been looking forward to this since last summer." As the cancellation letter had arrived early in the week of Good Friday, it looked like there wouldn't be time to set up another trip, but radio announcements on the Pittsburgh stations asking for last-minute help were heard by James Lee, president of the Gulf Oil Corporation, who got his company to ante up $5600 for air fare, meals, lodging, and sightseeing.

As the Gulf money came through less than forty-eight hours before the match was to begin, the problems of making last-minute arrangements were tremendous. Scotland Yard, at least one U.S. Senator, the American Embassy in London, and various others joined forces to get the U.S. team officially reentered in the event which it had just pulled out of. The only flight that could be booked was one that would get the team to London only a few hours before the Americans were to meet their first opponents. What's more, the plane itself had to land at Boston when it developed engine trouble and then had to circle over Heathrow Airport while some Easter week snow was removed from the runway.

Having lost the element of surprise they had going for them the previous July and without any sleep to speak of for two nights, the Americans were nonetheless ready to play, which they immediately demonstrated by knocking off Irish (25-0, 25-0) and French (25-1, 25-0) teams with ease. This brought the Americans face to face with the Terribles. The United States took the first game 25-1, lost the second 25-5, and brought it all down to a single game. Ray Jarrell of Whitesville, West Virginia, led off and proceeded to "hit 'em with a stick"—marblese for taking all twenty-five marbles in twenty-five consecutive shots.* For

the first time in history the international title (and the cup that comes with it) was brought to the United States.

The actual win and the exhibition victory that had preceded it helped give American marbles a whole new lease on life, with one of the most significant boosts coming from the media. The champs appeared on the Mike Douglas Show, word of the win was uttered by Walter Cronkite, and much more. Marbles had been given new and serious recognition as an international sport, and plans were being made to make sure that American teams were represented on future Good Fridays in England. Meanwhile, reports were filtering in from other nations that they would be entering the event to try to unseat the new international marbles power.

For women marble players, there was added significance in the fact that Ms. Regan was on the team. Her appearance effectively ended a ban against women that had been in force for as long as anyone could remember. As recently as 1970 a women's team from Brighton was turned down by the World Marbles Board of Control at Tinsley Green. At the time of the ruling a "spokesman" for the board issued this statement to the press:

> Marbles are traditionally a male sport and the Board feels it is one of the few remaining exclusive to men. Playing marbles requires a player to bend double in order to flick the tolley and we feel that ladies in this position are open to ridicule at the very least.*

great moments like the famous "half marble" of Bud McQuade when he took the first national championship in 1922. During the winning match McQuade split one of the marbles in the ring in two with one half coming out of the ring and the other staying in. The officials ruled that he would have to knock the remaining half out of the ring to win his point so he carefully hit it low and hard and it leapt out of the ring like a golfer's chip shot.

* Its blatant sexism aside, the statement was at odds with the truth. Women had already made deep inroads into marbles in England and without ridicule. A prime example is Lady Docker, who in 1955 at age forty-four defeated a seventeen-year-old bottle filler named Pauline Phillips for the national women's championship. Lady Docker played from a gold cushion and made sure you knew which was her shooting arm as it bore a gigantic emerald bracelet.

* Only time will tell for sure, but chances are that Jarrell's stick will go down in marbles history as one of those never-forgotten

However, all of this good news on the marbles front should not cause partisans to let their guard down and allow the dark forces that lurk in the wings—prosperity and its expensive toys, the urge to bulldoze over prime playing areas in the name of more parking spaces, park and recreation officials reluctant to think small, and so forth—to gain the upper hand again.

Indeed, if when the first sap rises and the forsythia is about to bloom, kids weren't to come out for their first cold-fingered match of the season, childhood would be diminished and no quantity of pricey new electronic games, well-appointed "rec" rooms, or Six Million Dollar Man Bionic Module Kits (or whatever they are called) could offset the loss. One of the most direct means of forestalling such a grim day is for more people to get down in the dirt and start playing marbles. Now.

Entering the Ring

The first step in taking up marbles is selecting a good shooter or taw. Shooters normally range in size from a half to three-quarters of an inch in diameter, and you will probably want to try several in this size range for feel. In general, the size of the shooter depends on the size of your hand.

In case you don't recall (or never knew) your shooter is a special marble that you properly call a shooter, not a marble, and which you will not want to give up until a better one comes along. Don't plan to offer it up in a game you play for keeps. Shooters are generally made of glass, steel, or agate with the latter being the best by tradition and generations of universal acclaim. In terms of the economics of the sport the agate (or, on the street, aggie), which today is only made in Germany from real agate or limestone, is extremely expensive, running about $2 apiece. Because of their expense you will not find them in your local toy store unless it happens to be a place like F.A.O. Schwarz or Neiman-Marcus, which are among the few places that always seem to have them in stock. Traditionally aggies are passed along through families but occasionally show up in antique shops, auctions, or garage sales when there is no heir to pass a bag of them along to.

(Should this send you scurrying to the attic to paw through an old jar of marbles to see if there is already an aggie or two under your roof, here is how they are identified: (1) they are heavy and obviously made of stone, (2) they have bands of color (usually alternating with white) which *circle* the orb, and (3) they are opaque, so hold them up to the light to check. If the marble in your hand is translucent it is most probably one of the many imitation glass agates which have been produced over the years.)

In addition to your shooter you will need a bag of common marbles (most are five-eighths of an inch in diameter and made of glass) which you will need for many marble games. They can be purchased almost everywhere.

Next you will want to master basic shooting. Holding your shooter is easy. Put it between your index and second fingers with your hand open, double up your hand folding your thumb under the shooter so that when you close your hand it is resting on the upper joint of your thumb. Now touch one or more knuckles to the ground (whatever is most comfortable and natural feeling) and you are ready to shoot with your cocked thumb. As you push out with your thumb to shoot, you will want to tighten up slightly on your index finger to give the shooter a bit of backspin (as you practice, you will see how important this backspin is in giving you control). As the shooter is released, follow through with your thumb as you would with a tennis racket or golf club. Once you can do this, you should begin sharpening your aim by shooting at your other marbles.

That's basically all there is to it, but there are a few tips which will come in handy to help you get good. Little has been written or otherwise publicly revealed on technique, but back in 1953 a boy named Shirley "Windy" Allen of Fairdale, West Virginia, who had won the nationals in 1951, sat down with an adult collaborator and wrote a twenty-page booklet called "The Game of Marbles," which is a classic work on technique and strategy. Here are some of the most important pointers from that booklet:*

● "Dwell on the aim you intend to get. As in billiards when you shoot with the cue, you first size up the shot you are going to make.
● "*Do not shoot hard.* . . . It takes a great deal of practice to get the right speed, but as my first coach Ted Cook always told me, 'roll that marble in.'
● "If your thumb is inclined to blister, it means that you're squeezing that shooter too tight in your hand when you're letting it go.
● "If the ring you are shooting on is sort of a hard surface, you'll need a band-aid across your knuckles."

After obtaining a serviceable shooter and a bag of marbles and learning how to use them, the next thing you will need to get into (or back into) marbles is a basic vocabulary which should include these terms:

For keeps: Playing without giving back your opponent's marbles which you knock out of the ring.

For fair: Returning all your opponent's marbles at the end of the game. The decision to play for "keeps" or for "fair" is decided by mutual consent at the beginning of each game. All games in the national tournament are for "fair."

Slip: Call made when your shooter slips from your hand and rolls a short distance, allowing you to shoot again. In most play the slip cannot roll within ten inches of the ring line.

Dubs: Hitting two or more marbles out of the ring with one shot.

Snooger: A close miss.

Knuckling down: Resting one or more knuckles on the ground when shooting.

Lofting (or Popping): Shooting in an arc through the air to hit a marble.

* There was another reference work remembered from my childhood called "How to Be the Marble King on Your Block," put out by Marble King. Considerable effort was put into trying to find a copy of that work but to no avail—Marble King Company President Roger Howdyshell doesn't even have a copy. Memory has it that this little booklet had some good information in it. The only point that is clearly remembered, however, is to watch out for distracting shadows when shooting.

Stick: When your shooter stops inside the ring line after hitting a marble out.

Bowling: Rolling, as opposed to shooting, your shooter across the ground. Generally, a novice technique.

Fudging: Cheating, usually.

Histing: Raising one's hand from the ground when shooting, or . . .

Hunching: Moving one's hand forward when shooting.

Eggies: Borrowed marbles or the act of borrowing marbles.

Spinning: The ability to make your shooter hit another marble making it travel while causing the shooter to lose momentum and stay in the ring or "stick."

Pot: The hole.

Pitch and Lag lines: Two parallel lines. At the beginning of play the participants toss their shooters at the lag line from the pitch line and whoever lands closest goes first.

Match: The agreed-upon number of games needed for a win. It can be one, three, five, or any odd number of games.

It must be emphasized that this just scratches the surface of marble-game terminology, but it should be enough to get you started. In addition to these game terms you should be aware of the names for the marbles now in common use. These tables should help.

Shooters are variously called:
Taws
Bowlers (large shooters)
Moonies
Types Now in Use (by Material)
Metal
Steelies (usually ball bearings or balls from pinball games)
Stone
Aggies (shooter of agate or limestone, scarce but obtainable)
Black Beauties (Rare shooters made of black agate or obsidian)

Clay
Crockies (fewer and fewer of these are still used as they roll toward antique status)
Plastic
Plastics (Used in packaged games, they are very unsatisfactory marbles—for one thing they don't click right when hit—and for that reason have yet to be honored with a nickname)

Target Marbles are called:
Ducks
Stickers
Dibs
Hoodles
Kimmies
Immies
Pee-wees
Mibs (or Miggs)
Crockies
Commies (or, Commons, Commoneys, etc.)
Types Now in Use (by Material)
Glass
Solids (or Little Solids, solid in color and also used for Chinese Checkers)
Rainbows (Common multicolored marbles, usually 5/8 inch in size)
Rainbow Reelers (large rainbow used as a shooter)
Milkies (marbles with a lot of translucent white glass)
Clearys (Clear glass, usually colored and with air bubbles)
Pureys (Clearys without any air bubbles)
Cat's Eyes (Clear with a wedge of color suspended in their centers)

It is important to know your marbles because there is a varying scale of values which goes with them and which you should be aware of to protect your interests. The scale at a given moment depends on local supply and demand and can change quickly when a rack jobber stocks the local candy store with a gross of Marble King Cat's Eye bags or Taiwanese Bowlers. However, it is safe to say that just about everywhere a purey is worth at least a half-dozen clearys, steelies are worth more than any glass marble (save for rare

antiques) and real aggies are worth hundreds of glass marbles. The best way to determine the local scale of values is to check the situation out with the kids in your neighborhood.

Now for the games themselves.

Ringer. This is the most important marble game in the United States and Canada, and is the game played in the nationals, for which reason it is the game that kids with immortality on their mind play. Over the years the official tournament rules for this game have become long, detailed, and written to cover all sorts of contingencies, including marbles splitting in half when hit. These rules appear in their entirety in Appendix IE starting on page 187 and should be studied by those wanting to play this American classic by the book. Detailed rules notwithstanding, the gist of ringer is relatively simple: the player shooting the most of thirteen marbles out of a ring ten feet in diameter wins the game. The thirteen marbles are placed in a cross inside the ring and play takes place after the players have lagged to see who goes first. Each round begins as the lead player knuckles down outside the ring line and tries to knock a marble out of the ring while keeping his shooter inside the ring. As long as his shooter stays in and he continues to knock the other marbles out, he keeps going. When he misses the next player begins. In the street version two to six can play ringer, but in tournament play only two can play and the first one to remove seven marbles from the ring wins.

Beyond ringer there are scores of marble games (more than fifty of which appear in Fred Ferretti's *The Great American Marble Book,* including such special games as *Last Clams,* a New Hampshire game played only in the snow, and games like *Newark Killer* that are specialties of a single city or area). One may wish to learn more games in time, but for now here are three of the most popular games now being played.

Chasies. Usually for two players, this is the marble version of follow-the-leader. The lead player shoots his shooter in any direction and the second follows

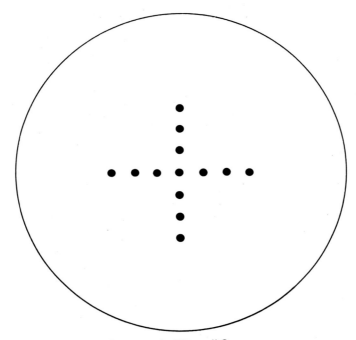

Diagram of a "Ringer" Course.

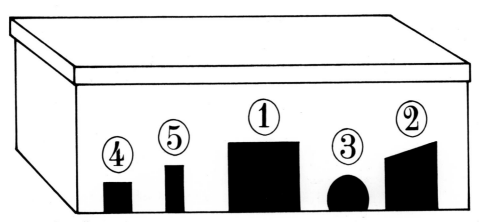

Example of a "Box Game."

A modern marbles tournament at a Pittsburgh shopping mall. (Courtesy of Walter Lease.)

trying to hit the first shooter. If the second player hits the first shooter, he keeps the hit marble and then shoots, again in any direction from that point. If the second player misses, the lead shooter tries to hit the second shooter at the point where it lays. This continues until one player is out of marbles or an agreed upon limit is reached. This game can consume large amounts of time and cover a lot of terrain. Ferretti has issued one important caveat for chasies: "It is a game which demands use of one's best shooter—an *aggie* or *steelie*. It is wise to keep an adequate supply of ordinary *immies* in one's pocket so that the possibility of having to pay a debt with one's shooter is to be avoided." Important advice!

Potsies. A ring game like ringer, which is by definition a game played for keeps—often for high stakes. An unlimited number of players each contributes a given quantity of marbles which are put inside a large circle on the ground arranged in any number of configurations depending on the whim of the players (a cross, a circle, concentric circles, a star, square, or whatever). As in ringer, the players lag for position in the lineup and keep shooting as long as they are knocking marbles out of the ring, while keeping their shooter inside the ring. The first player who obtains the majority share (the number of marbles in the pot divided by the number of players, plus one) wins and takes all the marbles left in the pot. The game is usually played with twenty-five, fifty, or a hundred marbles depending on the marbles wealth of the participants. (Potsies is also called *twenty-five-a-dub,* *fifty-a-dub,* and so forth, depending on the size of the pot.)

Black Snake. One of the commonest of hole games. In this game seven holes are dug at irregular intervals to form a course. Each player must land his shooter in each of the seven holes taking in turn as many shots as needed and then return through the same seven holes to the starting point, at which point he gains the status of "black snake." Once you have become a black snake you have the right to shoot at

U.S. Team Captain Larry Kokos takes home the International Cup from the British. (Courtesy of Walter Lease.)

other players' shooters. If you are hit by a black snake (even if you are also a black snake) you are eliminated from the game. And should a black snake land in a hole while trying to knock out another player, the black snake is out of the game. Normally this game is played for fair as it is only played with shooters. One reason for its popularity is that it provides good practice in shooting skill.

There are variations galore on just these three games which cover many situations—for instance, in the cement-surface version of black snake the "holes" are circles drawn in chalk, and indoor potsies can be played with a "ring" formed by a natural boundary in a patterned rug (whether it be a hexagon or whatever). The latter variation is often called *Persians* for obvious reasons. In addition to the host of games played with marbles alone there are a number which require other equipment, such as the old box game known by too many names to catalog here in which you shoot at the side of a box (shoe, cigar, etc.) into which holes of various sizes have been cut. Each hole has a point value based on its size and the object is to see who gets the highest score. Of course, the smaller the hole the more points you get.

While tournament ringer and other "serious" games are quiet and carefully regulated, there is another kind of game which involves as much wit and noise as it does skill. These are games like potsies and black snake which allow "shouts" by mutual consent of the players. "Shouts" were well described by an old shooter named Robert Pearman in a nostalgic newspaper article in a Kansas City newspaper a few years back as follows:

> The game of marbles, as it was played by a select group in my youth, was more of a shouting contest than a shooting contest.
> For instance, if you could say, EVERS AND UPS AND PEAKS AND CLEANS IN THE RING, before an opponent could rattle off NO EVERS AND UPS and NO PEAKS AND CLEANS IN THE RING, chances are that you'd come out way ahead of the game. In the final analysis it was more important to talk first than shoot straight.

The major shouts in this kind of contest are easily translated. EVERS allows you to move around the ring and UPS permits you to lift your shooting hand off the ground while NO EVERS AND UPS prohibits these options. PEAKS AND CLEANS IN THE RING gives you the right to smooth out the path in front of your shooter. COW TRAILS shouted at the right moment grants you license to dig a trench with your finger in front of your opponent's shooter and, still in the realm of dirty tricks, if you holler BURIES, you are allowed to step on your victim's shooter and push it into the ground. Worse still, you can yell GRINDINGS and work the other person's marble into the ground with your heel (making NO GRINDINGS an all-important precautionary call). DROPS lets you pick up your shooter and drop it like a bomb. Finally, there is the all important cry of FINS (or FENS depending on the neighborhood you live in), which immediately suspends all rules and shouts by others while you plan your shot and shouts—a most important call.

What is so appealing about shouts is that they add an extra dimension of creativity to your playing— who is to say you can't make up your own shouts, as there are really no limits to this kind of play—and *they* allow *you* to cheat in an honest and above-board manner. You can bellow out HINCHING or FUDGIES and get away with such transgressions—a real tonic to the soul in a world where the rules to so many games, from Little League baseball to Scrable and, for that matter, tournament ringer are so carefully legislated and enforced.

Meanwhile, a growing number of devotees see another dimension to the marble which is that of an antique work of art. In the period from approximately 1840 to the middle of the 1920s some stunningly beautiful marbles were produced, mostly in the Lauscha area of what is now East Germany (an area which before World War II was also known for beautifully crafted glass Christmas-tree ornaments, artificial eyes, and paperweights). Swirls, ribbons, goldstones, onionskins, and other types of marbles from this period are eagerly sought for and collected by antiques specialists today.

In aesthetic terms this was a Golden Age for marbles, and once one has seen a few from this era, it is easy to get hooked on looking for more. Those who have studied them usually end up describing them with the kind of reverence normally reserved for the Elgin Marbles or the Pietà. For instance, Barbara Jones describes a type of glass swirl of the Victorian era in her book *The Unsophisticated Arts* as glass spheres holding . . .

> a twisted spiral of filaments, thin music translated into colored glass, crimson with pale blue, fire with canary, emerald with rose. The similar sphere of the eye, however closely juxtaposed to the harder crystal, peers in vain through the twined colors to see a heart.

Of all the classic varieties, however, few can approach the legendary German sulphides in interest, value, or beauty. The sulphides were each carefully made by hand and each contained within it a tiny figure fashioned from china clay, kaolin, or gypsum and dried slowly in a kiln at precisely 25 degrees Centigrade. The commonest figures were cats, dogs, sheep, eagles, and other animals. The figure was then inserted in hot glass, allowed to cool, shaped, and polished. Because a small amount of air always got between the figure and the surrounding glass, an effect is produced which give the figures a hazy, silvery look which is quite pleasing to the eye. Some of the figures are complex and finely executed—hence rare—including such things as angels, scenes from children's stories, and religious events. A magazine devoted to antique glass reported a while back that a special sulphides with the bust of William McKinley, issued immediately after his death in 1901, would fetch $100 as a collector's item. (A few aging craftsmen continued to produce limited numbers of sulphides until about 1950, but they are gone now, and it is safe to assume that the skill has been lost.)

Marble collecting is booming right now, as adults discover the many variations to which this simple object has been subjected over the years. There is already an important reference book in the field (*Collecting Antique Marbles* by Paul Baumann) and, as this was being written, a group of enthusiasts was in the process of creating a national marble-collectors society which would put out a newsletter, sponsor permanent museum displays, and produce reference manuals. Besides the types already mentioned, collectors dote on such rarities as early stone marbles, hand-decorated china marbles (many of which date back to German craftsmen of the 1700s), and marbles made of such semiprecious materials as jade, topaz, aquamarine, and amethyst. Rare marbles, by the way, don't have to be that old. One of the most highly sought-after items in marble collecting is a series put out by the Peltier Glass factory in Ottawa, Illinois, for a short period in 1926. The series features the faces of such comic strip favorites of the time as Little Orphan Annie, Moon Mullins, Skeezix, Smitty, and Andy Gump.*

Incidentally, one of the reasons why certain early marbles are so rare today is because of a game dating back many centuries called Conqueror. Here is how it is described with presumed pain by Paul Baumann in his work, *Collecting Antique Marbles*:

> One player lays his taw on the ground and the other throws his own taw at it with all his force. If the taw thrown at breaks, the other taw is known as the Conqueror of one. One half of the broken taw is then taken as a trophy by the more fortunate marble owner. If neither taw breaks, then the other is set down to be thrown at. When one taw breaks another which has previously broken other marbles, all of these marbles which it had broken earlier are also added to the winning taw's score. For instance, if my taw had broken twenty marbles previously and it breaks your taw which had also broken twenty marbles previously, then my taw will rank as the Conqueror of forty-one.

Fortunately, for the sake of art and collecting, the game of Conqueror is now out of vogue.

---

* *Be forewarned*: Dabbling in marbles as antiques is no simple matter. Even an elementary knowledge of, say, spirals will mean learning the intricate differences between divided cores, latticinio cores, solid cores, micas, and more.

Chapter 7

The Frisbee Culture

Question No. 1. *Take the total age of the Library Bar starting team at IFT 17; add the mold No. of the special run Pro made for Ann Arbor; divide by the number of times "Wham-O" appears on a third period Pluto Platter; add the number of time outs allowed per team in Ultimate; subtract the number of cents deposit on the Frisbie tin; multiply by the number of apes appearing on the Amsun "Planet of the Apes" disc; add the number of players currently holding "World" distance titles.*
—First part of the *"Flying Disc Trivia Quiz"* appearing in the June 1975 issue of Flying Disc World.

Unlike the objects discussed thus far in the book, the Frisbee is a totally modern device with no clear precedents in antiquity. It is a legitimate child of the twentieth century, coming to flower in the Plastic Age following World War II.

The earliest known Frisbee was a pie tin from the now defunct Frisbie Pie Company of Bridgeport, Connecticut. Somewhere along the line—probably in the twenties—people began to independently discover that these tins were a cheap form of amusement because they scaled beautifully with a little practice. In 1946, when the vets began to swell the colleges of New England, it became very popular to flip the Frisbie tins back and forth across the grass on warm afternoons. The tins were especially popular at Yale. (Many people have been led to believe that the fad actually began at Yale way back in 1827 when a student named Elihu Frisbie—or John Frisbie in some versions of the tale—hurled a church collection platter across the campus to protest compulsory chapel. But this story has been shown to be an outright hoax concocted by those who obviously felt the object was in need of a more fascinating past.)

Despite its initial popularity in New England as a pie bonus, it was not until 1948 that a West Coast man, Walter F. Morrison, with no apparent knowledge of the Frisbie, fashioned a rather crude flying disc out of plastic and began selling them under the name Flyin' Saucer. He did well selling them on his own and in 1955 attracted the interest of a small company, the Wham-O Manufacturing Co., whose main product at the time was a line of wooden slingshots. In 1957 Wham-O began manufacturing the discs under license from Morrison and soon found that it was not going to be an overnight sensation like the Hula Hoop, which the company introduced at about the same time.* Convinced that the disc had a

* The company, which still sells slingshots, has been in on a number of major and minor fads over the years, including such mor-

future despite a slow start, the company kept making them and in the process began to make some changes. With a slight spelling modification from -ie to -ee, Wham-O adopted and registered the original and strikingly appropriate name which was shouted by early users as a warning in much the same manner that golfers yell "Fore!" The Frisbee was then redesigned for better aerodynamics and grip and then Wham-O began marketing it as a piece of sporting equipment rather than as a toy or novelty. As anyone who has been near a beach, college campus, public park, picnic grove, or vacant lot since knows, the determination to stay with the Frisbee paid off. To date, more than 100 million Frisbees have been sold worldwide, and that total does not include many millions of variations and knock-offs produced by Wham-O's competitors.

Much of the Frisbee's appeal and one of the reasons it has transcended the faddish appeal of, say, the Hula Hoop is its remarkable versatility in providing sport for two or more. In the early days of the sport, most people were content to scale the discs back and forth as an end in itself—just as many casual users continue to do. "A ball looking for a game," snapped some of its critics who completely missed the point that was becoming apparent, which is that it was a "ball" for all games and the reason for certain totally new games like Guts Frisbee.

Since the disc culture is so integral to the major form of Frisbee competition, it is important that these games be summarized here and now so that those who don't regularly follow Ultimate Frisbee or Frisbee Golf are not lost. (The detailed rules to those games marked with an A. appear in Appendix IG.)

Frisbee Golf. Played much like regular golf, this game has become the most popular Frisbee copy of an existing ball game (although Frisbee Tennis and Frisbee Hockey are quite popular in some areas). Players begin at tee areas, curve around or scale over hazards and "hole-out" by hitting predetermined objects which are usually poles or baskets. As stated in written International Frisbee Association (IFA) doctrine, its growing popularity can be traced to a number of factors ranging from its appeal to all ages and levels of ability to the fact that course design and construction is usually quite inexpensive. But the most important factor seems to be the strategic challenges of which the IFA says, they

> exceed ball golf because of the wider range of flight patterns available to the Frisbee Golfer (rollers, curves, hovers, skips, etc.). Also playing a part in the technical challenge of the sport is the effect of the wind and the great number of delivery styles which may be used (backhand, sidearm, overhand wrist flip, etc.). The strategy of shot placement is of course equally challenging in both games.

This form of Frisbee now boasts its own national championships (first held at the Rochester Frisbee Club Course in 1974 in Rochester, New York) and at least one municipal course (established in 1975 in Oak Grove Park, Los Angeles County). *A.*

Guts Frisbee. A very popular form in which teams of one to five potential decapitators (five in most tournament play) face off along goal lines fifteen yards apart across a "neutral" zone. The object of Guts is to send forth a shot so hard and fast that the other team cannot make a clean one-handed catch. A bad throw on offense or miss or bad catch by the defense gives the other team a point. The winning score is twenty-one points and the winning team must have a two-point edge.

Perhaps the most popular of all of today's Frisbee games, it is also one of the oldest. The Frisbee's leading scholar, Dr. Stacil E. D. Johnson who is both a psychiatrist and the author of the definitive treatise,

---

tal fascinations as the Superball, Monster Bubbles, The Water Wiggle, and Silly String. Wham-O's biggest flop was something called Instant Fish, a certain type of fish egg that hatched when put into water for several hours. The idea looked great on paper but miscarried when the male fish the company had bought refused to fertilize the eggs.

Top performers playing Ultimate Frisbee at the 1975 World Frisbee Championships. Kerry Kollmar, 1975 Freestyle Champion, is on the left and John Cohn is on the right. (Courtesy of IFA.)

Frisbee, has traced it back to a primitive tin-era version which was played on an intercollegiate level as early as 1954 when a Dartmouth College team took on and defeated a team from Montreal. *A.*

Ultimate Frisbee. A field game, Ultimate pits two seven-person teams against each other on a sixty- by forty-yard playing field for forty minutes. The object of the game is to score a goal by passing the Frisbee into the other team's end zone. The Frisbee changes sides when there is an incomplete pass or it gets intercepted. It is an all passing game, in which there is no running with the Frisbee. A goal is worth one point.

The game was developed by a group of students at Columbia High School in Maplewood, New Jersey, in 1968 and quickly spread to other high schools and then to the colleges. Looking for omens? A number of colleges now play Ultimate on the intercollegiate level with the first having been played between Rutgers and Princeton on November 6, 1971. It was played between the same two teams, on the same spot that the first intercollegiate football game had been played 103 years earlier. *A.*

Maximum Time Aloft (MTA). A competitive exercise in which players attempt to keep the disc in the air for the longest amount of time. Each player makes a "boomerang" throw, and time is counted from release until it is caught with a clean one-handed catch. World's record: fifteen seconds by Canadian Ken Westerfield.

Distance. As with the javelin or discus, distance is measured from the foul line to the point where the Frisbee first touches the earth. A handful of Frisbee experts have scaled their discs to distances in excess of a hundred yards. World's record: several conflicting claims but most acknowledge John Kirkland's 336 feet.

Accuracy. Contestants attempt to place their Frisbee through a Hula Hoop at increasing distances (usually 15, 25, and 35 yards).

Throw, Run and Catch (TRC). Each player throws a "boomerang" attempting to cover the longest distance to get to a point where he can still catch the Frisbee. The distance measured is that between the point where it is thrown to the point where it is caught. Record: 174 feet, 6 inches by Ken Headrick.

Freestyle Frisbee. Players are judged on a one-to-ten scale for a specified period, usually five minutes, of Frisbee performance. Grace, style, and creativity are major factors here.

The Field Meet. A competitive tour de force in which two teams compete in six events (Distance, Accuracy, Frisbee Golf, Freestyle, Guts, and Ultimate). *A.*

There are many more games including some indoor games such as *Frisbee Lag*, penny pitching in which the Frisbee replaces the penny, and *Friz-Banger*, an indoor one-on-one version of Guts frequently played in the halls of college dorms. New games are coming out with regularity, adding to the fun. For instance, *Conversion* made its debut in the pages of *Flying Disc World* in 1975 and is already attracting much attention. This is a field game played with a football goal post in which the object is to put your disc through the uprights in such a way that the player on the other side of the goal is unable to make a one-handed catch. Another new entry is something called RIFRAF (Relay Internationale de Frisbee Runners and Flingers) in which teams race along a thirteen-mile course tossing a Frisbee back and forth as they go.

Given its relative infancy as a plaything, one might not expect the Frisbee to have the kind of rich culture that accrues to the yo-yo or marble, but it does. In fact, it is easily contended that among the subcultures addressed in this book only that of the kite is in the same league as that of the Frisbee today in America.

Support for this contention lies in the fact that the Frisbee not only has its own hierarchy, literature, tournaments, cast of characters, and the like; but is constantly showing up in the oddest places.

Evidence. There is a Frisbee course at MIT (another, "Frisbee Techniques and Special Applications," was to have been given at the University of Oregon, but was withdrawn when taxpayers who keep an eye on the state-supported school protested). . . . There is a World's Champion K-9 at Frisbee, one Ashley Whippet, who has appeared on at least a half-dozen network TV shows including one with Mike Douglas. Douglas won $200 from Bobby Riggs when he bet him that his next guest could catch a Frisbee in his mouth better than Riggs. . . . A (very) modern version of *Henry V* staged in New York had actors tossing Frisbees about the stage. . . . At least two Soviet cosmonauts are full-fledged members of the International Frisbee Association. . . . Frisbee devotees number in the millions and include such names as Richard Burton, Julie Andrews, Neil Armstrong, Gregory Peck, and President Ford, who within days of taking office was out on the South Lawn tossing one around with members of his staff. (Ford's style is far superior to that of the President before him who, when presented with one at the 124th graduation at the U.S. Naval Academy, tossed it upside down.) Elliott Gould and Donald Sutherland on location making a movie in England had sixty Frisbees air-expressed to them, and when Indianapolis 500 drivers were delayed by rain at the start of the 1973 race, people began flipping them around the infield.

In addition to the millions of players and fanciers worldwide, the flying disc has attracted attention from other, often unlikely, sources. Two Philadelphia physicians, Dr. Halley S. Faust and Dr. Mark L. Dembert, actually broke into the august pages of *The New England Journal of Medicine* with a paper on "Frisbee finger," a painful scraping of the middle finger caused by too much Frisbee throwing. They report that the affliction can only be cured by giving up the sport until it has healed. The doctors also solemnly point out that the problem is at its worst in urban areas where the edge of the disc has been made more abrasive as it comes in contact with pavement and curbs.* This report caused another doctor to respond in a subsequent issue of the *Journal* with this bit of doggerel:

> *I do not argue with the contention*
> *Abstention is the best prevention*
> *So have it printed on each disk*
> *You toss this plate at your own risk.*

Another, and even more outlandish, source of attention has come from the United States Navy, which took a long, hard look at the Frisbee as an article for war—at a cost to the taxpayer of a cool $375,000. The work, which included extensive wind-tunnel tests, a special Utah test site complete with tracking cameras, and much paperwork was aimed at determining if the Frisbee would be a suitable vehicle for delivering flares to battle areas. As reported in the official report, "Adaptation of the Frisbee Flight Principle to the Delivery of Special Ordnance," it was ultimately discovered that this special application was not feasible, and the day of the battlefield Frisbee was not yet at hand.

And then there are those who have used—better yet, exploited—the plastic saucer as a symbol for some profundity or other. One such work is an essay penned by Albert L. Weeks, an associate professor of English at New York University, which appeared on the "Op-Ed" page of *The New York Times* in 1971. In a painstakingly wrought 1000 or so words he manages to make the Frisbee an outward and visible sign of everything from pop culture to the Aquarian Age, to drugs, to the inflamed political rhetoric of the time, and more. Weeks's labored case reaches crescendo with lines like this:

> Today's extremes of dropping out and freaking out—in other words, leaving and breaking off from reality—are

* Further medical examination of the subject appears in a special paper by Dr. Roger Woods in Johnson's *Frisbee* entitled "Medical Aspects of Frisbee." Woods, a neurologist who is medical director of International Frisbee Tournament and head of his own Institute of Frisbee Medicine at Santa Monica, acknowledges Frisbee finger and several other problems like Frisbee elbow, but is quick to point out that the disc is generally healthful, safe, and fun.

like the Frisbee which, when faced with the realities of aerodynamics, simply stalls out and falls feather-like to the ground.

But the most fascinating part of the Frisbee culture is the hard-core of true aficionados who annually vie for the Julius T. Nachazel Trophy (named for a mysterious contestant who at an early contest flung his Frisbee into the woods and was never heard from again), who can date discs within months of their production day by arcane differences in color, measurements, and mold markings, and can recite the "Ten Commandments of the Disc." (Sample commandment: "The most powerful force in the world is that of a disc straining to land directly under a car, just beyond reach. This term is technically termed 'car suck.' ")*

Various types inhabit this subculture. In Frisbee letters, for example, there is Dr. Stacil E. D. Johnson, a psychiatrist from Pacific Grove, California, who worked for years on his book *Frisbee.* His case is an interesting one. At thirty-five he was picked up in the medical draft by the Navy and assigned as a psychiatrist working with Marines who had just come back from the war in Vietnam at Camp LeJeune, North Carolina. This grim assignment put him in need of therapy of his own, so he turned to playing with and studying the Frisbee, which in turn led him to working on the book.

Judged on scholarship alone, the result is a monumental work which includes such individual labors of love as painfully detailed sections on weather and the Frisbee, the physics of disc flight, and the care, repair, and transport of the Frisbee. However, there is more here than dry scholarship and how-to information, because his fervent love for the disc pokes out between the book's covers. At the back of his book there is an exchange of letters between the good doctor and the folks at the famous Forest Lawn Memorial-Parks and Mortuaries in California. In Johnson's letter to the cemetery he asks that upon his death he be cremated and that his ashes then be mixed with enough of the best polyethylene to make twenty-five Wham-O Pros which would be distributed to his best friends and family. Johnson's vision is of a day when he will live on as, "my remains will waft through the air between the hands of those whom I have loved so much. . . . " Forest Lawn's rather terse response was that it could cremate him but could not carry out the rest of his request. (Speaking of this proposed last fling, one of the book's reviewers unfeelingly commented, "Dr. Johnson becomes the first Frisbee tosser on record to flip his own lid.")

As the Boswell of the Frisbee, Johnson is in a class all by himself.* Another class of some size are the top performers, a growing group of sportsmen and women. The two biggest names in Frisbee today are John Kirkland and Vic Malafronte, both champions and record holders in various aspects of disc performance, who have become well known nationally since they traveled for a year with the Harlem Globetrotters as a warm-up act and began giving other professional demonstrations. Like diving, gymnastics, and other style-heavy sporting activities, top-flight Frisbee freestyling as performed by this dynamic duo is better seen than described. However, one J. D. Reed who has studied these superstars in action and wrote about them in *Sports Illustrated* gives us a pretty good feel for the magic of their act:

> The Frisbee is doing impossible things. Malafronte throws it so that it floats over Kirkland's face. Kirkland blows on it, bounces it into the air with his fingers, leaps, does handsprings, catches it behind his back, whirls and throws it back—all in one fluid, almost Oriental motion. Frisbees walk on edge across the polished floor in elaborate question mark patterns, arriving exactly at the shoe tips of the other player, to be booted into the air and caught between the legs. Several Frisbees, thrown together like nested clay pigeons, go spraying out; huge arcing Frisbees whip over the seats, sail between the beams, dance by the huge exhaust fans in the ceiling.

* All ten appear in the *Appendix.*

* Appendix II contains remarks on the need for more of this type of scholarship.

The great John Kirkland in action. This top performer not only teaches a course in Frisbees (at MIT, no less), but was one of the first flying disc "pros" in the world. (Courtesy of IFA.)

Not to take anything away from Malfronte, who is certainly one of the top performers in the world, the evidence points to Kirkland as the Frisbee's first Superstar and the sport's most avid spokesman. Among other things, he is working on a book on the Frisbee (which will concentrate on its metaphysical aspects), designing his own super-disc, which he forecasts will be the best ever, teaching the MIT Frisbee course, and spending almost as much time in the air as his discs, as he flies around the country to lecture and demonstrate. He holds several world's records, including fastest clocked flight (84 mph.) and is a consistent winner or runner-up in many of the events on the tournament trail.

He is also very serious about "his sport," and if it weren't for the fact that his conversation is sprinkled with references to higher math, Zen, literature, and such, you might think you were talking to Pete Rozelle about football. He is not entirely one-sided, either, as he is also a jazz drummer, student of aeronautics (beyond those of the Frisbee), and a three-corner billiard player of some note.

We talked by phone one night in early 1976 for an hour or so and what follows is part of that interview presented here to give an insight into the world of a Frisbee superstar.

Fris-Whiz

Q. How did it all start?

Kirkland: It was in the summer of '56 when I was at summer camp, and there wasn't much there more exciting than tetherball. A Frisbee fell into my hands, and I got a lot of enjoyment out of it. I kept going back to it over the years as something I liked, but it wasn't till much later that I really got into it.

Q. What changed you from a casual user to a man whose life has become tied to a plastic disc?

Kirkland: A lot of things, but much of it had to do with finding a true extension of myself. It's like being a little kid in the dark with a flashlight who turns the light on for a second and extends his reality to the end of the beam. The Frisbee is my beam. Another thing that became important was the immediate feedback of the thing—knowing right away how well you did.

And also, the business of getting better and better, discovering my own rhythms and learning to work with a partner have all been important. It's my dance.

Q. You make it sound very personal and internal. Is it?

Kirkland: It is. But it's also something I'm intensely competitive about as well as something which I work hard to communicate with others. I teach it here at MIT and lecture and demonstrate all over the country. I love to teach what I feel and whether it's at a resort in the Catskills or at the University of Alabama, people wake up to what can be done with one and want to start doing it themselves, and not just to fool around with it for a few minutes but to learn how to express themselves with it. You know last year was the biggest year for Frisbees in history, and this year is going to be bigger. People are learning to discover themselves through the Frisbee.

Q. Do you practice a lot, and what element of the game are you working on now?

Kirkland: I spend a lot of time practicing, and I spend a lot of that time getting smoother in my catch and delivery, working so that I can take it and release it in one perfect move. When people see Dr. J., New York Nets' basketball star Julius Irving, do one of his fantastic shots, they stop and say "What the hell was that?" For those people time has stopped for a moment and reality has been suspended. Well, that's what I work to do for the people who come to watch me.

Q. Are there major differences in playing style?

Kirkland: Sure. People suit it to their needs, and you get different expressions or as I like to put it, it is as plastic in utility as it is in manufacture. If you take Guts as an example, I look upon it and play it as a form of high-speed, close-in freestyle. Others do it as a very aggressive, macho, rev-up-the-team kind of thing. This describes the great Guts teams of the Upper Peninsula of Michigan where both Guts and, significantly, hockey are so popular.

Q. I understand that you have a collection of more than five hundred different discs from all over the world. Forgetting which is the rarest collector's item for a moment, if you could only have one disc to actually play with, which one would you pick?

Kirkland: Actually I have the largest collection in the world, which contains over 1600 different discs, some of which are extremely rare. But if I had to pick one for general use in all events, it would have to be the Wham-O Super Pro.

Q. When you work with another pro like Malafronte or Ken Westerfield in a demonstration, do you have a set of moves that is all worked out ahead of time?*

Kirkland: It's not choreographed as, say, ballet is but we work out sections and think about what we're going to accomplish in each section. The proper analogy would be to jazz, where you have a framework but you are liable to have to improvise to get to where you want to be. We move in and out of the sections and might start off with some freestyling, work with four on the floor, start throwing baskets, do two at a time and then go back to a little freestyling.

Q. How many Frisbee pros are there now working?

Kirkland: There are ten of us now making a living or coming close to it.

Q. Tell me something about your Frisbee course at MIT.

Kirkland: We study all aspects of the Frisbee. I'm finding out something very important through the course, which is that the Frisbee has tremendous transfer to other activities, and there are shortcuts which can be taught which enable people to quickly develop their coordination. This is important to a lot of MIT students who because they had a bad early experience with athletics sublimated those drives into their studies which they did so well they got into MIT. For a lot of these guys I find that building confidence and coordination with a Frisbee turns them back on to physical things and soon they're not only playing

One of the most dreaded logos in all of organized Frisbeedom, that of the almost-unbeatable Rutgers Ultimate Frisbee team. (Courtesy of Rutgers Ultimate Frisbee Team.)

---

* Kirkland and Malafronte aren't the only two making a living by the disc. Ken Westerfield and Jim Kenner, for instance, do the same in Canada under an arrangement in which they work as demonstrators for Irwin Toy Ltd. (Wham-O's licensee there) in the summer and Molson's Ale in the winter. Before this job security came along, they spent two years roaming their country putting on demonstrations wherever they could find a crowd and then passing the hat for contributions. These two were also instrumental in starting the Canadian Open Frisbee Championships, which began in 1972.

Frisbee, but are running, playing tennis, and so forth.
Q. Have you actually been able to demonstrate this coordination development?
Kirkland: At the beginning of the course I taught one control group how to juggle. Then I taught them all how to Frisbee well and got a second group to start juggling, and the second group learned how to juggle in about half the time of the first.

Not all the big guns in the sport are as deeply involved as Kirkland. One force of certain magnitude who is able to maintain his status as a full-time college student while being part of the Frisbee elite is Irv "Dr. I" Kalb. He is one of the original group which created Ultimate Frisbee while at Maplewood High in 1969. He not only brought the game to Rutgers University but has been the prime force in turning that school into the top-ranked Ultimate power in the nation. He has also helped move Ultimate to other parts of the country and takes some pride in knowing about some fifty colleges and universities where the game is now played seriously. He is also one of the nation's top freestylers, or jammers, who normally works in tandem with Dan Roddick, former *Flying Disc World* editor who is now the Director of the IFA. One move that Kalb has developed for his freestyle act that nobody else has yet been able to master involves the small indentation (the "navel," or as Kalb calls it, "puddle") at the top of the Frisbee. His partner sends him the Frisbee upside down, and he catches it—in an amazing display of timing and coordination—by putting his finger in the puddle. Kalb doubts he'll ever turn full-time pro, as he thinks his ultimate future lies in computers, but he is one of the first to put himself through college with a Frisbee (he fetches sums like $200 for putting on demonstrations). Incidentally, Kalb, like Kirkland, says that if he were only allowed one disc to work with he would also choose the Super-Pro, specifically an edition of that model made for the International Frisbee Tournament.

Although their number is not yet as great as the number of top-rated males, there is an increasing number of women who are both highly skilled in the use of and serious about the Frisbee. Jo Cahow, Women's World Champion for both 1974 and 1975, didn't even begin using one until 1971 when she hooked up with the Humbley Magnificent Champions of the Universe, a group of Frisbee fanatics in the Ann Arbor, Michigan, area. She not only became the best woman player in the world in a remarkably short period of time but also found her nine-to-five calling: she works fulltime at the IFA's headquarters, where she is assistant to the director and where, among other things, she is helping to promote Frisbee as a woman's sport. She says, "There are only about a dozen or so serious women players today, but I feel there'll be a lot more before too long, especially as those with an interest in gymnastics and modern dance realize how much these things have in common with freestyle Frisbee."

Other women to watch: Monika Lou (women's distance record holder at 234 feet), Gail McColl and Patty Hipski.

Another aspect of the subculture is its institutions: tournaments, organizations, periodicals, clubs, and such. Clearly the strongest single force in organized disc throwing is the International Frisbee Association itself, which was created in 1967, not surprisingly, by Wham-O, which supports and promotes it to this day. It boasts some 70,000 dues-paying members, stages the annual World Frisbee Flying Disc Championships at the Rose Bowl, regulates and records proficiency ratings (Novice, Amateur, Expert, Master, and the elite and coveted World Class Master rating) and publishes *Frisbee World.** There is more to the IFA than all of this serious business, as attested by the name of the organization's executive director, Harvey J. Kukuk, who has never been seen by anyone. (Kukuk's

*The magazine began in January 1976 after a merger of the old *IFA News* and *Flying Disc World*, with the editor of the latter, Dan "The Stork" Roddick, in charge of the new offering. While the new magazine is more impressive than either of the two that made the merger, it effectively puts much of flying disc journalism in one place and under the watchful eye of Wham-O. One hopes that an independent journal will surface to complement *Frisbee World*. One possible contender: *The Circular*, put out by the New York Flying Disc Institute.

Jo Cahow, who was women's world champion in 1974 and again in 1975. Besides being the top woman player in the world, she works at International Frisbee Association headquarters as Assistant to the Director. (Courtesy of IFA.)

Cover of the first issue of Frisbee World, *which debuted in January, 1976. It replaces the two pioneers of Frisbee journalism:* IFA News *and* Flying Disc World. *The quality of writing in the new entry is high, as evidenced by the opening to an article entitled "Frisbee Behind Bars," which reads: "Leavenworth Federal Penitentiary is known throughout the world as the worst place a person can wind up. There are at least two reasons, however, why this is not true. One is that the institution is not located in Texas, and the other is that Frisbees are allowed inside." (Courtesy of IFA.)*

name became nationally prominent for a moment when the IFA attempted to bestow the coveted Harvey J. Kukuk Golden Frisbee Award on California Governor Edmund G. Brown, Jr., shortly after he took office. It was returned as "an unsolicited gift," an example of Brown's policy of not accepting things of value from special-interest groups while in office.)

There are other organizations—ranging from the United Kingdom Frisbee Association to the Olympic Frisbee Federation, which has been put together primarily to lobby the sport into the Olympic Games—and a number of events and tournaments on the flying-disc circuit. The biggest are the American Flying Disc Open held each August in Rochester, New York, the IFA's World Championships held in the Rose Bowl in August, the World Invitational Flying Disc Championships held each May at Rutgers University, and the International Frisbee Tournament (IFT), held in July in Marquette, Michigan. For Juniors (fifteen years old and younger) there is the International Junior Frisbee Tournament held in September in a different location each year. Incidentally, the stakes at these events are not to be sniffed at. The winning team at the Invitational Guts Tournament (which follows the IFT in Michigan) gets to split $5000, and the individual winner at the American Open in Rochester gets to drive home in a new car.

These events range in tone and style from the "Wide World of Sports"-y Rose Bowl event, which apes rather than parodies the New Year's Day football extravaganza, to the IFT, which pokes fun at the big-money sports through traditions that include a tournament queen (who must be older than sixty), a 1946 Studebaker official pace car, a precise opening moment (12:01) and the opening cry, "Gentlemen, start your Frisbees!"

In addition there are clubs and teams which often have colorful names. In Guts Frisbee the biggest power around are the teams headquartered at the Library Bar in Houghton, Michigan, which compete under the name of the bar. Other guts groups of note include the WABX Air Aces, the Highland Avenue Aces, the Berkeley Frisbee Group, Stroh's Strokers,

Indiana Gutsmasters, West-End Scrap Metal, the Foul Five and the Half-Way Bar. Nicknames are also a big thing in this sport making it heavy with names like "The Stork" (who is Dan Roddick, a top performer who now runs the IFA), "The Flash," "Thor," "Sky King," and "No Nickname."

Perhaps because serious pursuit of the Frisbee is new and the players are striving hard for respectability, they have created for themselves a complex, technical jargon of their own which some insiders (Kirkland, for one) feel has already gone too far and like other jargons is becoming more of a barrier than an aid to communications. There are more than a hundred terms in the glossary to Johnson's book alone, and more coming along all the time. Examples of the extent of the Frisbee language are the names for the nine periods of flight outlined by Johnson: 1. Whelm (release), Wedge (insertion), Well (climb), Wax, Waft (float), Wane, Waste, Warp, and Was (the touchdown).

To bring the phenomenon full circle, it should be noted that a number of the faithful are already avidly at work cataloging, classifying, and collecting flying discs. In fact, in order to satisfy the growing demand for collector's items the IFA now sells classic and standard models in odd colors from its Collector's Corner, and eye-opening prices are being paid for rarities—$30 was paid for a rare Wham-O Olympic from the first mold at a 1975 collector's auction, and John Kirkland paid $57 for his rare Pipco "Li'l Abner" model a few years back. Kirkland feels he got a real deal at that price, as only six of these discs are known to exist (the deal between the maker and Al Capp never went through, so only a handful of samples were made). Collectors say it is just a matter of time before the first $100 disc is sold, a price that would certainly be reached if another mint Li'l Abner or the right Wham-O "Speedee" (the rarest of all true Frisbees) came on the market.

There are leading authorities in this disc subspecialty, including Johnson (who, for instance, actually has a chart in his book which allows you to establish the date when a Wham-O Pro was made),

Bruce Koger of Chicago, Illinois making a freestyle catch. He was 1975 men's world champion. (Courtesy of IFA.)

Roger Barrett, Kirkland, Malfronte, and the IFA's Roddick. These people are able to speak breathlessly of odd models, obscure color variations, mold differences, foreign variations, and the like with the same kind of esoteric facility that a philatelist uses to describe nineteenth-century postal rarities. Listen as Roger Barrett describes one section of the Wham-O museum in a "Curator's Report" in an issue of *Flying Disc World*:

> Section I is of course my favorite. One of its prizes is an indigo (yes, indigo!) Flying Saucer executed in fine material. The catch? —it was made in Hong Kong. Another gem is a set of Speedies in apricot, white and green . . . sorry no maroon yet. Then there is a beautiful gold disc with pictures of angels and rocketships. What's that you say . . . Empire? Premier?, no this item comes from Japan. There are Empire Zo-lars in both red and blue . . . soft Pipcos in four colors, in the wrapper . . . an unpigmented Mystery Y regular with just a few strands of red at the center. Perhaps the best item in the case was bought in Dallas in 1959. It is a green "Flying Saucer" made by the Plastic Fittings Co. of Dearborn, Michigan. . . .*

As such words suggest, there are many collectible flying *objets d'art*. The most sought-after are the "antiques" —those produced before 1960—but there are highly prized items in such specialized areas as foreign models, Wham-O's, and sales-premium discs such as those which have been put out by Burger Chef, Pepsi, Keds, and Oreo.

What makes all of this especially fascinating is that it is one thing to collect exquisite antique marbles with Victorian swirls; but quite another to dote on the endless variations on the polyethylene flying disc of a supposedly "throw away" culture. In the world of Frisbee collecting a disc is liable to become a

---

*It would take too many pages to explain the significance of all the "finds" in these few sentences. But one name that begs to be explained is the "Mystery Y." This is the name that has been given to a fine disc which has the image of two players in the mold, one with a Y on his shirt. The mystery comes in because nobody has been able to figure out who created it.

collector's prize before it's even broken in. Already the Wham-O Pros of the late '73-early '74 period, which were thinner than other models because of the shortage of plastic during the Arab oil embargo, are being collected as historical oddities. An even later item surely destined to be coveted in the future is the first issue of the Wham-O Super Pro 141-G, which had just been withdrawn from the market as this was written. After a few thousand had been made and distributed, the company found that they were of an inferior plastic and prone to cracking. (The trick here is going to be figuring out the difference between the first model—bound to be called the "cracker"—and the later, corrected model with the better plastic.)

P.S. About that trivia question at the beginning of the chapter; it seems that nobody has yet come forth with an answer (at least none that the folks at the IFA had heard of), which goes to show that the Frisbee culture is so rich that it overwhelms its own members.

Disc Tips
From the experts I spoke with the consensus seems to be that the best set of opening instructions on the use of the flying disc are the terse ones writ in plastic on each Wham-O: "PLAY CATCH—INVENT GAMES/TO FLY, FLIP AWAY BACKHANDED/FLAT FLIP FLIES STRAIGHT/TILTED FLIP CURVES—EXPERIMENT!"

Between this and something as ambitious as Kirkland's course there is much else to be learned. Here are some tips:
- Irv Kalb: "One thing you must always keep in mind is that the edge away from the hand in which the disc is held must always be lower than the one in your hand."
- Both Kirkland and Kalb agree that one thing holding people back is the inability to realize what can be done with a Frisbee. Seeing a pair of top-notch freestylers in action can remedy this situation.
- Always point your hip in the direction in which you want the Frisbee to travel.

- Once you have gained mastery over the basic beginner's throw, the backhand, begin to experiment with other throwing grips such as the sidearm two-finger grip (two fingers under, thumb on top), which is the basis for most trick shots.
- Develop tricky and interesting catches as well as throws. One impressive number is the trailing-edge shot in which you allow the disc to get behind you and then catch it from behind.

Chapter 8

Tabletop Universe

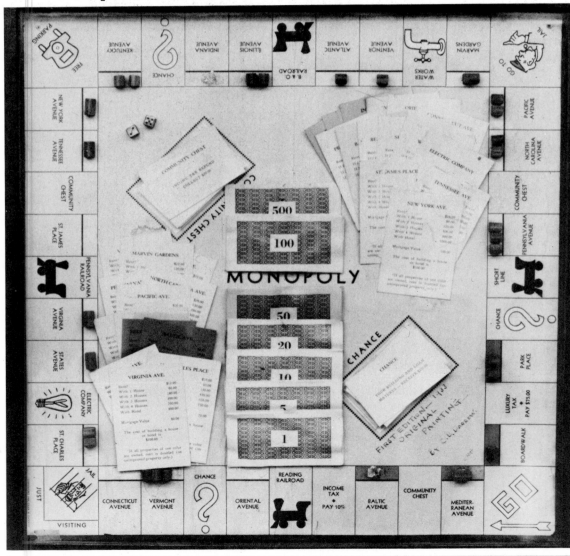

. . . The name of the game is _____
(fill in the blank.)

"Group Therapy" . . . "Ghetto" . . . "Ulcers" . . .
"Credibility Gap" . . . "Ratrace" . . . "The Howard
Hughes Game" . . . "Smog" . . . "Victory over
Communism" . . . "1776" . . . "Petropolis" . . . "Beat
Nixon" . . . "The Energy Crisis Game" . . . "Anti-
Monopoly" . . . "Population" . . . "Extinction" . . .
"The Godfather Game" . . . "Pro Draft" . . . "The
College Game."
*— The names of just a few of the games that have
been on the market in recent years.*

Currently some $300 million is spent annually on
board games in America, a sum that takes in a lot of
games and game players. And while a lot of kids still
spend a lot of time with them—starting with "Candy-
land" and other preschool games—the number of
adults at play on a board is tremendous and apparently growing by the day.

The reason for this is not only that adults have
more time for leisure and more money for recreation,
but that the people who develop and design them
have learned to slip something extra into the package
besides funny little markers, dice, cards, and multicolored boards. Increasingly the game-box cellophane
is wrapped around a fear, fantasy, or other major pre-
occupation of some sort. And even though the subject
of these games is as often as not something we have
little or no control over, the game gives us some real
control (mixed to varying degrees with the factor of
chance) over that piece of the real world it apes.

Let's say you're neither poor nor Black and want a
safe one-evening lesson in being poor and Black, you
can buy "Ghetto" ($25 a copy at better stores); or if
you want to painlessly drive home the realities of a
racially divided society, there is "Blacks and Whites,"
a game in which Blacks begin with $10,000 and
Whites with a million and the two play with different
stacked decks of cards. The frustrated football fan can
try to rebuild the New York Jets in an evening with
"Pro Draft," the exasperated environmentalist can
buy a copy of "Smog" or "Dirty Water" and expect,
finally, to have an impact on the problem (even if it is
only simulated), and the over-bossed office worker
who doesn't even have control over his or her coffee
break time can head home for a few rounds of "Dip-
lomacy," in which he or she may end up in control of
Europe.

Not all board games are concerned so much with
the real world as, say, "King Oil" or "The World
Commodity Futures Trading Game," which fact bears
a note of explanation. Basically all board games break

(Courtesy of Milton Bradley Co.)

The Checkered Game of Life was the first game published by Milton Bradley. It came out in 1860. A modern version of the game was published in 1960 and is still on the market. The game is much the same, but the ultimate goal has changed. In the original one worked toward a "happy old age" while in the new version one goes after 1 million dollars. (Courtesy of Milton Bradley Co.)

down into two categories: those which simulate some portion of the real world and games which are exercises unto themselves and copy nothing else. However, aside from the extremely successful game of *Scrabble* and several other word and math games, the tremendous growth in tabletop gaming has been with those which simulate.*

It seems that Americans have long had a special fascination for tabletop simulation, and all the early successes were of this type. Some of the early hits include W. & S. B. Ives's "Mansion of Happiness," "Banking," which was George Parker's (of Parker Brothers) first game, and Milton Bradley's first, "The Checkered Game of Life," which the company he founded is still selling today (with modifications) as "The Game of Life."

Yet ranging from the earliest examples, like 1844's hit, "The Missionary Campaign, or the Siege of the Stronghold of Satan, by the Christian Army," to the latest in which you are liable to draw a card that reads "You constantly resort to stereotyping sex roles; lose one turn," there is only one game that stands head and shoulders above the rest. Indeed, while the Great American Novel is still waiting to be written, the Great American Board Game has already been created.

During the Great Depression, in 1933 to be exact, an unemployed heating engineer named Charles B. Darrow fashioned a tabletop parlor game for the amusement of his family. The "board" was a hand-painted piece of oilcloth, the game markers were carved from lumberyard scraps, and the cards needed to play it were typed on cardboard strips. The idea of the game was to gain as much as you could as a real-estate speculator/developer. Darrow patterned his model of a real-estate market on the streets of Atlantic City, New Jersey, where the family had spent vacation time before the onset of hard times. He called it "Monopoly."

*There are some gray areas here. For example, is chess a military-simulation game or a game of skill built around a military metaphor? Still, the definitions do work in most cases.

It was not only a hit with his family but with friends and neighbors, who soon began pestering him for copies. He started making them at home by hand at the rate of two sets a day but soon found that the demand far outstripped his ability to produce them, so he had some run off commercially. Still he couldn't keep up with the increasing orders. Lacking the capital to go into large-scale production, he went to Salem, Massachusetts to try and convince Parker Brothers to go into partnership with him. Years later, Edward P. Parker recalled Darrow's fateful visit:

> After Darrow left, the executives played the game several times, and although we personally enjoyed it, everyone felt it could never be a popular success. It violated several of what we thought were elementary rules for a family game. We always felt that 45 minutes was about the right length of time for a game, but *Monopoly* could go on for hours. Also, a game was supposed to have a definite end somewhere. In "Monopoly" you kept going around and around. The rules involving mortgages and rents seemed much too complicated. The decision to turn it down was unanimous.

Darrow was not only told that the game was rejected but that in the company's opinion it contained fifty-two basic errors. Rebuffed but still undaunted, he got the money together to have 5000 more games produced and immediately sold the whole lot to John Wanamaker's department store in Phialdelphia, which planned to feature "Monopoly" as a big Christmas 1934 item. A report on the Wanamaker deal got back to Salem and the company hastily reconsidered. Early in 1935 Parker Brothers made Darrow an attractive royalty offer for rights to the game. What happened next is best described in this paragraph from "90 Years of Fun," the company's official history:

> "Monopoly" was the biggest thing that ever hit Parker Brothers. And more importantly, it rescued the company from very serious financial straits caused by the Depression. By mid-February, the plant was producing 20,000 sets a week. Before Christmas, so

The Mansion of Happiness holds claim to being the first board game published in America. The picture shows a relatively late 1894 edition published by Parker Brothers, which had bought the firm of W. and S. B. Ives which brought out the original in 1843. Like many offerings of the last century, Mansion of Happiness was determinedly uplifting and moral. (Courtesy of Parker Brothers.)

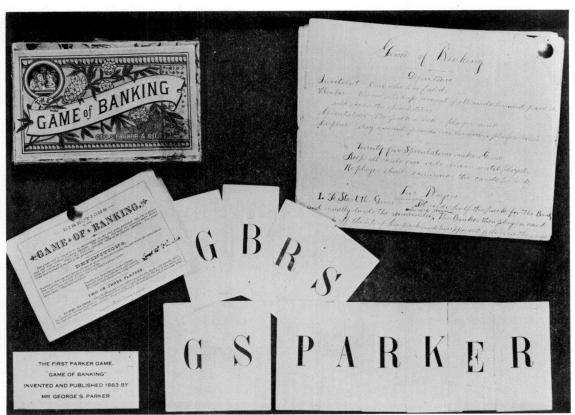

The Game of Banking, *George Parker's first game. Most 19th-century board games were like* Banking *in that they emphasized thrift or some other virtue and shied away from the idea of gambling. (Courtesy of Parker Brothers.)*

40 years of Monopoly. Shown here is the 1933 first edition of the game and the special edition published in 1973. The differences are ever so slight. (Courtesy of Parker Brothers.)

many telegraphed orders had poured in that they had to be filed in laundry baskets lined up in the hallways. A bookkeeping firm in Boston was called in to help with the mountains of paper work. They took one look and refused the job at any price.

Despite this initial success, Parker Brothers felt that the game was destined to be short-lived— perhaps selling well for three years. Orders did indeed begin slowing in late 1936 and early 1937, suggesting that its popularity had peaked early, but this was followed by a quick upturn, and the sales curve has yet to turn down, let alone level off, in all the years since. Some eighty million sets have been sold to date making it by far the best-selling copyrighted game in history and the world's most popular board game.* The hottest new game on the market is a decoding exercise called "Mastermind." As it has posted worldwide sales of ten million sets in its first three years on the market it just might give "Monopoly" a run for its money.

Meanwhile, Darrow, who passed on in 1967 at the age of seventy-eight, was set for life. Except for the hours he put into another far less successful game called "Bulls and Bears," which came out in 1937, he never worked again. He soon became a millionaire (and then a millionaire several times over) and spent the rest of his life raising orchids, visiting foreign countries, dabbling in photography, and tending his three-hundred-acre farm. He not only realized the Great Depression dream of a rags-to-riches idea but the dream of countless thousands of game designers who have tried to come up with a second "Monopoly."

With eighty million sets of the game at large, it should come as no surprise that all sorts of wild and interesting things have happened to the game. Does it seem odd that when the world's largest "Monopoly"

game was staged for charity in 1971 in Sunnyvale, California, that a real jail was used and the gigantic dice were thrown from fire escapes? Or, that the record for playing the game underwater, at least at the time of this writing, was set at a two-hundred-hour session in Mississippi in 1975 when two students broke the old 144-hour mark? Or, that when the Third World Monopoly Championship was held in Washington, *bone fide* national champs were there from fourteen nations (the contest was won by a real banker from Dublin named John Mair)?

There is so much of this stuff—records for hours played in a moving elevator, computers working to figure out the best opening-game strategy, the Russians who allegedly stole a half-dozen copies of the banned game from an American trade fair where they were on display, and the major flap that ensued when Atlantic City considered changing the names of two streets which also appear on the game board—that even the Monopoly put-ons begin to sound real. One such work, "Great Moments in Indoor Sports" by Sally McClusky, which appeared in the *Washington Star-News*, told of such plausible people and events as the two gents in a retirement home who played the longest game in history (from 1946 to 1952); "Stalemate" Agnes Mulligan, "who liked to have a card in every color and would not trade" and Diamond Fred Ogden:

> The greatest stylist of the game . . . whose winnings were so phenomenal that he used to light his cigars with money and give hotels to the cleaning lady. When he had another player at his mercy, he would hire him, at $1,000 a round, to move his pawn for him.

Understandably, this seemingly endless fascination for "Monopoly" has helped spawn a number of games with similarities to the original, especially the illusion of wealth which so many have called the key to Monopoly's success. One recent entry which owes a debt to Darrow is "Petropolis," a game in which wealth is counted in millions (rather than "Monopoly's" paltry thousands) and in which one vies for con-

*As of this writing, Parker Brothers was trying to decide who should get the 80-millionth copy. The choices that the company had narrowed their decision to were a top leader of the Soviet Union (where the capitalist game is banned), the Smithsonian, or Atlantic City.

The late Charles B. Darrow, who made a fortune for himself by inventing Monopoly while out of work during the Depression, gives away a $500 bill. (Courtesy of Parker Brothers.)

trol of oil-rich nations rather than mere pieces of New Jersey real estate. This game, invented by French photographer Baron Arnaud de Rosnay, gathered a lot of attention when it first came out because the first editions, with their silver-plated markers, leather deeds and such, cost $790 apiece.

While the people at Parker Bros. may see most of the "Monopoly"-like games as a form of flattery, this is clearly not the case with "Anti-Monopoly," a game they are attacking in court on the allegation of copyright infringement. "Anti-Monopoly" is like the original but has as its goal the completely opposite one of busting rather than building trusts. To read its rules is to give you the impression that you are reading a position paper from Ralph Nader's Center for the Study of Responsive Law. Sample: "The monopolistic practices of monopolies, trusts and oligopolies are designed to produce exorbitant profits for those companies by price-gouging."

The man who created this game in which "trustbusters" compete for "social credits" is Ralph Anspach, a San Francisco State University professor of economics, who did it to instruct the young in the realities of trusts. Now that Parker (actually General Mills, which owns Parker) has locked legal horns with Anspach, things have gotten serious. Anspach now claims that he has evidence suggesting that Darrow "borrowed" the game from one or more homemade, unpatented board games of the period. (One deposition from a Charles Todd alleges that he taught Darrow the game and wrote out the rules for him and accidentally misspelled Marven Gardens as "Marvin" which is the way it appears in the game.)

Leaving this unpleasant business to be sorted out in court, the fact remains that the "Monopoly" mystique increases daily, and it would seem to be helped more than hindered by "Anti-Monopoly." In fact, several reports on the revisionist game say that the monopolophiles are its biggest buyer.

The sizable "Monopoly" cult is certainly one of the largest and most influential in board gaming, but it is by no means the only one. Tabletop baseball (especially American Professional Baseball Association, or

The front of the Parker Brothers plant in Salem, Massachusetts in the early days. The company now has close to 500,000 square feet of plant space devoted to game production. (Courtesy of Parker Brothers.)

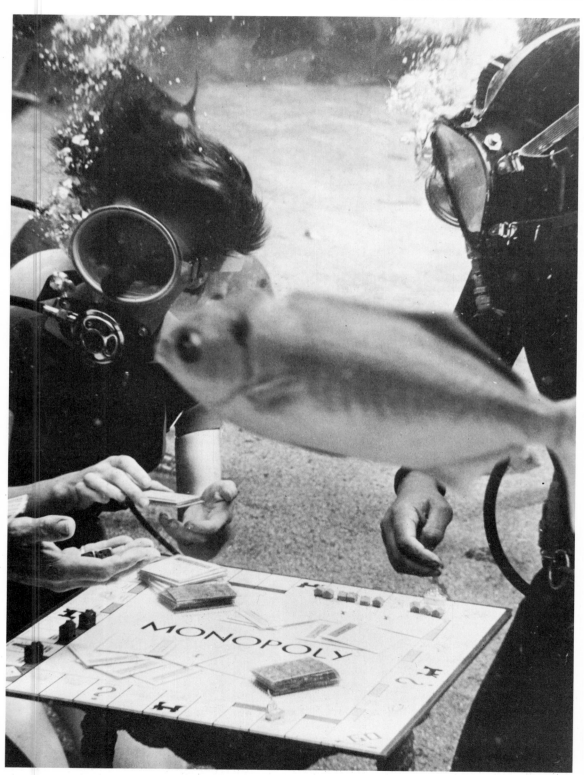

As teams form to vie with each other in the new sub-specialty of underwater Monopoly, *one thing that should be kept in mind is that the special waterproof edition of the game costs $500.00. (Courtesy of Parker Brothers.)*

Well-known anti-capitalists prepare for a friendly game of Monopoly (which is actually banned in the U.S.S.R. as a "decadent instrument of capitalism") in a San Francisco wax museum. (Courtesy of Parker Brothers.)

View of one of the largest Monopoly games ever played. This one is taking place in a shopping center in Flint, Michigan

in June, 1972. (Courtesy of Parker Brothers.)

AMERICAN SPORTS.

A new card game embodying all the popular sports of the day, which are illustrated on a set of cards. Embracing the following :

Toboggan Slide, Trap Shooting, Polo, Cricket, Sailing Regatta, Archery, Rowing Regatta, Lacrosse, Snow-shoe Race, Soap Bubble Party, Polo on Wheels, Base Ball, Croquet, and Bicycle Race. Other cards have illustrations of first, second, and third prizes. Put up in elegant style.

Price, each, 25 cents.

(Courtesy of Milton Bradley Co.)

APBA) players constitute a major subculture with its own newsletters, tournaments, heroes, and fanatics. One in the latter class is David Eisenhower who, while his father-in-law was still in the White House, drove to APBA headquarters in Pennsylvania to get the new cards for the game (new ones come out for each baseball season) so he wouldn't have to wait for them to come through the mail. Another man spent $1500 on telephone calls in a fourteen-month period making trades in an APBA league that allows trading. This cult is one of the few with its own novel, the highly praised *Universal Baseball Association, Inc. J. Henry Waugh, Prop.* by Robert Coover. In the 1968 novel Waugh creates his own league, which increasingly pulls him away from the real world.

But not all of the game-playing tribes have goals as mild and plausible as real-estate acquisition and winning the World Series on paper.

Armageddon Anyone?

It has long been claimed that the most interesting classified advertising in the world is to be found in the personal sections of London newspapers. The claim is kept alive by the occasional ad placed in one of them by a broker in mercenaries looking for recruits to support a lucrative uprising or by an archaeologist seeking financial or physical help for a promising dig. However, I'm convinced that the honor of "most-fascinating classifieds" belongs to an obscure American magazine called *The General.* I support my contention by quoting the first sentences of a few typical examples:

- Above average adult wargamer wants tough ftf (face to face) combat in Bay Area.
- Wanted: German who can beat my Spad 13. Will shoot the wings off your plane.
- Tired of fighting for nothing? Fight for a cause! We have opponents and a cause that is true. Joint the Black Death's glorious army of liberation.
- Prayer: God of Wargames, please send me face to face opponents!
- *Achtung!!* Announcing the formation of Der

"Hans Rudel," 1st SS Raumsturmgeschwader of Der Totenkopf SS's new RaumWaffe (space weapon).
- Wanted: Teenage boy to battle allies in the D-Day invasion.

Each issue of *The General* carries a hundred or so such ads with most of them coming from high school students, college students, and full-fledged adults. *The General* is just one of a score or more periodicals now being published which are completely dedicated to the art and science of tabletop wargaming. In case you haven't heard, wargaming has been growing since the late 1950s in the United States at a speed not even rivaled by the real arms race. The result of the boom is that there are in the nation today something like 100,000 hard-core (hard corps?) wargamers and hundreds of thousands more casual players. The hard core is roughly identified as being made of those with a number of games, who read the journals, probably belong to a club, and spend at least one full day a week in combat.

In 1975 the Avalon Hill Company of Baltimore, which is the leading manufacturer of war games and the publisher of *The General*, sold some 350,000 games, grossing more than $2 million in the process. Except for a few sports and other simulations, the Avalon Hill (A-H to gamers) line of twenty-six games is war-related including such titles as "Richtofen's War," "Blitzkrieg," "D-Day," "Stalingrad," "Gettysburg," "Waterloo," "Panzer Leader," "1914," and "Midway."

To give you an idea of what one of these games is like and show what the designers see in it, here is a partial description of a recent offering from the press release which announced it. The full name of the game is "The Rise and Decline of the Third Reich."

THIRD REICH is the final word in simulation scope. It features a mapboard stretching from Ireland to the Urals, and from Norway to the Suez. Indeed, just one of its "squares" includes the entire area fought over during the Battle of the Bulge. Each turn represents 3 months

Trek.

No. 4287.

A new game of skill and strategy, suggesting the tactics of the South African War. While the object and rules of the game are simple and easily understood by children, yet it affords to older people full scope for unlimited skill and scientific study. It is replete with fascinating problems and interesting combinations.

Trek will undoubtedly be the best selling game of the year. Complete in handsome cardboard box.

*Price, $1.00.

Size 17 x 19.

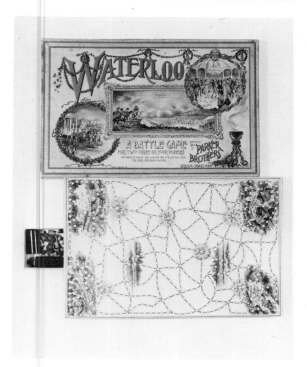

As these classic illustrations show, topical war games are hardly new. (Courtesy of Milton Bradley Co. and Parker Brothers.)

of actual time—quite a jump when compared to the hourly turns of a BULGE game, for instance.

All phases of warfare are covered in THIRD REICH. Naval, air and ground forces all play important roles. Players marvel at the historical patterns which most games follow as Poland and the Benelux countries fall to the German blitzkrieg followed in rapid succession by Norway, France, and the Balkans. Only after the invasion of Russia falters in the seemingly endless Russian steppes do the Allies begin on the long road back from defeat. Armor breakthroughs, submarine warfare, strategic bombing, fleet actions, and attrition all are represented in a game that leaves the players almost as exhausted as their forefathers must have been in the actual conflict.

Yet, unlike other games, history does not always repeat itself. The German player can avoid the strategic blunders of Hitler and pursue other strategies. With luck, an extremely clever player might just win the golden ring of world conquest which Hitler's Germany so narrowly missed.

Those who play such games appear to be a varied lot who defy very much generalization. There are war lovers here no doubt, but so too (under the same rubric which says you don't have to love murder to love to read murder mysteries) are the pacifists and former war protesters. As a matter of fact, Randy Reed, AH's game designer, applied for but didn't receive C.O. status. Avalon-Hill's research indicates that 70 percent of its clientele are between twelve and nineteen years old, and the rest are adults. According to its promotional material, Walter Cronkite and other celebrities are devotees of such games as "Battle of the Bulge" and "Waterloo."

Some have anguished over the question of to what extent do these games glorify war—or just as bad or worse—make it seem somehow logical? And for all those critics who have looked on it all with a nervous, skeptical eye, the faithful insist that the games are just games and hardly training grounds for world conquest. Players often remark that the games are as apt to point out the futility of war as a means of resolving issues or territorial disputes. Be this as it may, there is a side to this kind of game that has less to do with war *per se* than with the fantasy of tremendous power and control over world events—to be able to hopscotch the world looking for seminal moments, to be in charge in the guise of Grant, Eisenhower, Rommel, or whomever. This is potent stuff for Walter Cronkite, let alone a young mail-room clerk.

Unlike these war games and the many other entertainment games that show up in so many retail outlets from toystores to bookstores, the "new" simulation games list entertainment as but one of many functions. Designers of these games have added a whole new range of complexities to games, which are now separated into two broad categories: "manual" games, which are portable like "Monopoly," and "machine" games, or those which depend on computers. These designers are supported by a series of concepts, theories, and premises which add up to a way of thinking in which the game becomes a purposeful tool and technique for dealing with reality.

At present there are a few thousand of these games—with new ones being announced every week—being played in almost as many realms for goals as diverse as preparing civic administrators for natural disasters, helping high school students unscramble the vagaries of installment buying, testing urban-development theories, training air-pollution control administrators, and teaching the art of collective bargaining.

Creating, supporting, and evaluating this burgeoning game population is an increasingly large body of thinkers drawn from many disciplines who have their own professional organizations, periodicals, and scholarly meetings at which formula-laden papers are presented. While the term "game" may connote superficiality or frivolity to some, it does not to those researchers and academicians who call themselves "gamers" and who belong to the National Gaming Council and subscribe to *Simulation and Games—An International Journal of Theory, Design and Research.*

The gamer's universe extends into a variety of institutions. Government agencies have developed new games under contract, colleges work to develop new ones, research firms have installed game-design groups, and publishing firms market them. Certain computer-game development efforts have been huge, involving research teams, consultants and million-dollar budgets. Illustrative of the number of private groups and firms with designers on their payrolls was an announcement by the Department of Housing and Urban Development a few years back which asked for game designers to bid on a contract to develop a game to be used by community groups in learning about the urban decision-making process. Although the contract was to be a small one by Federal standards, seventy-three groups bid on the contract.

The use of games for reasons other than entertainment is not new—war games have been played by military planners for centuries, going back to the ancient Chinese game of encirclement, Wei-Hai, a game of military strategy attributed to the military thinker Sun-Tzu. By the latter half of the last century in Prussia the war game had emerged as a trusted and sophisticated arm of military planning—and was given at least partial credit for Prussian victories in the wars of 1886 and 1870-71 because they had suggested and led to the anticipation of conditions realized in combat. To varying degrees, games were used by most of the major powers during and between the two World Wars. The Japanese, for instance, successfully gamed Pearl Harbor, but unsuccessfully prepared for Midway with games. Most recently, the U.S. Department of Defense has used gaming techniques extensively, ranging from relatively simple role-playing games, in which hypothetical crises are set up and acted out by players, to ultrasophisticated, computer-assisted games in which detailed battles and thermonuclear exchanges are played out.

While "serious" gaming is not new, what is new is that in the last decade or so games have emerged as a force in a variety of nonmilitary areas. There is no single event, thinker, or theory which can be credited with the trend to play games outside the parlor and war room; however, there are certain trends which together have ganged up to prompt it. For one, the tremendous amount of thought and money that has gone

The Auto Game.

No. 4340

An inexpensive method of learning something about the Automobile.

Price, each, $0.12; postage, $0.08

He Cut off his Nose to Spite his Face.

This man is a Grammar Master of the old school. He does not believe in the "New Methods." He will not send for our **Illustrated Catalogue of School Aids and Material,** although if he would mention that he reads the "Ads" in the POPULAR EDUCATOR we would mail it to him without charge. Said a prominent teacher the other day: "I never dealt with any other firm as prompt and business-like in all their methods as Milton Bradley Co., Springfield, Mass., and their material is always excellent." The majority of teachers use it, and you will surely want some of it this year. Do not attempt to begin school without our Catalogue. Send 12 cents for our new Number Builder for desk-work in figures. Remember that we shall soon publish a Manual for Primary Work in Ungraded Schools.

MILTON BRADLEY CO.

October, 1889 **Springfield, Mass.**

Conflagration.

No. 4047

An exciting board game representing the race of the different pieces of apparatus to the fire.

Price, each, $0.12; postage, $0.08

(Courtesy of Milton Bradley Co.)

into military gaming and continues to do so (about $80 million a year these days) has led to all sorts of refinements in game design, play, and theory. Technological innovation has also helped—the computer, for example, has added a whole new dimension to gaming; it serves as a remarkable "gameboard" able to contain complex models into which a player's move can be fed and its effects quickly computed. Another factor was the push to put games in the classroom which began in the early 1960s when a group of academicians, led by Dr. James Coleman of Johns Hopkins, suggested that some of the interest and motivation shown on the athletic field might be transferable to the classroom through academic games.

One cluster of modern-day "Monopolys"s is a collection of urban games which have been fashioned to help others understand and study urban processes and problems. Some of them are as far removed in their degree of sophistication from Darrow's 1933 game as the Apollo program was from the first airplane. Most of these games first appeared in the late 1960s and serve as well as any other set of games to display the variety liable to crop up in any subject area. There are a score or more urban-simulation games now being played and they carry such titles as, "New Town," "Old Town," "Build," "City Model," "SIMSOC," "SIMPOLIS," "SITTE," "Sunshine," "Metropolitics," "Impact," "Fun City," "Urban Dyne," and "Yes, But Not Here."

Perhaps the most popular of the manual urban games carries the ponderous acronym "CLUG" which stands for "Community Land Use Game," which was developed by Allen G. Feldt of Cornell University. It simulates decision-making in an urban situation and is played as three to five teams try to build a city and remain solvent while doing so. Its main purpose is to show the players the basic factors affecting land use decisions.

Play starts with each team in possession of $100,000 in cash which will be used to develop land, construct buildings, speculate in land, or start new industries. The game is played on a board on which

highways and utility plants are located. Its rules are the generalized ones of urban economics; for instance, a residential property built on the board by a team will only return a profit if it is located near where there is a job for its occupants at one of the industrial sites on the board. The teams play at developing the land on the board for as many rounds as seems appropriate to them or their teacher, and there is no clear and definite end to the game.

By far the largest game audience in the country is in the classroom, where a large variety of games are played by groups ranging from elementary schoolers to graduate students. An example of an elementary school game is "Caribou Hunting," a game designed by Abt Associates of Cambridge, Massachusetts. It is a simulation of Eskimo hunting strategies intended to show the importance of social structure and strategies in resolving a cultural problem: i.e., how to kill enough caribou to survive the winter. The game begins as students are picked for one of three teams (two teams of Eskimos, one of caribou) which will play on a board representing ten square miles in Pelly Bay in Northern Canada. They move about the board following specific factual rules; for instance, on land the caribou can move faster than the men but in water Eskimos in kayaks can make better time than swimming caribou. The hunters must learn to cooperate and make the best use of their equipment—bows and arrows, spears and kayaks—to attain their objectives.

Manual games for the classroom show great variety and ofttimes reflect considerable imagination. "Panic," for example, is a game in which the students assume roles played by economic pressure groups during the Depression. "Destination" is a game for junior high school students in which players solve travel problems to gain an understanding of geographical concepts. "Life Career" simulates the labor market and puts students in the shoes of hypothetical individuals with certain goals to show the kinds of decisions (and the factors which impinge on those decisions) that a person in our society must make at various points. Other games come packaged in series, such as one that offers seven American

Not all board games published turn out to be big sellers, and true flops are not uncommon. The Tiny Tim Game of Beautiful Things *was such a flop. (Courtesy of Parker Brothers.)*

history games beginning with "Colony," an examination of trade relations between Britain and the American colonies, and ending with "Development," a game in which the superpowers court the favor of neutral nations.

Much more sophisticated games are finding substantial interest on the college campus, including some that have very specific users in mind, as indicated by such names as "The Cornell Hotel Administration Simulation," "The University of Massachusetts Poultry Farm Management Game," and "The Purdue Dairy Management Game."

To give a feel for the true variety in today's simulations here are a few more examples of games people are playing these days:

"The Energy Environmental Simulation." At $4000 a copy, this is far from a mass-production item. The purpose of the game, produced by the Atomic Energy Commission, of all people, is to keep the world operating for a given period of time without running out of energy. Part of the game's appeal is that it has all sorts of electronics associated with it giving the players various lights, levers, buttons, and buzzers to work with as they attempt to keep the world from running out of power.

"A Social Simulation of the Arab-Israeli Conflict." A structured recreation and acting out of the forces at play in the Middle East. The game takes eighty players with assigned roles and about eighty hours to play, spread out over a period of about a month and a half. It's a research simulation played to find leads for avoiding further conflict in the area.

"The Sticks and Stones Game." A management game in which up to four teams with appointed leaders compete in building a platform out of sticks that will support a stone. The game provides a structure for the investigation and discussion of supervision, dealing with others, and strategy. In this game building the platform is a broad simulation of the process of completing a job.

"Settle or Strike." A union/management collective-bargaining game which focuses on contract talks at the hypothetical Lastic Plastic Co. The game was developed under the sponsorship of the Communications Workers of America, which now distributes it for union representatives, management executives, and schools.

These efforts are not necessarily unique nor are they the far-out fringes of game application; rather they are presented to illustrate that there are increasingly few areas of pedagogical interest which have not been abstracted, simulated, and packaged as a game. This conclusion is further underscored as one browses through a few of the dozen or more game bibliographies and directories where one finds references to games simulating research procedures, campus unrest, international economics, advertising campaigns, ecological systems, and the management of a household.

Like other new techniques which have gained rapid popularity, this kind of gaming has attracted long lists of positive claims, advantages, and testimonials, especially as a classroom technique. Recent literature on gaming reveals a number of assertions about learning games—among them, that they are teachers of realism, are intrinsically motivating, develop skills, make concepts easier to grasp, teach both competition and cooperation, promote critical thinking, help "slow" students, also help bright students, are antidotes to passivity, are efficient, illustrate the role of chance in human affairs, show how the individual can affect the environment, teach problem-solving techniques, encourage mental flexibility, and illustrate the rewards and penalties exacted by society.

Although there is basis for most of these claims, they have prompted their share of skeptics. For instance, the editor of an educational journal, *Media and Methods*, acidly remarked, "Simulation games will revolutionize teaching (what won't?). Students will freak out on them (thus solving the drug problem), low tracks will suddenly become hypermotivated, teachers will become guides (referees, one supposes), and we will lock-step towards Nirvana with a pair of dice in hand."

All of this business about serious, purposeful gaming has taken us a bit off course from our examination of lighter, primarily diverting games. However, the differences between "serious" and "parlor" games are often not as great as you might think, as more and more games aren't that easily categorized. For instance, several versions of the aforementioned "New Town" have been marketed, ranging from a simpler, less expensive model for the parlor to a much more elaborate model for the professional planner. A few years back Field Marshal Montgomery and a German general refought part of World War II for the instruction of a BBC TV audience, not as part of a major computer simulation, but on Avalon Hill gameboards. And while it is hard to miss the entertaining possibilities from a new board game called "Seduction," it is harder to find a label for parlor games like "Group Therapy" and "Compatibility," which are hardly pure fun and frolic.

Each chapter of this book so far has attempted to include some helpful how-to information on the subject at hand; however, this is impossible to do in the case of board games since there are so many games with different rules, principles, and objectives. To compensate for not being able to provide tips on winning games, here is some solid information on designing your own games. Although the odds hardly favor it, there is always the chance that someone will use them to create the next "Monopoly."

Designing Your Own Games

There are probably as many formulas for designing games as there are people who have created them, but few designers ever bother to sit down and compile the steps of their art so others can learn. One who has is Samuel "Skip" Livingston formerly of the Johns Hopkins Academic Games Program, who has not only created his own games, acted as a game design consultant and evaluator, but has also written and taught on the subject of designing them.

SOCIAL HOURS.

AN EVENING'S ENTERTAINMENT FOR FIFTY GUESTS.

The popularity of the evening party of last season has suggested a more elaborate collection of material and directions for the entertainment of a company of guests of various ages and social tastes.

There are games, tricks, puzzles, rebus cards, fortune cards, age cards, etc., etc. A large and elegant box with illuminated label. Price, each, 50 cents.

PHRENOLOGICAL CHARACTER GAME.

An amusing and sensible entertainment for an evening party of children and adults. It embodies about one hundred quotations from the poets and gives very amusing chance characters to the players. The hits are at times so truthful and at other times very contrary to the facts, that great fun is afforded the players, and yet while the hits are oftentimes very sharp they are never offensive. Entirely novel in idea and method. Pithy, pointed, and pertinent. Price, each, 25 cents.

(Courtesy of Milton Bradley Co.)

GAME OF ROBINSON CRUSOE.

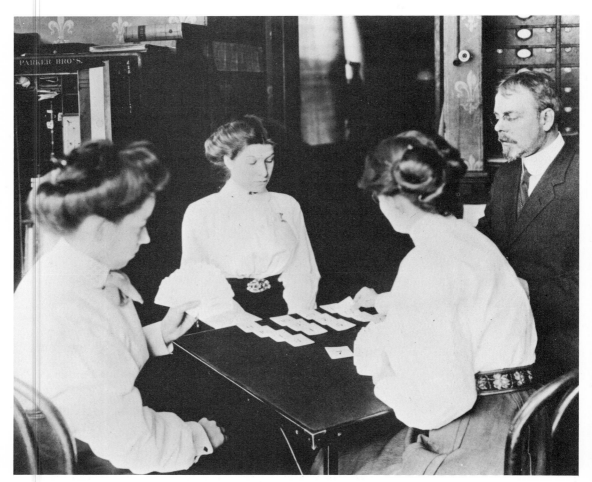

Gamesman George Parker at play with one of his own games, circa 1906. (Courtesy of Parker Brothers.)

Drawing from conversations with Livingston and from his writing, here is a basic list of the simulation-game design tenets for those who might wish to try their hand at creating a game. His rules are intended to work on games ranging from simple ones like "Monopoly" to complex computerized offerings.

1. Determine what you want your game to demonstrate, pick the real-life situation you want it to simulate, and identify the roles of the participants. In any good game, players only represent those persons whose decisions affect the game's outcome—in other words, there are no passive or dummy roles.

2. Identify each player's goals and choose a "measure of success" for the game. This measure may be a concrete item like votes, land, casualties, or dollars, or an abstract one like credits or points.

3. Determine the resources that will be available to each player—that is, those things which can be used to influence the game in his or her favor. Again, such things can either be concrete items like money or property or abstractions like prestige or ability. Once these are identified, you must figure out their relative importance and ability to influence events.

4. Figure out the interactions between the players—the way in which each player's move affects the other players and their chances for success.

5. Establish the sequence of events in your game. This may be a series of repeating cycles or a single event and may have a natural conclusion or be of indefinite length. (If the game is of indefinite length, you will have to devise a means of ending it. It could be timed, like a football game, or ended when one player has reached a certain score, as in tennis.)

6. Plot the external factors, or those outside the player's control, which will affect the game. These would include chance factors and the actions of people in the real-life situation who are not represented by players. For example, if weather is a factor in your game, you might wish to determine it by using dice, cards, or spinners, but you will want to try to match the probabilities implied in the real world situation, e.g., no blizzards in June.

7. Identify the physical factors of your game and organize them on a playing board. (If physical factors are unimportant, there may be no need for a board.) If, for instance, the most important physical attributes of the game are geographic, then your board will probably be a map.

8. Once a first version of your game is done, experimental play is required to work the bugs out of it. In revising and refining your games, two important basic considerations should be kept in mind: (a) *realism*, which demands that the choices of strategy, results, and final outcome of play in the game correspond fairly closely to those of the situation being simulated, and (b) *playability*, a hard quality to define outright but one which will be helped by editing out such pitfalls as: idle time for players, complex calculations which must be made during the game, complicated or confusing materials and rules that are easily misunderstood or likely to be violated by mistake.

In addition to these eight basic steps, Livingston cautions that perhaps the hardest conflict the simulation game designer faces is that between simplicity and accuracy. In order to be playable, the game must simplify the real life situation, but oversimplification destroys realism. One path suggested by Livingston for resolving this conflict is to make the game playable at different levels of complexity—adding complications which make the game more realistic after the players have mastered simpler versions of the game.

Chapter 9

Extra Innings

. . . Looking in on the state of tiddlywinks, croquet, horseshoes, paper airplanes, skates, and jump ropes.

Those things which have concerned us thus far are just some of the simple diversions worthy of great adult exploitation. There are more—many more in fact—which we should be aware of. As a starting point for understanding and enjoying still more of them, accounts will now be made of another handful, presented in no special order.

Still, the handful that follows fails to account for so many other greats which space does not permit to be depicted in the detail they rightfully deserve. This task must be left to others—scholars, fans whomsoever—to perform in other works. Make no mistake about it. There is much to be done. For instance, there is certainly need for a major examination of hopscotch, starting with such tantalizing evidence as the lines of what appear to be ancient "beds" (scotches or shallow cuts) on the floor of the Roman Forum, leading all the way up to today's hotly contested Chicago Hopscotch Tournament for Mothers. So too there is ample opportunity for making important contributions in such areas as bean bags, jacks, boomerangs, pogo sticks, darts, and Ping-Pong.

The Noble Tiddlywink

Tiddlywinks is an exacting pastime. It taxes every fiber of the brain and exercises every muscle of the body.
The world is now looking to tiddlywinks to get back to the primeval simplicity of life.
—Two statements from the Rev. E. A. Willis, retired minister and former Secretary-General of the World Tiddlywink Congress.

Few games labor under the disadvantages that tiddlywinks does because it is so commonly disregarded as an infantile game with a silly name. That image, however, flies in the face of reality. Consider the following sampling of evidence:

- Serious winkers consider it a tactical struggle of great complexity meant only for good minds (more on the game shortly).
- Oxford and Cambridge Universities, both long-time hotbeds of the sport, have been locked in a debate which has lasted for more than one hundred years over the correct spelling of the name, with Oxford favoring the less common "tiddliwinks."
- There are at least two known journals devoted to the game: the British *Winking World* and America's *Newswink.*
- The highest team honor in Britain is a trophy called the Silver Wink, which was donated to the sport by no less a person that Prince Phillip. This royal person, by the way, was once asked to join a team composed of a famous group of English madcaps called the Goons (which included Peter Sellers), an offer which he turned down with the utterly plausible explanation that, "While practicing secretly I pulled an important muscle in the second, or tiddly, joint of my winking finger."

Tiddledy Winks

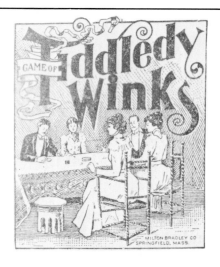

We offer two editions of this Popular Game which are all right in price and quality. They have the best imported bone winks.

BEST EDITION.

No. 4285
Price, $0.25; postage, $0.08.
Size, 4 7-8 x 5 3-4

1 Glass Cup, 6 set of winks each of four colors, 6 pieces of felt for the players to flip their winks. Best edition to be had at this price.

No. 4284 A   15 CENT EDITION.
Size 4 5-8 x 5 7-8   Price, $0.15; postage, $0.07

10 CENT EDITION.
No. 4284
Price, $0.10; postage, $0.05
Size, 3 1-2 x 4 7-8

GHEAP EDITION.
No. 4052
Size 2 1-2 x 3 1-2
Price, $0.05; postage, $0.03

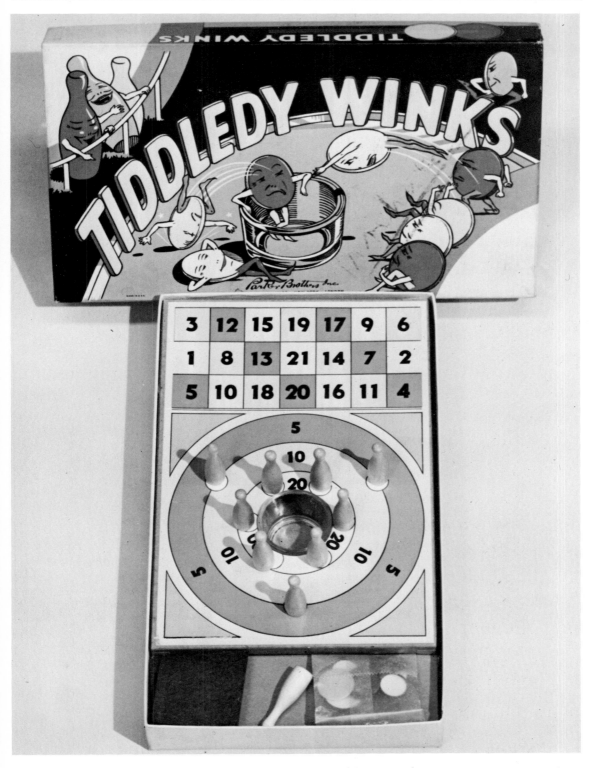

Few games have been offered in as many different packages while changing so little as this enduring classic. Here from different eras are offerings from Parker Brothers and Milton Bradley Co. (Courtesy of Parker Brothers and Milton Bradley Co.)

The game is played internationally with British teams roaming as far afield as India and Russia (where it is called "The Game of Fleas") to do battle. In 1975 Bill Renke of MIT beat English champ Alan Dean, which was a significant blow to the pride of the British who consider themselves the best in the world. (For what it's worth: the official title of the French rules for the game is "*les regles officielles du tiddly.*")

Great aficionados of the game include Terry-Thomas, King Alfred (871-901 AD) of England, and Ch'eng Ti, a first-century B.C. Chinese Emperor.

In parts of the world, the right tiddlywink happening can make headlines. When, for instance, several miniskirted competitors so distracted other players in an English regional tournament that the game had to be halted so they could change into slacks, one of the local papers carried the banner, "REPLAY! THE SQUIDGER [shooter] FLICKER'S KNICKERS WERE SHOWING."

The game itself (full rules in Appendix IK.) is played on a three-by-six-foot mat where one uses a squidger to shoot with. One's ultimate goal is to put all your winks [plastic discs] into a cup $1^7/_8$ inch in diameter, called the pot. Unsophisticated players don't realize, however, that "potting winks" is just one tactic employed by winners and one that is usually employed toward the end of a game. *Squoping*, or *freezing* your opponent's winks by putting one of your winks on top of his, is another potent tactic as are *boondocking*, sending enemy winks far from the cup, and *nurdling*, putting opposition winks too close to the cup to be able to pot easily.

The best players can do some remarkable things popping these little discs. One MIT champ, where most of the best American players come from (although Cornell, Utah, Harvard, and the Canadian colleges have had their share), in a demonstration made 996 pots out of 1000 shots, during which he rang up one string of 332 in a row. Then there was the fabulous "septenary squoop"—claimed to be the first on American soil—which took place in 1962 in a

Harvard versus Columbia contest when one wink tied up seven others.

Yet with all of this richness, tiddlywinks is still only seriously enjoyed by a small—some say, growing—number of devotees who virtually to a person believe the rest of the world is missing out. The general consensus in tiddlywinking circles is that all of this might change if the game was given a new name. The present one not only sounds silly but has less than an uplifting set of connotations. In old England the term was used for an unlicensed public house, such as a brothel or beer hall. It can also mean puny, idling, and cheating, while tiddle can mean to tickle and tiddly means very small or trivial.

The American journal *Newswink* has discussed this issue in its pages, and occasionally readers suggest alternative names that would attract a larger public to the sport. Perhaps the best ideas came from one devotee who feels that either "Football" or "Sex" might do the trick as a new name.

Classy Croquet

We'll never get over what Lewis Carroll did to us. All those hedgehogs and flamingos; it gives us an Alice in Wonderland complex.
—Croquet player quoted in the British press in reference to the zany game about which Alice complained, "They don't seem to have any rules in particular . . . At least, if there are, nobody attends to them."

Thus far we have concerned ourselves with things enjoyed by the average man, woman, or child, but now we come to a game of a different stripe. To be sure, Woolworth's sells croquet sets, and the masses play at it in the crabgrass, but there really is something different about those who are really into croquet—notably that they tend to be well-heeled, well-placed sorts with gardeners to keep their courses in tip-top shape.

In the United States, interest in the game tends to center in places like the posher Connecticut sub-

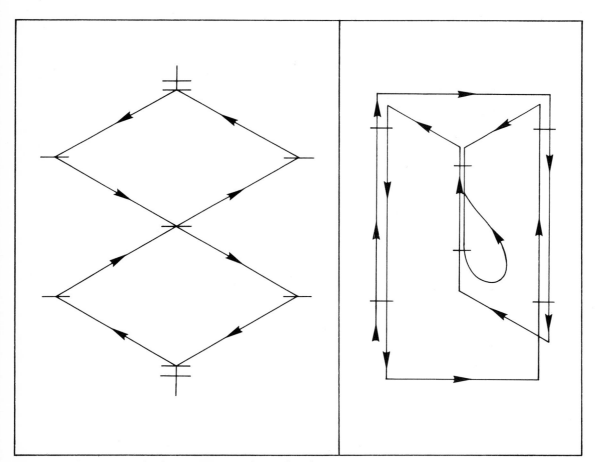

American Croquet Course (left). British Croquet Course (right).

urbs, Southhampton, and Palm Beach, where there is a $50,000 course at the Colony Hotel. In such places, the game is played with lignum vitae mallets (many of which come from the firm of John Jacques of England, which has been making them for people of means since 1795) and boxwood balls and taken ever so seriously by the players, who include the present and past likes of W. Averell Harriman,

Richard Rodgers, H. G. Wells (who actually wrote a book called *The Croquet Player*), and Sir James Barrie.

If an American elite is mad about playing the game, Britons of high social standing commonly go bonkers over it, with occasional devotees going off the deep end. Not too long ago the editor of a British croquet magazine had to be removed from his post

(Courtesy of Milton Bradley Co.)

(Courtesy of Milton Bradley Co.)

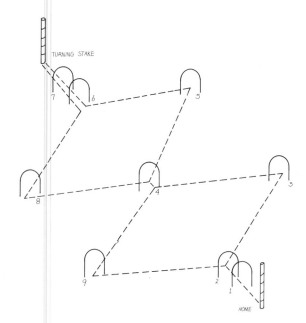

TURNING STAKE

7   6   5

8

4   3

9   2   1

HOME

American Croquet Course.

because of his ranting about the wrong types playing the game.

Despite the similarity of the types who play, the games played in the two countries are quite different. Americans play a nine-wicket game with a liberal eighth inch between the ball and the wicket and the British go through six much stickier wickets with only a sixteenth of an inch on each side (and sometimes only a thirty-second of an inch in tournament play). Also, the courses themselves are laid out differently.

There are other differences too. For instance, in style the British feel the Americans play too aggressively—sending opponents' balls off into the rhododendrons and such—instead of relying on more civilized tactics developed over the decades at tea parties and in rectory gardens.

Differences aside, it is a good game for the players (and one of the dullest of all games to watch) and worthy of a larger, more diverse following, such as it enjoyed during its American heyday in the late nineteenth century. (The American rules are to be found in Appendix L.)

The Humble Horseshoe

[The Revolution was won] on the village greens by pitchers of horseshoe hardware.
—The Duke of Wellington on the types who beat the British in the American Revolution

Although the sport didn't begin in America—it probably dates back to ancient times when Greek or Roman soldiers created it, killing time with discarded horseshoes—it has over the years become the most American of pastimes, with an estimated 30,000 "serious" pitchers, tens of thousands more dabblers, national championships and tournaments, a national players association, its own folklore, and a patron saint in Harry Truman, who took to horseshoes the way Ike took to golf.

Unlike croquet, pitching horseshoes is a distinctly working-class avocation, and its great centers of

GAME OF PITCH-A-RING.

One of the many variations on the horseshoe/quoits theme. (Courtesy of Milton Bradley Co.)

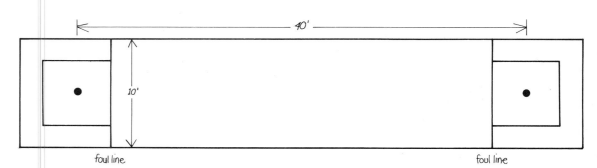

Diagram of a Horseshoe Court.

activity are in the industrial outbacks of Ohio, Pennsylvania, Indiana, and New Jersey as well as certain rural areas. At its best, it is a game of great precision, and national champions are able to turn about 85% of their pitches into ringers. Because ringers cancel each other out, big tournaments are affairs of attrition in which it is not uncommon for a winner to have walked five or six miles between the pits and to lose ten or so pounds. Like croquet, it is more fun to do than to watch (see Appendix for rules).

The Soaring Paper Airplane

As for me, when the world goes wrong, when the work I have to do tomorrow morning is especially laborious and when the things that So-and-so said to me yesterday afternoon were peculiarly galling, I seldom turn to any of these things. I turn instead to paper aeroplanes.
—*H.G.G. Herklots from his 1931 book of essays,*
Paper Aeroplanes.

Back in those simpler, hot old days before they started air conditioning and hermetically sealing the nation's office buildings, it was common to see paper airplanes soaring on the afternoon thermals of Madison Avenue, Constitution Avenue, and other great centers of paperwork. Without the ability to

push a paper plane out the window, the art for office-bound adults as an antidote to boredom was foundering, and it seemed as though it would only live on in schools, where most of us first learned to turn three-ring, lined composition paper into sleek expressions of aerodynamic art.

Then, suddenly, on December 12, 1966, *The New York Times* carried an ad from *The Scientific American* magazine announcing the first International Paper Airplane Competition. The idea came from the late advertising genius Howard Gossage and *Scientific American* publisher Gerard Piel, who hit upon it one day at lunch. Ostensibly conceived to promote the magazine—which it did quite well—there was a second motive to their madness, which was never admitted in so many words but which was nonetheless clear. This second motive was to poke some fun at the Supersonic Transport (SST) which the nation's aerospace poobahs were just beginning to insist the nation could not live without.*

The rest of what happened to the competition is history: editorials supporting it appeared everywhere, no less than 12,000 souls crafted planes and carefully

---

* The first ad for the contest appeared in the *Times* on page 38 while page 37 of the same edition contained a full-page ad from the folks at Lockheed encouraging the American people to push for the SST. The machinations which led to this critical placement—surely no accident—have never been revealed.

Gerard Piel, publisher of Scientific American, *launches an entry in the magazine's 1st International Paper Airplane Competition.*

shipped them to contest headquarters, and the final fly-off at the New York Hall of Science was covered by a total number of reporters equal in size only to the number that had covered the visit of Pope Paul to New York. "It was," as its promoters later claimed, "an event unique in aviation history."

While the event itself was significant, what is perhaps more important is that paper airplaning has come back to glory in its wake as a great white-collar workaday pursuit. This has been aided greatly by the fact that the people who ran the original contest published the classic *Great International Paper Airplane Book* in 1967, which not only discussed the art in great detail but which contained pages on which the winning entries (in categories ranging from longest-distance flown to origami) were outlined to be torn out, trimmed, folded, and flown. Immediately anyone with the price of the large paperback was in possession of a fleet of what were unquestionably the best paper airplanes ever designed. Paper aviation had taken a great leap forward, and thanks to the modern miracle of Xerography countless thousands more were copied and flown from those pages.

Not too long ago, while visiting the offices of a company in New York while researching a magazine article, I rounded a corner and came face to face with a graceful little plane fashioned of computer print-out paper of good stock. It was quite reassuring.*

A Tale of Two Skates

I think that the skateboard is going to be the biggest toy of the next two years and, who knows, the decade.

---

* On balance, however, there are far too few office sports outside of paper-airplaning, suggesting the need for new development in this area. One of the few new items to come down the pike in recent years is a kit containing a Nerf Ball and an inch diameter basketball hoop. Though marketed primarily for kids, it is gaining for something to mount over your trash basket for office basketball, which can be played with either the ball provided or wadded-up paper.

— Toy buyer for a major New York Department Store, December 1965.

In the spring of the year 1975, it came to pass that:

1. Roller skating as a pastime was clearly going into a downhill slump. For one, the Union Hardware Company of Torrington, Connecticut, which supplies about 40 percent of the declining market, laid off almost all of its workforce with no hope of calling them back at least until the fall. The plant manager, Bob O'Conner, told the *Washington Post*, "Kids aren't skating now." As always there were forces to blame—in this case the urban exodus to new suburbs where sidewalks are in short supply.

2. The skateboard returned from ten years of dormancy to such a degree that the phenomenon was termed one of the most sensational comebacks in toy history. Coming out of Florida and California where the fad first returned, they moved across the land like so many lemmings.

Although the correlation between these two turns in popularity was not direct, it was indeed ironic that as one form of skating was going into eclipse another was coming out.

For roller skates the development was in keeping with history. The nation was hit with its first roller skating boom in the 1870s, which was monumental and resulted in wooden rinks being erected in almost every town of any size in America. According to Inez and Marshall McClintock in their *Toys in America*, over $20 million was tied up in rinks, an amount which, of course, bought a lot of planks in those days. In the mid-1880s the craze died with the same suddenness with which it had appeared, and the rinks came down. Then at the turn of the century skating came back—aided in great measure by vastly improved new models with ball-bearing wheels, say the McClintocks—and a new generation of wooden rinks got built. About the time World War I got underway, skates were out again but came back heavily in the 1930s when it became a big sidewalk pastime (more, mostly enclosed, rinks came along too), which it has remained until the recent fall-off. Given this history, it is hard to really believe that skates and their culture—the all-important skate key, asphalt-scabbed knees, "snapping the whip," skate tag, and so forth—are dying. The odds would seem to favor the belief that they are napping, to wake suddenly again in the future (although one hopes not as they are depicted in the film *Rollerball*).

Just as technology once brought the roller skate out of the doldrums (i.e., the ball bearing), an advance in the state of the art has been one of the prime forces behind the return of the skateboard. When the first came on the scene in 1965, it took only weeks before safety groups, medical societies, and the like were up in arms over skateboards calling them, among other things, "child cripplers" and "suicide kits," for the reason that their wheels (made of Chicago clay) were not well suited for taking corners, causing many falls and injuries. The new, vastly improved skateboards now in vogue have urethane wheels with good cornering ability.

The Universal Jump Rope

I would offer tempting odds that there is not an able-bodied man, woman, or child who has not, at some time or another, succumbed to the challenging fascination of a turning rope.
—*Peter L. Skolnik from his book* Jump Rope!

Probably the most striking thing about the jump rope is its virtual universality, showing up in the remotest corners of the earth. In addition to the rope per se, it carries with it an unwritten body of knowledge which moves around the world seemingly carried on the wind. Rope games played by kids centuries ago in England show up today with the same rules on the sidewalks of Philadelphia; jump rope rhymes and jingles that can be heard on the streets of Belfast or Birmingham are heard with only minor variation in Levittown and Watts, and certain basic rope tricks are as identical from nation to nation as sneezing.

Jump ropes have been around for a long, long

time, although little is known about their earliest history. Much that has been written about ancient jumping is more conjecture than fact. For instance, one thought that has appeared in print a number of times is that jumping may stem from the ancient belief that crops would grow as high as a person could jump and that the rope began an adjunct to this ritual of the planting season.

In any event jumping rope has long been popular among children—especially girls*—and has of late been gaining added respect as adults of both sexes realize that jumping rope is an inexpensive, diverting, and effective aid to staying in shape.

Jumping takes many forms, from simple standing in place solo jumping to things like "Double Dutch," the difficult exercise in coordination in which you jump as two confederates turn two ropes inwardly like a gigantic eggbeater. It also has a rich terminology of its own and scores of games, stunts, and exercises, some of the most important and universal of which are:

Visiting. In which one turns the rope and jumps as others, one at a time, "visit" to jump for a while inside the same rope.

Double Dutch. As described above, the object here is to survive inside the eggbeater of ropes for as many turns as possible. It is so popular in New York City, for example, that there is an annual citywide competition.

Calling In. Two players turn a large rope as a third comes in and jumps for a specified number of turns (usually three) calling another player in on a specific jump (usually the second). The two jumpers jump once together and the first jumper runs out and the second calls in a third.

Drop the Handkerchief. Again two players turn a large rope as a third runs in and while jumping drops her handkerchief and on the next jump picks it up.

---

* In *Jump Rope!* Peter Skolnik points out that much evidence suggests that jumping rope was originally a boy's pastime, but that as boys moved into organized, competitive sports the girls took it over. He also believes that girls developed ways of keeping the rope to themselves, for example, creating rhymes with feminine content.

This skill game is also played with a stone when it is called Baking Bread.

Relay Jumping. Often played in school gym classes, teams of jumpers compete with each other on separate ropes held by two players. In each round a successively harder feat is attempted by each member of each team with one point being scored for each completion.

High Water, Low Water. Like high-jumping, two hold the rope stationary as the others jump over it. The rope is moved higher on each round until there is a winner.

Beyond jumping and jumping games *per se*, the jump rope brings with it a rich and varied collection of rhymes which show up all over the world. Often one child will carry a remarkable sampling of these rhymes. When, for example, a Washington D.C. school principal who was collecting rhymes asked a group of fifth-graders for their favorites, she found that most handed in fifteen or more and one girl was able to summon up 150 different rhymes before slowing down.

Of late the true extent of the repertoire of jumping rhymes has begun to be demonstrated as adults—for reasons ranging from pure fun to pure scholarship— have begun putting together collections of them. Skolnik lists 250 in his book but his is not the only book. Others include three with the same title, *Jump Rope Rhymes*, by Patricia Evans (Porpoise Books, 1954), Florence Radcliffe (the D.C. School System, 1969), and Edwin H. Adams (Silver Quoin Press, 1947), and *American Nonsinging Games* by Paul G. Brewster (University of Oklahoma Press, 1953). In addition, scholarly articles on the humble rhymes have appeared in such learned locations as *American Anthropologist, Western Folklore, The New York Times Magazine, Keystone Folklore Quarterly*, and the *Journal of American Folklore.*

With such attention by serious collectors and scholars, it should come as no surprise to find out that the rhymes have been given interpretations which remove them from the realm of innocence (fortunately kids don't do too much browsing in the *Keystone Folklore Quarterly*, where they might see their secrets bared), and it now seems that the rhymes often serve purposes beyond that of providing mere words to jump by. Scholars who have a closer look at them are finding that they are often outlets for deep emotions and repressed desires. On this, Francelia Butler, a University of Connecticut English professor and collector of rhymes, has written:

> I am convinced that through the act of skipping, of overcoming the demonic power of the rope, the child achieves a bodily and psychic loosening of emotional strictures. The rhymes, ancient in origin, durable and widely distributed, are a way for unconscious elements in the personality to surface. This is apparent . . . in widely diverse countries and cultures.

As an example, she points to a rhyme she collected in Northern Ireland which shows how an older child contends with the frustration of having to tend for a younger one:

> My wee brother is no good.
> Chop him up for firewood.
> When he's dead
> Cut off his head
> Make it into gingerbread.

This chant from Northern Ireland is far from rare, as these other less than cheerful rope songs demonstrate. They deal with such assorted villains as dictators, teachers, and older brothers.

> Hitler, Hitler
> I've been thinking,
> What on earth have you been drinking?
> Smells like whiskey,
> Tastes like wine,
> Oh, my gosh!
> It's iodine.
> (Evans, ca. 1945)

I had a little brother,
His name was Tiny Tim,
I put him in the bathtub
To teach him to swim.
He drank all the water,
He ate all the soap,
He died last night
With a bubble in his throat.

In came the doctor,
In came the nurse,
In came the lady
With the alligator purse.

"Dead," said the doctor,
"Dead," said the nurse,
"Dead," said the lady
With the alligator purse

Out went the doctor,
Out went the nurse,
Out went the lady
With the alligator purse.
                (Baltimore Sun, *June 12, 1966)*

Jaybird, Jaybird, sitting on a rail,
Picking his teeth with the end of his tail.
Mulberry leaves and calico sleeves,
All school teachers are hard to please.
                (Florence Radcliffe, 1960s)

Johnny on the ocean,
Johnny on the sea,
Johnny broke a milk bottle
And blamed it on me.
I told Ma,
Ma told Pa,
Johnny got a whipping
And a ha! ha! ha!
How many whippings did he get?
1, 2, 3, etc.
                (Skolnik)

I won't go to Macy's any more, more, more,
There's a big fat policeman at the door, door,
    door.
He takes you by the collar and makes you pay a
    dollar.
I won't go to Macy's any more, more, more.
                (Radcliffe)

In the rhymes of grim or hostile content, there are certain figures which appear again and again: Tiny Tim, the hapless little brother; Johnny, the older brother who always gets caught; and "the big fat policeman." Mysteriously, however, the most universal of all these figures is the "lady with the alligator purse" who in rhymes from all over shows up when there is sickness or death. Another example:

Mother, mother, I am ill.
Call the doctor over the hill.
In came the doctor,
In came the nurse,
In came the lady
With the alligator purse.
                (Radcliffe)

Another class of rhymes that seems to be more than just words to jump rope to are those which, in the mind of a child at least, can be suggestive and risqué.

Postman, postman
Do your duty.
Here comes (fill in name)
The American Beauty.
She can do the rhumba,
She can do the splits,
She can pull her pretty dress,
Right up to her hips.
                (Evans)

Salome was a dancer,
She danced before the king.
And every time she danced,
She wiggled everything.
"Stop!" said the king,
"You can't do that in here."
Salome said "Baloney!"
And kicked the chandelier.
(Evans)

John *and* Mary
Up in a tree,
K-I-S-S-I-N-G.
First comes love,
Then comes marriage,
Then comes Mary
With a baby carriage.
(Skolnik)

A few jump-rope rhymes have actually become controversial. For instance, three jumper's jingles were among the specific items which came under fire by objecting parents in the famous Kanawa County, West Virginia, textbook controversy of 1975. The three rhymes which show up in a Webster/McGraw-Hill Series are:

Sally drank marmalade
Sally drank beer
Sally drank everything
That made her feel queer.
A-whoopsie went the marmalade
A-whoopsie went the beer.
A-whoopsie went everything
That made her feel queer.

Fudge, fudge
Call the judge.
Mama's got a newborn baby!
It's not a girl,
And it's not a boy.
It's just a newborn baby!
Wrap it up in tissue paper
Put it on the elevator.
One, two, three
And
Out goes she!

I was standing on the corner,
Not doing any harm.
Along came a policeman
And took me by the arm.
He took me around the corner,
And he rang a little bell.
Along came a police car
And took me to my cell.

Another curious aspect of the rhymes is their striking ability to remain intact, with minor variations, over long distances and periods of time. *Washington Star-News* writer Diana McLellan was amazed to find her daughter and friends still jumping to rhymes which had been topical years before, such as the classic:

Charlie Chaplin went to France
To teach the girls the hoochi-koochi dance.
First on the heel,
Then on the toe,
Do the splits and 'round you go.
Salute the Captain,
Curtsy to the Queen
And touch the bottom of the submarine.

Ms. Butler has discovered a rhyme still in use in locations as far apart as Virginia and Northern Ireland which she has traced back to the Roman Era. It is an odd little rhyme (which she feels contains "an element of fear") which goes like this:

All in together, girls,
No mind the weather, girls.
I spy a lark, sitting in the dark.

Others, however, remain regional or national because of their content. This New Deal Era chant unearthed by Skolnik is entirely American:

W.P.A.
W.P.A.
You're let out,
Go and get your pay.

So too, one can guess that some of the rhymes which a Reuters reporter heard in China in 1972 will have a hard time breaking into the jump-rope hit parade in the West. One began with the line, "The Revolutionary Peoples are going to win."

Aside from providing cadence for jumping and expressing social concerns, there are many special rhymes which are variously used for fortune telling (such as divining the name of one's next boyfriend), counting, and calling in or moving out a jumper. An example would be the old favorite: "Keep the kettle boiling / Never miss a loop," in which the old jumper goes out on the word "loop," runs around the ender (one of those holding the rope), and the new jumper comes in. The same thing happens in this long-time hit: "House to rent, inquire within / As I move out, let [name of next jumper] in."

All in all, the jump rope, which is so unremarkable and simple when not in use becomes so remarkable when placed in the right hands—those skilled jumpers with an ageless repertoire of games and stunts and an amazing collection of rhymes. It is an underrated pastime which the adult world (save for rhyme scholars) has overlooked for too long.

Author's Afterword

During the researching of this book, I was struck time and again by the fact that many of the simple things under discussion were once the province of adults and children rather than, as has been the case until very recently, children alone.

I am at a loss to explain exactly why or when this occurred. But much of the damage was done in the years of this century before World War I, when putting away childish things seemed to be the order of the day for adults. I think that a major reason for this may have been the concurrent rise of new pursuits for adults — the automobile, aeroplane, scientific tinkering, and organized sports. To play at marbles or to fly a kite was suddenly immature, and such things were only proper in the context of grander pursuits. For instance, a 1911 work, *The Library of Work and Play*, in telling kids of kites says, "In these days when a man is seen flying a kite, people very naturally imagine him to be an aeronaut, studying the science for the purpose of improving or inventing a flying machine of some kind — for which there seems to be ample room." Other toys were allowed in adult hands when and if they taught a scientific lesson to kids — such as using a top to demonstrate physical laws.

If this thesis is correct, it would now seem that those very things that pulled adults away from childish sport are becoming increasingly hard to enjoy. The price of gasoline for pleasure driving, manned flight (save as a passenger), big science, greens fees, and more are all conspiring to bring the average man and woman back to the simpler things.

And if, as we are told, things continue to get more complex, the trend should continue and increase.

Action-Packed Appendices

Appendix I

A. Some Kites to Make

The following are intended as an introduction to kite building, as they represent only a sampling of the scores of designs available. All of these are designs which originally appeared in the pages of *Kite Tales*, which has kindly granted permission for their use here.

1. Eddy Kite

Materials: Two straight-grain white pine or spruce sticks free of knots and each 30 x $^3/_8$ x $^3/_{16}$." Cotton string for kite framing, bow string, and bridle. Colored tissue paper or Percale cotton cloth or sheet plastic such as from trash bags. Thin wire nail. Elmer's Glue.

Study the plan carefully then mark each stick as shown and saw notch in stick ends as shown in detail.

Assembly:

1. Join sticks on marks using thin wire nail. Clinch or bend nail over where it protrudes but do so carefully to avoid smashing spars. Lash spars lightly at crossing point if you wish to keep in alignment until framing line and covering is applied.

2. Square cross-stick with upright and then tie string through notch at (A). Then pass string through notch at (B) and once around stick and back thru notch and then on around kite in a similar fashion. Check carefully to be sure that side of kite (A) to (B) is same as side from (A) to (D), and then tie end of string at point (A).

3. Place trued frame on paper or cloth. Place a weight on upright stock and then trim paper or cloth to at least ½" beyond string outline. Do not use glue on string, only on edge of your paper or cloth. Run a light line of Elmer's Glue along extreme edge which you have folded over the framing line and press down securely and let dry thoroughly before handling kite. Plastic covers may be applied with contact glue or rubber cement.

4. When kite is dry and firm, sit in a chair and with the kite upright between your knees, bend the upright stick gently and firmly to create a "belly" or "pocket" in the plastic wings on each side of the upright spar.

5. Now "bow" the cross-spar by placing a knotted string in the notch at one end, drawing it up tightly enough to form a bow and securing the other end of the string in the notch at the opposite end. For a 30-inch spar, the bowing line should be about 10 percent of the 30-inch distance at the center of the kite, or about 3 inches.

6. Now tie each end of the bridle line to upright stick as shown, puncturing the cover at the proper points.

When tied, it should be 31 inches long from front to back, allowing for a small loop to which the flying line or leader may be attached. Locate the loop for the flying line at a point 11½ inches from the front tie-on point. Always start with a piece of string for the bridle that is long enough to adjust down to the proper bridle length, including the loop for the flying-line attachment.

This is a tail-less kite and should launch from the hand if enough wind velocity is available. You can add a tail to the kite if you wish, but basically it shouldn't need it unless winds overpower it.

Adjustments, forward and back, may be necessary if kite shows looping tendencies. Always flatten the angle some if the kite fails to climb well. It is advisable to loosen bow string when kite is not in use to prevent strain on the frame and for easier storing.

(From the Autumn 1975 *Kite Tales*, based on the plans of AKA member Paul Thomas of York, Pennsylvania. This is basically a simplified Eddy. A more complex and ambitious lesson on Eddy construction appears in the autumn 1972 issue of the same magazine.)

2. Scott Sled

Materials: Three $^1/_8$-inch dowels 36 inches long (preferably of birch), one roll of Scotch plastic tape, 40 inches of polyethylene 36 inches wide, monofilament line, and three small swivel hooks (available where fishing tackle is sold). It is a good idea to use cheap polyethylene for your first, "trial" model; however, cloth, Tyvek, and Zepherlite make fine and durable sleds.

Assembly:

1. The silhouette shown is that of the Scott Sled laid flat. It measures 40 inches from wing tip to wing tip and 36 inches longitudinally.

2. The long strips indicate the supporting dowels, or slats if you prefer, and the small rectangles on the dowels indicate the plastic tape to hold them in place on the fabric. The large triangle is the vent, a controversial matter, since some sleds fly without it. We suggest you use it.

Note: The vent lower point begins 5 inches from the trailing edge. It extends upward to a point fifteen inches from the trailing edge. If you wish you may border the vent with plastic tape to make it more fun and prevent tearing.

3. The squares at the wing tips indicate a reinforcement of tape at the point where the bridle is fastened. Many builders use a strip of filament tape, which is very strong and won't tear through since it is reinforced.

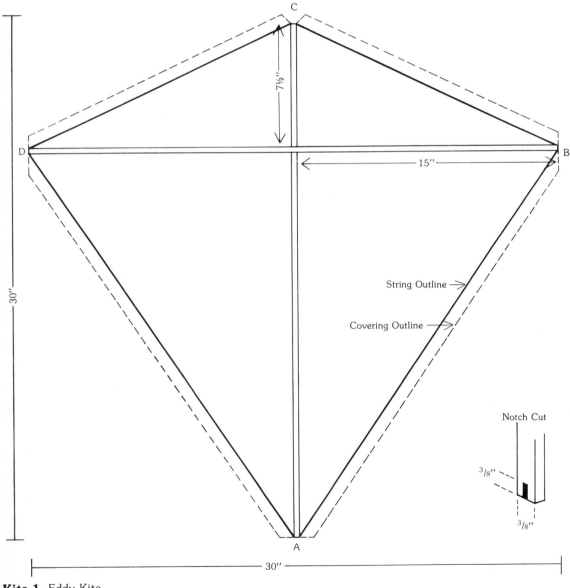

C

7½″

D ← 15″ → B

String Outline →

Covering Outline →

Notch Cut

³/₈″

³/₈″

A

30″

30″

Kite 1. Eddy Kite

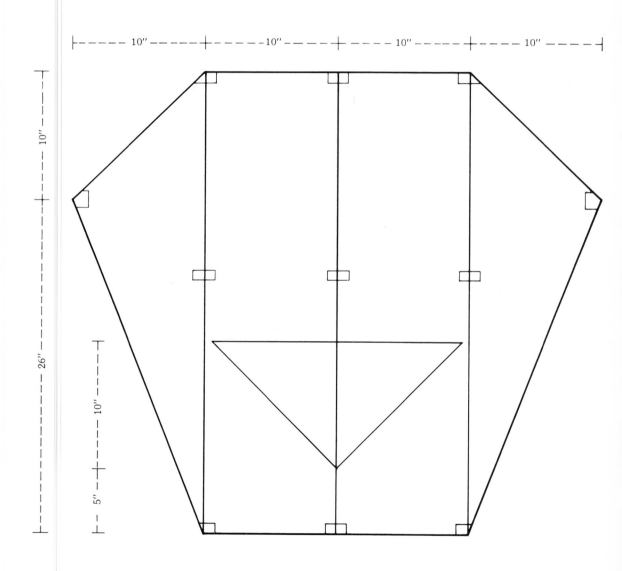

Kite 2. Scott Sled

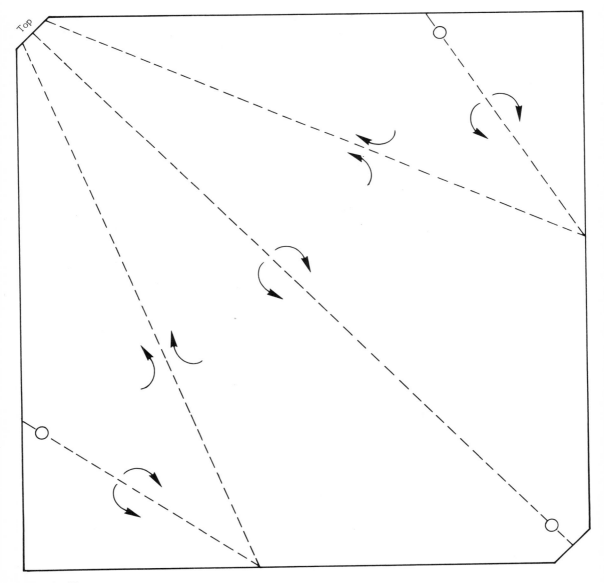

Kite 3. Chiringa

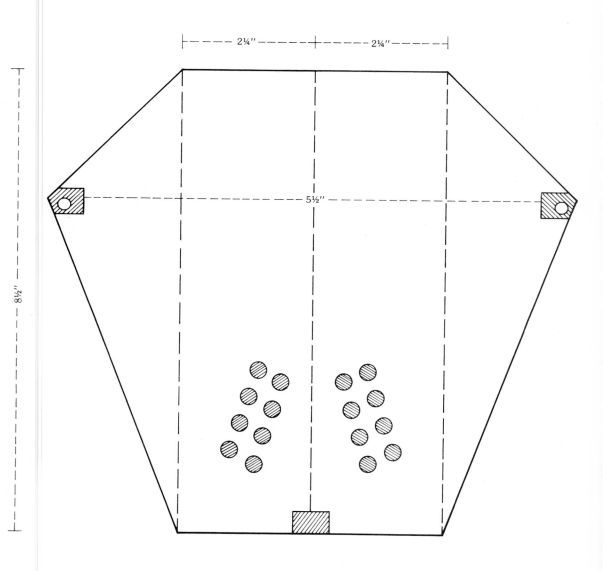

Kite 4. "Mini Sled"

4. Tack or tape down the polyethylene sheet on a suitable cutting surface, mark it out, and cut the vent opening first. Then cut the general shape, using a sharp knife or razor blade.

5. The bridle (single piece from wing tip to wing tip) should be long enough to permit the entire kite (in flying configuration) to rotate entirely through the bridle loop. This means about 80 inches overall or 40 inches for each bridle lead. Monofilament line makes the best bridle for a Scott Sled. After tying the bridle ends to the wing tips, hold the latter firmly together and draw the bridle to an exact center point and tie a small loop in it.

6. It is highly essential to use very small swivel hooks, one or two in tandem on the bridle attachment to prevent the bridle from twisting. Insert the loop of the bridle through the eye of the swivel and then pass the swivel through the loop and draw tightly. A similar swivel on the flying line will then easily snap on the bridle swivel.

7. Sleds do not normally require a tail. However, in high winds one may be desirable. Use a light streamer of plastic surveyor tape or crepe paper strip from 6 to 8 feet long. Shorten or lengthen according to flight behavior. It can be taped to the center of the trailing edge of the kite.

(From *Kite Tales*, Summer 1972.)

3. Chiringa

Materials: Any square piece of paper from 6 to 20 inches will work. Paper should be medium in weight — newsprint is too light, construction paper too heavy — a spool of thread and a strip of crepe paper ½ inch wide and 10 feet long.

Assembly:

1. Using the diagram itself, or one like it drawn on another piece of paper, cut out the kite along the solid lines.

2. Fold on the dotted lines in the direction of the arrows, starting at the center.

3. Cut or punch holes at the three places marked with a small O.

4. Upper two holes are for bridle. Tie the ends of a piece of thread at least 15 inches long through each hole, but not too tight to cut paper.

5. Fold kite and pull bridle above top. Tie knot in bridle about an inch above top of kite. Make sure knot is centered in bridle. Attach a spool of thread to end of bridle. This is the flying line.

6. Tie a piece of thread through the bottom hole to attach the tail. Attach two 5-foot pieces of crepe paper

about ½ inch wide to the tail thread. If the wind is above 8—10 mph. double the length of the tail.

7. The Chiringa will fly in almost any wind from 2 to 20 mph. If it doesn't, the bridle is too short, the bridle point is off center, or the kite is inside out — the outside fold of the center crease must face the flier.

(From *Kite Tales*, Winter 1970.)

4. The "Mini Sled"

Materials: Same as Chiringa, except that you will need two 8-foot-by-1-inch crepe paper strips.

Assembly:

1. Using the diagram itself or one like it drawn on another piece of paper, fold along center dashed line.

2. Cut along solid border line so that the two sides are exactly alike.

3. Using paper punch, punch out those holes with the kite still folded.

4. Reinforce corners with tape and attach 16-inch thread bridle.

5. Tape on two 8-foot x 1-inch crepe paper tails.

6. Fold forward along both side dashed lines.

7. Fly it on line attached to the center of the bridle.

8. If kite is unstable in good wind, tape the loose ends of the tails together. Various patterns of holes work, as long as both sides of the kite are the same. The length of the tails may be varied for different wind strengths.

(Plan by Howard Norville in Winter 1970 *Kite Tales*.)

B. Kite Books

Barwell and Bailey, *How to Make and Fly Kites*, Van Nostrand Reinhold Co.

Brummitt, Wyatt, *Kites*, Western Publishing Co.

Fowler, H. Walter, Jr., *Kites*, The Ronald Press

Garber, Paul E., *Kites and Kite Flying*, The Boy Scouts of America. (This 1931 classic is out of print.)

Hart, Clive, *Kites: An Historical Survey*, Frederick A. Praeger, Inc. (This complete history has recently gone out of print.)

____, *Your Book of Kites*, Transatlantic Arts, Inc.

Hiroi, Tsutomu, *Kites*, Manichi Newspapers, Tokyo. (The text of this lavishly illustrated work is in Japanese.)

Hunt, Leslie, *Getting Started in Kitemaking*, Bruce Publishing Co.

____, *25 Kites That Fly*, Dover Publications. (A reprint of a book originally published in 1929.)

Neal, Harry Edward, *The Story of the Kite*, Vanguard.

Newman, L. and J., *Kite Craft*, Crown.

Wagenvoored, James, *Flying Kites*, Macmillan Co.

Yolen, Jane, *World on a String*, World Publishing Co.

Yolen, Will, *The Complete Book of Kites and Kite Flying*, Simon and Schuster

——, *Young Sportsman's Guide to Kiteflying*, Thomas Nelson, Inc.

C. The Whole Kite Catalog

Assembled here are just about all of the major and a number of minor sources and their addresses that will come in handy as you get deeper and deeper into kiting.

Associations.

American Kiteflyers Association
P.O. Box 1511
Silver City, N.M. 88061.
(Probably the most important address in kiting. Membership in this nonprofit, worldwide organization is $5 per year, which includes four issues of *Kite Tales*.)

International Kitefliers Association
321 E. 48th St.
New York, N.Y. 10017
(Will Yolen's group, in which membership is free and membership benefits are almost entirely spiritual.)

Maryland Kite Society
7106 Campfield Rd.
Baltimore, Md. 21207

Kites and Kite Supplies.

(Unless otherwise noted, these are retail outlets for kites and supplies. No attempt has been made to list the many *summer-only* kite stores which have sprung up in so many beach and resort areas in recent years.)

Airplane Kite Co.
Roswell, N.M. 88201
(Home of Ray Holland Jr.'s stable of kites.)

AKA Emblem
c/o Sharon Reese
P.O. Box 144
Carlsbad, N.M. 88220
(The only source for the official red, white, and blue cloth AKA patches and "Come Fly With Me" bumper stickers. The former cost $1.75, the latter $1—both postpaid.)

Asian Imports Ltd.
P.O. Box 382
Beverly Hills, Cal. 90213
(Easy-wind spools.)

Carol Frush Kite Shop
1525 State St.
Santa Barbara, Cal. 93101

Come Fly A Kite, Inc.
900 North Point
Ghirardelli Square
San Francisco, Cal. 94109
(Dinesh Bahadur's exciting shop, which at last count had spun off two branches: one in Picadilly Square in Santa Barbara and the other in the Carmel Plaza in Carmel. The store publishes a catalog for $1.00.)

Come Fly With Me
3212 Highland
Manhattan Beach, Cal. 90266

Condor Industries Ltd.
3914 St. Peters Rd.
Victoria, B. C.
Canada V8P 2J8
(The Space Platform and other kites.)

Davie Street Kite Shop
1783 Davie St.
English Bay
Vancouver, B.C.
Canada

Eureka Paper Tiger
Olla Podrida
12215 Colt Rd.
Dallas, Tex. 75230

Fly By Kite
99 W. 10th, Suite 120
Eugene, Ore. 97401

Flying High
36 Boyleston St.
Cambridge, Mass. 02138

Flying Tiger Associates
P.O. Box 48634
Los Angeles, Cal. 90048
(Reels and kite line.)

Gayla
P.O. Box 10800
Houston, Tex. 77018
(Manufacturer of low-price soaring kites.)

Gentle Earth
6723 Snider Pl.
Dallas, Tex. 75205

Go Fly a Kite, Inc.
1434 Third Ave.
New York, N.Y. 10028
(The father of American kite stores. If you can't get there, the store puts out an excellent catalog for 50¢.)

Go Fly a Kite
East Mall—Sunset Center
Amarillo, Tex. 79102

Heavenly Bodies
603 Front St.
Lahina, Maui
Hawaii 96761

High As a Kite
691 Bridgeway
Sausalito, Cal. 94965

Higher than a Kite
209 Osborne
Winnipeg, Manitoba
Canada

Hobby Saucer Kite Headquarters
Box 4563
Kansas City, Mo. 64127
(Sells novelty styrofoam kites.)

International Kite Co.
P.O. Box 3248
San Diego, Cal. 92103
(A special line of fighter kites can be mail-ordered from this company.)

KHK Corp.
P.O. Box 398
Delray Beach, Fla. 33444
(Sells the soft Kiddie Hawk Kite by mail.)

Kite and Gift
333 Jefferson St. No. 7
Fisherman's Wharf
San Francisco, Cal. 94133

The Kite Factory
P.O. Box 9081
Seattle, Wash. 98101
(Dave Checkley's company that puts out a line of fine and sophisticated kites.)

Kites International
1000 E. Northwest Hwy.
Mt. Prospect, Ill. 60056

The Kite Shop
1313 S. Country Club Dr.
Mesa, Ariz. 85208

The Kite Shop
542 St. Peter St.
New Orleans, La. 70166

The Kite Shop, Ltd.
1917 Kalakaua Ave.
Honolulu, Hawaii 96815
(Important new outlet which sells kites by mail, including kites which are exclusive to this store.)

The Kite Store
2nd and Bay Ave.
Beach Haven, N.J. 08008

Kite World Inc.
540 De Haro
San Francisco, Cal. 94107
(Kite wholesaler handling many lines . . . the people to call if you decide to drop out and open a kite place.)

Kiteflier
1350 Dixie Hwy.
Pompano Beach, Fla. 33060

Kites and Strings
740 Ventura Pl.
San Diego, Cal. 92109

The Kiteworks
Beach Rd. Vineyard Haven
Martha's Vineyard Island, Mass. 02568

L.G. Striegel Mfg. Co.
1223 Arcade Ave.
Louisville, Ky. 40215
(Sells only its own "Super-Kite.")

Lee's Custom Kites & Reels
1327 13th St.
P.O. Box 148
Clarkston, Wash. 99403

Let's Fly a Kite
327 Buffalo St.
Hamburg, N.Y. 14075

Let's Fly a Kite
13763 Fiji Way
Fisherman's Wharf
Marina del Rey, Cal. 90291

Let's Fly a Kite
1432 North Federal Hwy.
Dania, Fla. 33004

Let's Fly a Kite
1510-G Walnut St.
Berkeley, Cal. 94708
(I have heard that this store may have changed its
name to Above and Beyond.)

Lucy in the Sky
2203 Hermosa Ave.
Hermosa Beach, Cal. 90254

Lure of the Kite
Village Fair
South Coast Hwy.
Laguna Beach, Cal. 92651

Marblehead Kite Co.
28 South St.
Marblehead, Mass. 01945

Mylar Star Kites
3519 Caribeth Dr.
Encino, Cal. 91316

Nantucket Kiteman and Lady
P.O. Box 1356
Nantucket, Mass. 02554

Outermost Kites
Union Square
Provincetown, Mass. 02657

The Passport
Highway 42
Box 2
Ellison Bay, Wis. 54210

Peter Powell Kites of America
1914 Sands Dr.
Annapolis, Md. 21401

Quicksilver Kites
1622 Castro St.
San Francisco, Cal. 94114

R.A. Simerl Instruments Div.
238 West St.
Annapolis, Md. 21401
(Wind-measuring instruments.)

Rayco Reels
7320 West Lloyd St.
Wauwatosa, Wis. 53213
(Reels only.)

Rogallo Flexikites
Kitty Hawk, N.C. 27949

The Sale Shop
13107 Harbor Blvd.
Garden Grove, Cal. 92643

San Francisco Kite Factory
2231 Judah
San Francisco, Cal. 94122

Seattle Air Force
166 South Jackson
Seattle, Wash. 98104
(Offers some interesting equipment—including a reel for left-handed people—and sells through the mails.)

Stratton Air Engineering
10859 Portal Dr.
Los Alamitos, Cal. 98104
(The specialty here is airplane kites.)

Synestructics, Inc.
9559 Irondale Ave.
Chatsworth, Cal. 91311
(Tetrakites, Kite Links, etc.)

Tom Joe
International Acrobatic Kites
1891 Caspina Ave.
Long Beach, Cal. 90810

Troyer Kite Supply
4174 Kent Rd.
Stow, Ohio 44224
(Reels.)

W.O. Weathers and Sons
17707 East Howard St.
Milwaukie, Ore. 97222

Windy City Kite Works Ltd.
1750 North Clark St.
Chicago, Ill. 60614
(First large kite store in the Midwest.)

Zepher Kite Shop
305 Front St.
Beaufort, N.C. 28516

D.   More on the Yo-Yo
Both Duncan and Festival offer booklets of yo-yo tricks at 50¢. Write to:

Giant Book of Duncan Yo-Yo Tricks
Flambeau Plastics Corp.
Baraboo, Wis. 53913

Yo-Yo Secrets
P.O. Box 909
Pawtucket, R.I. 02862
Your best bet if you want to find out when the next Duncan demonstrator will be in your neighborhood is to write to Dolores Brown at the Flambeau Plastics address.

There are very few published works of any substance dealing with the yo-yo. Two that are worthwhile:

Cohen, Martin, "The Swinging World of Yo-Yos," *Boy's Life*, December 1971.
Malco, George, "Will There Ever Be Another Yo-Yo Champ?," *Lithopinion*, Summer 1970.

E. Official Ringer Marble Rules*
Ringer is played in a ring 10 feet in diameter, with 13 marbles arranged in the center in the shape of a cross. The object is to shoot these marbles out of the ring, the player shooting the largest number of marbles out of the ring in any game being the winner of that game.

No less than two and no more than six may play in one game of Ringer except in tournament championship matches, where only two play. All tournament play is for fair, and marbles must be returned to owners after each game.

Equipment. The playing surface shall be a smooth, level area of ground, hard clay or other suitable substances. The *ring* is inscribed upon the area 10 feet in diameter and all play within this ring. (*Note:* The outline of this ring shall not be so deep or wide as to check the roll of the marbles.)

With the center of the ring as a point of intersection, mark two lines at right angles to each other to form a cross, which shall be a guide for placing the playing marbles. Place one marble at the center and three on each of the four branches of the cross, each marble 3 inches away from the next one.

The *lag line* is a string drawn tangent to the ring and touching it at one point. The *pitch line* is a straight line drawn tangent to the ring, directly opposite to the lag line.

Playing marbles shall be round and made of glass. All marbles in any one playing ring must be of uniform size.

*These are the official rules set down by the National Marbles Tournament, which have been in force since 1922 when the first nationals were held in Atlantic City.

The standard size shall be $5/8$ inch in diameter. Slight variations may be allowed by the referee for manufacturing fault.

Shooters shall be round and made of any substance except steel or any other metal, and shall not be less than ½ inch or more than ¾ inch in diameter, as determined by the referee.

Plan of Play. The *lag* is the first operation in Ringer. To lag, the players stand toeing the pitch line, or knuckling down upon it, and toss or shoot their shooters to the lag line across the ring. The player whose shooter comes nearest the lag line on either side wins the lag.

Players must lag before each series of games. The player who wins the lag shoots first and the others follow in order as their shooters were next nearest to the lag line. The same shooter that is used in the lag must be used in the game following the lag.

On all shots, except the lag, a player shall *knuckle down* so that at least one knuckle is in contact with the ground, and he shall maintain this position until the shooter has left his hand.

Knuckling down is permitted but not required in lagging. Starting the game each player in turn shall knuckle down just outside the ring line, at any point he chooses, and shoot into the ring to knock one or more marbles out of the ring.

A player continues to shoot when he knocks one or more marbles out of the ring—provided his shooter remains inside the ring. When a player's shooter passes outside the ring, whether or not he has scored on the shot, he shall cease to shoot, but he shall be credited with the marbles he has scored.

After a miss a player picks up his shooter, wherever it lies, until his next turn, and then is permitted to take rounders and shoot from any point of the ring line.

Playing regulations. Marbles knocked out of the ring shall be picked up by the player who knocks them out.

Whenever a marble or shooter comes to rest on the *ring line*, if its center is outside the ring, or exactly on the ring line, it shall be considered out of the ring; if its center is inside the ring, it shall be considered inside the ring.

If a shooter knocks out two or more marbles in a combination play he shall be entitled to all points on the shot.

When a shooter slips from a player's hand, if the player calls "slips" and the referee is convinced that it is

a slip, and if the shooter did not travel more than 10 inches, the referee may order "no play" and permit the player to shoot again. The referee's decision is final.

The game shall end when one player has knocked seven marbles from the ring.

Scoring. For each marble knocked out by a player, he shall be credited with the score of 1.

The player having credited to him the largest number of marbles at the completion of the game shall be the winner of that game.

In games where more than two players are engaged, if two or more players lead with the same score, those in the tie shall play a new game to break the tie.

A player refusing to continue a game, once it is started, shall be disqualified, and if only two players are engaged, the game shall be forfeited to the offended player. The score of the forfeited game shall be $7-0$.

Officials. The officials shall be a referee and a scorer, if a scorer is available, otherwise the referee shall also keep score.

The referee shall have complete charge of the play. He shall interpret these rules and have power to make a decision on any points not specifically covered by these rules. He shall have the authority to order from the ring or its vicinity the coach or other representatives of any player who conducts himself improperly.

The scorer shall keep a record of the game, noting the score of each player, shot by shot, and at the end of each game shall notify the referee of the score and the referee shall announce the winner. The scorer shall assist the referee in enforcing the rule against coaching, and call to the attention of the referee any infraction of the rules.

Penalties. A player shall *not:*

Lift his hand forward until the shooter has left his hand. This violation is known as "hunching."

Smooth or otherwise rearrange the ground or remove any obstacles. He may request the referee to clear obstructions. PENALTY (for all these violations): If any marbles were knocked out or dislocated on the shot, they shall be restored to their place, and the player shall lose his shot.

Change shooters during the course of the game. He may choose a new shooter on each lag, provided he uses that shooter in the subsequent game. PENALTY: The player shall be removed from the game.

Communicate in any way with his coach during the course of a game. PENALTY: Forfeiture of all marbles he knocked out of the ring, said marbles to be returned to the game and placed on the cross.

A coach shall not give instructions to either his own or any other player engaged in a game. PENALTY: Coach shall be ordered from the playing field if, after being warned once, he continues this violation.

Players must not walk through the marble ring. PENALTY: After a player has been warned for violation, the referee *may* require the forfeiture of one marble on a second offense, said marble to be returned and placed on the cross.

Additional Rules.

Lagging: Players shall lag together. If either shooter strikes the backboard, or the marbles or rack in the ring, that player loses the lag. If both shooters strike an obstruction the players lag over.

Backspin: Each player shall be responsible for the results of backspin. If the shooter on its return strikes any part of the player's body he shall lose the turn but shall be entitled to any marbles knocked out on the shot.

Marble in Action: A player shall not pick up any shooter or marbles while in motion and shall not stop a shooter's or marble's motion. Violation of this rule shall be considered a foul and the player shall lose his turn.

Broken Shooter: A player may not change shooters during a game *excepting* that if a shooter is broken the referee may permit a change, if, in his judgment the shooter has been damaged enough to impair good shooting.

Wind Action: If before a shot, the wind moves a marble, the referee shall return it to its original position. However, any marble or shooter set in motion during a shot shall be allowed to continue until it comes to a full stop and if the wind carries it out of ring it shall be counted out. The marble or shooter shall be considered "dead" once it comes to a complete stop. If the wind moves it thereafter, it shall be returned to position.

Wrong Shooter: If any player carelessly shoots with one of the playing marbles he shall lose the shot and any marble knocked out with the illegal shooter shall be returned to its position.

Picking up Marbles: Each player may use his own judgment as to whether to pick up his marbles after each shot or wait until he finishes shooting excepting that any marble which bounces back into the ring must be picked up immediately.

Forfeited Game: Each player shall be responsible for keeping informed as to the progress of the game. If, before the actual completion of a game, a player mistakenly believes he has lost and throws his marbles into the ring he shall be considered to have forfeited the game.

Slips: The rule regarding slips shall be enforced strictly and whenever the shooter travels more than 10 inches it must be considered a shot. If a player picks up his shooter on a slips before it has stopped it shall be considered to have gone more than 10 inches and he loses his shot.

The Lag: Players shall lag before each set of games and the winner shall shoot first in all odd-numbered games.

F.   More on Marbles

For information on the National Marbles Tournament contact:

Oka Hester, National Director
Drawer W
Greensboro, N.C. 28206

Collectors can join the Marble Collectors Society of America for $10 a year. Write to:

Mr. Stanley A. Block
Marble Collectors Society of America
P.O. Box 222
Trumbull, Conn. 06611

The folks who run the international championships each Good Friday can be reached by writing to:

World Marbles Board of Control
c/o 14 Fermandy Lane
Crawley Down, Sussex
England

The booklet "The Game of Marbles" by Shirley "Windy" Allen can be obtained by writing:

Marble King, Inc.
Paden City, W.V. 26159

Two Pertinent Books:

Baumann, Paul, *Collecting Antique Marbles*, Prairie Winds Press, Leon, Iowa, 1970. (The book can be obtained by sending $7.50 to the Mid-America Book Company, Leon, Iowa 50144.)

Ferretti, Fred, *The Great American Marble Book*, Workman Publishing Co., New York, 1973. ($2.50)

G. Frisbee Games

I. Frisbee Golf. Set up your course using the natural lay of the land as a normal golf course would be set up, with hazards and "holes" which are clearly visible from your tee areas. Two of the most popular holes in use today are wire baskets and metal poles set into the ground. Most courses are set up with the traditional nine or 18 holes, but the holes are usually shorter from the tee than in ball golf.

The IFA rules for play are as follows:

1. Lie. Where the Frisbee stops after the throw constitutes the player's lie.

2. Tee Throw. Initial throw on each hole must be made from the tee area.

3. Fairway Throw. All throws after the tee throw, player's front foot must be touching the player's lie, at the time of release. (A run-up is allowed.)

4. Putt Throw. Within 10 yards of the hole a player may not touch any point in front of the player's lie before, during, or after the throw. (This means no falling putts).

5. Unplayable Lie. An unplayable lie is any Frisbee stuck over 6 feet high in a hazard (i.e., tree or bush). Next throw must be made from below the unplayable lie, not closer to the hole. (One-Stroke Penalty.)

6. Out-of-Bounds. Tee throw landing out-of-bounds must be thrown again from the tee area. Fairway throw landing out-of-bounds must be thrown again from the tee area. Fairway throw landing out-of-bounds must be thrown from point where Frisbee left the course (one-stroke penalty).

7. Each throw counts one stroke (unless penalty strokes are assessed).

8. Frisbee furthest from the hole throws first.

9. Low score on preceding hold throws first.

II. Guts Frisbee. The two teams (one to five players on each team) line up face to face along parallel goal lines which are 15 feet apart. Your team gets a point when the opposition makes a bad throw or misses a catch. The first team with 21 points wins and the winner must have a 2-point advantage. The official IFA rules:

1. Each team's honor and gamesmanship, as well as their skill, are vital components in each contest, and the players are the judges. However, if one team captain believes judges will benefit play, judges may be used.

2. *Throwing:* A good throw is one that traverses the 15 yards and crosses the goal line without touching the ground, and within the reach of the receiving team. A throw is judged high if the receiving team makes an optimum effort and cannot reach the Frisbee. It is wide if it is outside an end man's optimum effort. The throw must cross the goal line at less than 90 degrees.

3. *Catching:* A clean catch is when any member or members of the receiving team catches the Frisbee with only one hand. The Frisbee may not be trapped against any part of the body at any time. The Frisbee may be deflected and bobbled about as long as it is not touched by one person's two hands simultaneously, or trapped in any other manner. All members of the receiving team shall toe the goal line at the time of delivery. After delivery players are free to move anywhere during the attempted catch.

4. *Throwing Order:* To begin the game, any player on the throwing team may make the first throw. Subsequently, the person who catches the Frisbee will make the next throw. If the Frisbee is touched but not caught, the first person who touches the Frisbee must throw it. If the Frisbee is not touched, any member may make the next throw.

5. *Optimum Effort:* It is not necessary that the receiving team members jump for a high throw. A hand stretched as high as possible above the head is required. If the receiving player jumps, a Frisbee below his outstretched hand is a good throw. For optimum effort to the side, it is necessary for the outside man to move the outside foot and extend the outside arm to the maximum reach.

6. Bad throws are to be judged by the person who threw it. A bad catch is to be judged by the person who made it. In the event of an honest difference of opinion over a throw or catch, the throw will be taken over.

III. Ultimate Frisbee. Ultimate Frisbee is a fast-moving, competitive, non-contact sport played by two seven-man teams. The sport has a great deal of freedom and informality implicit in the rules. Primary among these is the spirit of sportsmanship which enables the honor system to be effective.

The object of Ultimate Frisbee is to gain points by scoring goals. The Frisbee may only be passed, and a goal is scored when a player successfully passes the Frisbee to a teammate in the endzone which that team is attacking. The team with the most points at the end of the game is declared the winner.

Equipment. The Wham-O Master is the official Frisbee to be used in tournament play. Individual players may wear almost any aids they wish, including hats, helmets, or gloves, as long as they do not endanger the safety of any other player. For example, shoes with cleats are permissible but ones with sharp spikes are not. No player may carry any sort of stick, bat, or racket.

Playing Field. The playing field may have any surface whatsoever, including grass, asphalt, sand, snow, or the wood of a gymnasium floor. The main playing field for the official Ultimate Frisbee game is 60 yards long and 40 yards wide. Both end zones are 40 yards wide and 30 yards deep.

If a pass is completed outside the lateral boundary, it is considered incomplete and the defensive team gains possession of the Frisbee. In order to be considered in-bounds, a player must land with both feet touching inside or on the boundary line. Should the Frisbee land outside the lateral boundary, it is returned to play on the main playing field at the point where the Frisbee went out of bounds. The player throwing the Frisbee in-bounds *must* have one foot on the line.

Officials. A referee or referees may officiate, and their decision must be final. If no referee is used, the two teams play on an honor system. Each team should provide one person to keep time and score.

Time. A game of Ultimate Frisbee lasts for 48 minutes of playing time, divided into two 24-minute halves. Halftime lasts for ten minutes. The clock starts after every throw-off when the receiving team touches the Frisbee. The clock stops after every goal, at the end of each period of play, for time-outs, injuries, fouls, and when the Frisbee goes out-of-bounds. The clock starts when the Frisbee is thrown in-bounds, or when both teams are ready to resume, and play continues at the location of the Frisbee when the play stopped.

Each team is permitted three time-outs per half and one per overtime period, each lasting two minutes. Time-out may be called by either team after a goal and before the ensuing throw-off. A team must be in possession of the Frisbee in order to call a time-out during play.

In the event of a tie at the end of regulation time, there will be an overtime period lasting five minutes. The captains flip a coin to determine which team will throw-off. If there is no winner at the end of overtime, overtimes are continued until the tie is broken at the end of one.

Throw-Off. Play begins with the throw-off. The captains of the two teams flip a coin to determine which team will throw or receive, or choice of goal. The teams shall alternate throw-offs at the beginning of each period. All players must be on or behind their own goal line until the Frisbee is released. The receiving team must stand on their own goal line without changing relative position.

A player on the goal line throws the Frisbee towards the other team. As soon as the Frisbee is released, all players may cross the goal lines. No player on the throwing team may touch the Frisbee in the air before it is touched by a member of the receiving team.

The receiving team may catch the Frisbee or allow it to fall untouched to the ground. If a member of the receiving team successfully catches the throw-off, that player has possession at that point. If the receiving team touches the Frisbee and fails to catch it, the team which threw off gains possession of the Frisbee where it is stopped. If the Frisbee is allowed to fall untouched to the ground, the receiving team has possession where it is stopped.

If the Frisbee goes out-of-bounds before crossing the goal line, the receiving team makes the immediate decision of: 1) gaining possession at the point the Frisbee went out-of-bounds, or 2) having the Frisbee thrown-off again. If the Frisbee goes out-of-bounds after crossing the goal line, the receiving team gains possession on the goal line at the nearest corner.

Each time a goal is scored, the teams switch direction of their attack, and the team which scored throws-off on the signal of the receiving team.

The Play. The team which has possession of the Frisbee must attempt to move the Frisbee into position so that they may score a goal. A player may propel the Frisbee in any way he wishes. *The Frisbee may never be handed from player to player.* In order for the Frisbee to go from one player to another, it must at some time be in the air.

No player may walk, run, or take steps while in possession of the Frisbee. The momentum of the receiver, however, must be taken into consideration. Should a player take steps obviously not required to stop, play stops, he returns to the point where he gained possession, and play resumes when both teams are ready.

The player in possession may pivot on one foot, as in basketball. The thrower may not change his pivot foot. Only *one* player may guard the person in possession of the Frisbee. The Frisbee may not be wrenched from the grasp of an opposing player, or knocked from his/her hand.

The defensive team gains possession whenever the offensive team's pass is incomplete, intercepted, knocked down, or goes out-of-bounds. A rolling or sliding Frisbee may be stopped by any player, but may not be advanced in any direction. After the Frisbee is stopped, no defensive player may touch it. Possession is gained at the point where the Frisbee is stopped. Any member of the team gaining possession of the Frisbee may throw it.

A player may catch his own throw only if the Frisbee has been touched by another player during its flight. Bobbling to gain control is permitted, but tipping to oneself is not allowed.

End Zones. Any time a team gains possession in the end zone which they are defending, the player may choose to resume play where the Frisbee is stopped, or at the goal line. A player may carry the Frisbee up to the goal line provided that he/she approaches it perpendicularly. The player may not pass the Frisbee as he/she approaches the goal line. If a team gains possession in the end zone which it is attacking, the Frisbee is *carried* perpendicularly to the goal line, and play resumes immediately from the goal line.

Fouls. A throwing foul is called only by the player fouled. It is defined as any physical contact between offensive and defensive players sufficient to deter the flight of the Frisbee. Contact occurring during the follow-through is not sufficient grounds for a foul. If the pass is completed, the foul is automatically declined, and play proceeds without stopping.

A foul is also called when physical contact occurs as a result of the offensive or defensive players playing the man instead of the Frisbee. This includes pushing, grabbing, clipping, holding, kicking, submarining, etc.

The player who is fouled calls "foul," play stops, and the player gains possession at the point of the infraction. Play continues when both teams are ready. Should a foul occur in the end zone, possession is regained at the goal line.

A stalling violation occurs when the player guarding the thrower calls out "stalling" and counts aloud 15 seconds. If the Frisbee has not been released at the end of the count it is turned over to the defense at that point.

Scoring. A goal is scored when an offensive player has two feet in the end zone after receiving a pass from a teammate. A player in possession may not score by running into the end zone. The team that scores receives one point.

Substitutions. Substitutions can be made only: 1) after a goal and before the ensuing throw-off, 2) to replace an injured player, or 3) after periods of play. Substitutions cannot be made during a time-out.

Clarifying Statements. There are no scrimmage lines or offsides in Ultimate Frisbee. The Frisbee may be passed in any direction—forward, to the sides, or backwards.

The term "when both teams are ready," used after time-outs, injuries and fouls, implies that the defender will hold the Frisbee until the defensive team is ready, and then hand the Frisbee to the thrower—the clock restarts. It should be common practice that the offensive team remains stationary until the Frisbee is given to the thrower.

Variations. Before the opening throw-off, the captains of the teams may agree on any additional ground rules necessary. The number of players, size of field, type of Frisbee, and length of game can be adapted.

IV. Frisbee Field Meet. The contest consists of six events, the results of which combine to determine the outcome of the competition:

1. *Distance:* Three players per team throw five throws each. The best throws of each player are added together to produce the team distance. The longer distance is the winner and the team scores one point.

2. *Accuracy:* Three players per team throw in the accuracy competition. Total scores are added for each team and one point is awarded to the winner.

3. *Frisbee Golf:* Three players per team play nine holes on the course and low total wins one point. (If no course is available the teams may design the holes as they play with the losing team calling the following hole.)

4. *Freestyle:* Each team enters one pair to do freestyle for 6 minutes. The teams flip the Frisbee for order of play and then perform for two 3-minute periods:

Team A—3 minutes
Team B—3 minutes
Team A—3 minutes
Team B—3 minutes

Each team also provides four judges. Each judge turns in a score for each pair from 1.0 (poor) to 10.0 (excellent). The scores from all judges are then totaled after the highest and lowest scores for each team are dropped (six scores remaining for each pair). Highest total wins one point for team score.

5. *Guts:* Two, five-member teams play one game to 21 points. Winning team awarded 2 points.

6. *Ultimate:* Game should consist of one 30-minute game using running time (clock never stops). Winning team awarded 3 points.

Scoring

Individual events	
Distance	1 point
Accuracy	1 point
Golf	1 point
Freestyle	1 point
Team Events	
Guts	2 points
Ultimate	3 points
	————
Total	9 points

Competition Procedure: The Frisbee Field Meet is designed to appeal both to players and spectators. To that end it must move along quickly and efficiently.

Prior to the beginning of the event, each team should submit a roster of the players they will be entering in each event. If the teams are of sufficient size, no single player should be in more than one individual event but may be in both team events as they are run consecutively.

If this restriction is followed the meet can move very quickly as all of the individual events may be started together. When judges are not available the players in each of the events are jointly responsible for that competition (measurement, etc.) and should report the results to the meet director.

After the individual events have been completed, the two team events should be contested—Guts followed by Ultimate. Total time for the entire event should be run about two hours.

H. The Ten Commandments of the Frisbee*

There are those who claim that the flying disc represents not a game but rather a way of life. Below are the rules by which that life is controlled. Together they form a concept of prediscenation upon which the Frisbyterian religion is based.

The rules have been widely recognized for many years but only now have they been codified. We have listed them so that we might better understand the forces that control our play. Hopefully, it will allow players to quickly identify situations in which they are inexorably involved and communicate that fact to other players through the use of rule numbers only. A shout of "Rule 4!" floating across the playing field should now be sufficient to produce an emphatic reaction from all players within earshot. Is it not true that:

1. The most powerful force in the world is that of a disc straining to land directly under a car, just beyond reach. (This force is technically termed "car suck.")

2. The higher the quality of a catch or the comment it receives the greater the probability of a crummy rethrow (good catch—bad throw.)

3. One must never precede any maneuver by a comment more predictive than, "Watch this!" (Keep 'em guessing.)

4. The higher the costs of hitting any object, the greater the certainty it will be struck. (Remember—the disc is positive—both cops and old ladies are clearly negative.)

5. The best catches are never seen. (Did you see that?—See what?)

6. The greatest single aid to distance is for the disc to be going in a direction you did not want. (Goes the wrong way—goes a long way.)

7. The most powerful hex words in the sport are—"I really have this down—watch." (Know it? Blow it!)

8. In any crowd of spectators at least one will suggest that razor blades could be attached to the disc. ("You could maim and kill with that thing.")

9. The greater your need to make a good catch the greater the probability your partner will deliver his worst throw. (If you can't touch it, you can't trick it.)

10. The single most difficult move with a disc is to put it down. (Just one more.)

I. Disc-ography

The all-important address of the International Frisbee Association is P.O. Box 664, Alhambra, Cal. 91802. Lifetime membership will cost you $3 (and includes membership card, certificate, proficiency manual, bumper sticker, and one year's worth of *Frisbee World*—$5 for six issues).

For those interested in tournaments and other Frisbee events, *Frisbee World* is your best source of information on dates and locations.

Dr. Johnson's book, *Frisbee!*, is published by the Workman Publishing Co. in New York and costs $4.95. Other references you may wish to consult are:

Petersen, Jim A., "Zen and the Art of Frisbee," *Oui* magazine, May 1975.

Reed, J. D., "They Are My Life and Wife," *Sports Illustrated*, February 24, 1975.

*These were originally published in the February 1975 issue of *Flying Disc World* and are reprinted here by permission of the magazine's editor, Dan "The Stork" Roddick.

Weeks, Albert L., "Frisbee: A Toy for All Seasons," *The New York Times*, August 2, 1971.

J. Names and the Games

Two important references on Monopoly are: Maxine Brady's *The Monopoly Book* (David McKay and Co., $5.95) which not only explains the game in great detail but suggests strategy and tactics which come in useful in establishing a winning game; and *90 Years of Fun*, the corporate history of Parker Brothers, published by the company. A book with much on the general history of board games in America is *It's All in the Game*, the history of the Milton Bradley Company, by James J. Shea and Charles Mercer (G. P. Putnam's Sons, 1960).

The great touchstone for all that has to do with Avalon Hill board games is *The General*, which costs $7.50 a year from:

Avalon Hill
4517 Harford Rd.
Baltimore, Md. 21214

K. Tiddlywinks

The game is played on a felt-covered table by two to four people playing as individuals or as two teams of two. Each player has a larger disc (usually 1 inch in diameter) and a set of three or more smaller discs or "winks" of the same color. In the center of the table is a low glass or plastic cup 1 $^7/8$ inch in diameter.

Each time a player puts one of his winks in the cup or pot, he earns an extra turn, and the first player with all three winks, or the first team with six, wins the game.

While this is about all the game amounts to in terms of rules, there is much more to it when experienced hands are snapping the winks around the table. For one thing, potting all your winks is usually attempted at the end of the game, and the early rounds are largely taken up with getting your winks into the best location and blocking your opponent(s).

L. Croquet

This game can be played with two opponents or with opposing teams of two or three members. With teams, partners do not play in succession but each alternates with an opponent.

The game consists of each player driving his ball with his own mallet through the wickets in their prescribed order. To begin play, the ball is placed one mallet's length in front of the first or "home" stake. The tour of the wickets continues until you return to the "home" stake. When singles are being played, the first one to touch the home stake wins while in team contests all members of the winning team must touch.

Here are the basic rules of play:
- The ball must be struck squarely with the mallet and not pushed or edged along.
- Every stroke counts, no matter how slightly the ball moves. However, if you completely miss the ball you may try again.
- You give up your turn if you go out of turn or play another player's ball (which must be returned to its original location.)
- You go again when your ball goes through a wicket or hits the turning stake. The ball has gone through the wicket if you can run the mallet handle along the driving side of the wicket without touching the ball.
- If you can hit another ball (either your own or that of a partner), you get two extra shots. You have three options for the first of these two shots: (1) to place your ball a mallet's length away from the ball you hit and take your first shot from there; (2) you may "roquet," or put your ball against the other and hit it so that both move; or (3) you can "croquet," by holding your ball against the other ball and with your foot hitting your ball so that only the other ball moves. A roquet or croquet uses up one of your two shots. The object of either of these two plays is to get an opponent's ball out of good position or to put a partner in a better position.
- No ball can hit the same ball a second time until it has gone through the next wicket in proper sequence.
- Should you wish, after you have gone through all the wickets, you can stop short of hitting the home stake and become a "rover" and roam about harassing opponents and helping partners. You must eventually hit the home stake in order to win, however.
- Boundaries should be established for your game, and balls driven beyond the edge of them should be brought back to the point where they left.

M. Horseshoes

The court shall include two 6-foot-square pitcher's boxes with stakes at their centers and shall cover an area 10 feet wide and 50 feet long. The stakes should be an inch in thickness and extend a foot above the ground and are 40 feet apart. The entire box shall be filled with clay which should be kept moist.

Two pairs of horseshoes are needed which should be the official weight (2½ pounds) and size (7 x 7 inches with no more than 3½ inches clearance at the opening of the shoe). The first person to throw is the winner of a coin toss and thereafter the first to throw is the loser of the preceding round. Each player throws his two horseshoes in succession. Any shoe delivered when the thrower's foot extends beyond the foul line does not count. The foul line is the front of the pitcher's box. The shoe can be thrown from any point in the pitcher's box.

In tournament play 50 points constitutes a game, while 21 is the norm in backyard games. In both 50- and 21-point games the following scoring system is used:

- Only one player can score in a round.
- The shoe closest to the stake scores 1 and if both your shoes are closer than your opponents you get 2.
- A ringer (a shoe that encircles the stake so that a ruler can be put against the calks at the bottom of the shoe and not touch the stake) scores 3 and a double ringer scores 6.
- All equals count as ties and no points are scored.
- If you have two ringers and your opponent one, you get 3 points.
- One ringer and closest shoe for the same player against a ringer for the second gives the first player 1 point.
- A shoe that is touching or leaning against the stake is a closest shoe and no more. A leaning shoe has no value over one touching the stake and would be considered a tie if they occurred in the same round.
- A shoe moved by an opponent's shoe counts in its new position.

Appendix II

Amplified comment on the lack of scholarship on the topics covered in this book.

Pursuant to the comment on page 122 concerning Dr. Johnson's work on the Frisbee, it is important to point out that despite his pioneering labors, far too little work has been done on the Frisbee, to say nothing of the kite, yo-yo, and other items discussed in this book. Other than Johnson, Gould (*The Top*), Hart (*Kites: An Historical Survey*), and scholars in the field of jump-rope rhymes, the picture is bleak indeed. And it is especially bleak in the area of doctoral theses, of which some 200 are produced each year in the United States in the area of physical education.

What appears to be happening is that the 50-odd institutions of higher education that grant Ph.D.'s in the area have put on blinders when it comes to suitable areas for research.

Keeping in mind that marbles, kites, tops, and the like have been almost excluded from scholarly research because they are too far out of the mainstream of serious athletic thought, consider what you can put into the American Ph.D. hopper if you stay in the right areas.

Historic Studies. Usually long and highly detailed, they are best typified by examples like "A History of Indiana High-School Basketball" (495 pages) and "A History of Sports at the Methodist Children's Home at Winston-Salem" (a 513-page opus that might prove too much for the home's athletic director).

Scientific and Technical. Typical recent titles in this realm include "An Electromyographic Study of Specific Muscles Used in the Lacrosse Cradle," "Selected Physical Factors Affecting the Success of the Forward Three and a Half Backward Two and a Half Somersault Dives," and "The Effect of Pre-Foreperiod Duration Upon the Response Time of Football Levelment."

Economic. For instance, recently a gent from the University of Illinois with the aid of an IBM 360 computer produced "An Economic Analysis of the Factors Influencing Football Attendance at the University of Illinois, 1926–1968." Incidentally, this 136-page dissertation concluded that the price of tickets, the amount of money in the pockets of students, and the win/loss record of the home team were the most important factors dictating attendance.

"Best Way" Theses. The large number of dissertations which dwell on such matters as the best way to praise an athlete, the best temperature for post-game showers, the best way to warm up for handball, and the best way to teach selected badminton skills to college women.

Philosophic. The trend here is theses which search for meaning and relevance. For example, a woman at the University of Southern California recently produced a work entitled "Meanings Found in the Acts of Surfing and Skiing"; another probed the meaning in square dancing, and still another looked into the effects of praise on athletes.

And then there are the studies which are hard to fit into precise categories, such as recent works on the influence of fatigue on missed jump shots in basketball and the effect of the menstrual cycle on the throwing ability of schoolgirls. In the catch-all "hard to categorize" area one is liable to find some of the most belabored work. One entitled "Criteria for Determining Success in Basketball" drones on for 99 pages to conclude that basketball success is a combination of — are you ready? — points made, assists, turnovers caused, and rebounds accomplished. No less dramatic a conclusion was reached in "The Effects of the University of Alabama Football Training on Reaction Time and Speed of Movement." It determines in 162 pages that, generally, you will come out of Alabama with quicker reactions and faster downfield speed if you played football for four years than if you didn't.

There seems to be no end to these theses in areas like football, basketball, baseball, and even bowling. The abstract for a recent bowling thesis, called "The Effect of Four Method Spare Conversion Involving Variations in Point of Aim on Bowling Achievement of College Women," says that the last 15 years has seen "a considerable increase in the amount of research involving aspects of bowling" and goes on to point out that the literature in the field of spare conversion is "overflowing."